112 Disney Lists

by

Tim Foster

Acknowledgments

Creating this book was a work of love, inspired by the dreams and imagination of Walt Disney, and all of the magic we've experienced at the parks and through the wonder of Disney films.

I want to thank and express my gratitude to all of the people who not only helped me put together this book, but who've also helped to create Celebrations Magazine.

Thanks to Lisa, Michelle, my mom and dad, and to the rest of my family for their support and love. Additional thanks go to all of those who have been a part of the Celebrations family over the years: Lou Mongello, Lori Elias, Steve Barrett, Nick Comande, Rachel Comande, Jamie Hecker, J Darling, Beci Mehnken, Allison Jones, J Darling, Cari Keebaugh, Chris Smith, Shaun Jex, Lindsay Mott, Catherine & Maredith Lusby, Mike Billick, Garry Rollins, Tim Devine, Kevin Carpenter, Ray Harkness, Jessica Clawson, and Becca Leap.

Most of all I'd like to thank you, our readers. Your friendliness and enthusiasm makes all of this worthwhile, and reminds us of the real reason why we do this; to share the magic of Disney.

Please visit us at www.celebrationspress.com to learn more about Celebrations Magazine and our other publications.

Photos on pages 164, 166, 168, 170, 172, 174, 176, 178, 180, 184, 186, 188, 191, 193, 195, 198, 199, 200, 201, 203, 205, 207, 208, 209, 211, 213, 215, and 278 © Disney

All other photos © Tim Foster

112 Disney Lists

CONTENTS

Superlatives

Top Ten Fastest Attractions in Walt Disney World

Walt Disney World might not boast the fastest roller coaster in the world (that title is currently held by the Formula Rossa roller coaster in Abu Dhabi, which reaches a top speed of 150 mph!), but you'll still find a number of attractions here that will more than satisfy your need for speed. So tuck your caps and sunglasses away in a safe place, get buckled in, and toss your arms up in the air as we race through the fastest attractions in all of Walt Disney World.

10. Mission: SPACE

Mission: SPACE is a centrifuge-based ride, simulating the sensation of motion through a combination of spinning and tilting. As such, it doesn't have a proper "speed," but it sure feels fast! In fact, Mission: SPACE was designed with the help of actual NASA astronauts, who say it's the most realistic simulation of space flight that they've ever experienced. You'll experience forces up to 2.4G, more than twice the force of gravity at the Earth's surface (effectively multiplying your weight by 2.4). Curiously, that's not tops at Walt Disney World; the Rock 'n' Roller Coaster subjects riders to a (temporary!) force of 4.5G, and even Primeval Whirl boasts forces of 2.5G. But it's the cramped quarters, realistic visuals, and sustained force that make Mission: SPACE the most thrilling space voyage you'll ever experience – until you hitch a ride on the Space Shuttle, that is!

9. Barnstormer Starring the Great Goofini

Naturally, this is the slowest of the Disney roller coasters because it was designed with little ones in mind. Your whimsical tour through Storybook Circus races along at a peppy 25 mph, brisk but not too scary! And along the way you'll get to see some of the acrobatic accomplishments of the Great Goofini himself. OK, some of them (actually, most of them) don't end so well, but hey, at least he tried.

8. Space Mountain

This classic attraction might seem fast, but that's mostly due to the compact design of the track and the tight turns – not to mention the fact that you can't see where you're going! Curiously, Space Mountain isn't much faster than the Barnstormer, clocking in at 27 mph.

7. Primeval Whirl

An innocent dinosaur kiddie ride? Hardly! Boasting higher (albeit shorter) spurts of g-forces than Mission: SPACE, Primeval Whirl tops out at 29 mph. (Too fast? You could always head on over to TriceraTop Spin instead...)

6. Big Thunder Mountain Railroad

It's back to the Magic Kingdom for this fun-filled romp through the Old West! We'll break through the 30-mph barrier as we race through an old mining town with its quaking caves and creepy dinosaur bones. Toss up your arms and give a big "yeehaw!" as your runaway train whisks you along at 30 mph – and even a bit faster in the afternoon as the sun heats up the grease on the tracks. (And be sure to hang on to yer hats!)

5. Twilight Zone Tower of Terror

30 mph straight ahead? Not so bad. 39 mph straight up and down? Now you're talking! The Twilight Zone Tower of Terror actually shoots you down the old elevator shaft at faster-than-free-fall speeds, thanks to a totally new ride system developed just for the old Hollywood Hotel. The innovative system consists of two massive motors (each 12 feet tall, 7 feet wide, and 35 feet long and weighing a staggering 66 tons), that sit atop the tower. The motors propel the elevator cars downward at speeds well in excess of those achieved during free fall. Now you know what all that screaming is about way up on the 13th floor!

4. Splash Mountain

Ironically, the fastest of the Magic Kingdom mountains isn't a roller coaster, but a flume ride. Splash Mountain is mostly gentle and relaxing, but that final plunge of more than 50 feet sends you into the briar patch at a blazing speed of 40 mph. Of course, it's not the speed you need to worry about. It's the big splash at the end. My oh my what a wonderful day!

3. Expedition Everest

Now we get to the true champions of the Walt Disney World thrill rides, and what better place to start than in the shadows of the fearsome Yeti? Expedition Everest sends you on a teeth-chattering trek through the Himalayas, but first you'll need to board a train for your journey to the base camp of Mount Everest. It promises to be a long journey, but fortunately(?) for you, you'll be taking a shortcut that passes through the Forbidden Mountain. Unfortunately, this same Forbidden Mountain is rumored to be guarded by the aforementioned Yeti, a fierce protector of the mountains, valleys, and forests, and he apparently doesn't take too kindly to mans' encroachment in these areas. Expedition Everest hurtles along at a blazing 50 mph, and as if that weren't scary enough, you'll soon encounter a broken set of tracks partway through your journey. At this point, you'll be traveling backward, reaching a top speed of 40 mph. Oh yeah, and it gets mighty cold at the top of those mountains...

2. Rock 'n' Roller Coaster Starring Aerosmith

The runner-up for pure speed at Walt Disney World is also the one attraction that features multiple inversions. The Rock 'n' Roller Coaster is a true thrill coaster, with an initial launch of your "limo" that takes you from 0 to 57 mph in 2.8 seconds, propelling you 200 feet straight ahead. You'll eventually reach a top speed of 60 mph as you race through a loop, a rollover, and a corkscrew, all to the thundering accompaniment of some classic rock tunes, courtesy of Aerosmith.

1. Test Track

Ironically, the fastest attraction in Walt Disney World is also the tamest of the Disney thrill rides. Most of Test Track takes place inside, with some thrilling hairpin turns, bumpy terrain, wicked braking maneuvers, and some (relatively relaxing) performance tests. But soon you're off to the high-speed tests, where you'll race through steep, banking turns, eventually hitting a top speed of 65 mph on the final straightaway – though it feels much faster than that. Fortunately, Test Track isn't nearly as scary as it sounds, and it's actually a thrill ride that nearly everyone can enjoy. Just be sure to take off your baseball cap first...

Top Ten Tallest Attractions at Walt Disney World

Going fast certainly puts the "thrill" in thrill ride, but to many people, going high up in the air is just as thrilling as going fast, if not more so. But first, we'll start out with an honorable mention. The Characters in Flight balloon at Disney Springs is the world's largest tethered gas balloon at an impressive 72 feet in diameter. Known as the Aéro30, the pastel blue balloon soars an astonishing 400 feet in the air (courtesy of 210,000 cubic feet of helium), allowing you to see up to 10 miles away. Does that qualify it as the tallest attraction in Walt Disney World? Perhaps not. The balloon itself (including the gondola) is a bit over 100 feet tall, which would place it ninth on our list, but the panoramic views can't be beat, and it's certainly the champ in terms of getting you up in the air.

10. Astro Orbiter/Rock 'n' Roller Coaster Starring Aerosmith

First up on our list is actually a pair of entries, each topping out at 80 feet: the Astro Orbiter in the Magic Kingdom and the Rock 'n' Roller Coaster Starring Aerosmith at Disney's Hollywood Studios. The Astro Orbiter gets points for allowing you to actually see how high you are off the ground you are (even though you're whipping around at an impressive 11 revolutions per minute), while the Rock 'n' Roller Coaster wins out on sheer thrills. As far as height goes, the Rock 'n' Roller Coaster might be scarier, and faster, but because you can't see how high you are (being immersed in total darkness) the concept of height doesn't mean a lot. (That's small comfort as you hurtle through the three inversions.)

Before we continue to the number nine entry on our list, we'll give an additional honorable mention to a few structures in World Showcase. While not attractions or park icons, the beautiful Campanile clock-bell tower in Italy, the American Adventure building, the Goju-no-to pagoda in Japan, the Eiffel Tower in France, and the Hotel du Canada all rise approximately 80 feet above the World Showcase promenade. While they are all smaller than their real-life counterparts (for example, the real Campanile tower is five times taller), they're still a wondrous sight to behold.

9. Splash Mountain

Back to our list, and next up is the first of the Walt Disney World mountains to make the list, Splash Mountain. It might be the smallest of the group at 87 feet, but the drop of 52 1/2 feet at a 47-degree angle sure makes it seem a lot taller!

8. Mickey's Sorcerer Hat

Even though it's gone, we're going to give another honorable mention to Mickey's Sorcerer Hat. While the former icon at Disney's Hollywood Studios didn't quite measure up to the original park symbol, the Earful Tower (which is taller by about eight feet), the Sorcerer Hat was certainly much more visible, rising a mighty 122 feet above Hollywood Boulevard.

7. The Tree of Life

For our next entry, we'll go over to Disney's Animal Kingdom for the first (but not the last) representative from Disney's wildest park. The Tree of Life rises 145 feet over Discovery Island, and even more impressive are the 325 animal figures carved into the base. In case you're curious, the Tree of Life's Magic Kingdom cousin, the Swiss Family Treehouse, doesn't even crack the Top Ten, coming in at a mere 60 feet (though unlike the Tree of Life, you can climb to the top of the Treehouse for a breathtaking view of the nearby surroundings).

6. Spaceship Earth

Next up is Epcot's tallest attraction, Spaceship Earth. The majestic geodesic sphere soars a mighty 180 feet above Future World, and for a time, when it sported a giant Mickey Mouse hand holding a magic wand, it was the reigning height champ. This feature was originally added for the millennium celebration, with the giant "2000" later changed to read "Epcot." The wand increased Spaceship Earth's height to 257 feet, making it the all-time tallest attraction in Walt Disney World. The wand was dismantled in 2007.

5. Space Mountain

The oldest of the Magic Kingdom mountains comes in at number five, rising 183 feet above Tomorrowland. While the attraction is totally self-contained, some of the earliest sketches had the track weaving in and out of the show building, which would have made for some very impressive views! As it is, the iconic shell is still an engineering wonder, with the support beams visible on the outside so as to provide a smooth interior surface for the projection of stars, meteors, and other visuals.

4. Cinderella Castle

It might surprise some people to learn that the very symbol of Walt Disney World, Cinderella Castle, isn't the tallest attraction in the parks, but it is undeniably the most beautiful. It can be seen up to two miles away, and at 189 feet it's the second tallest structure in the Magic Kingdom. What is the tallest? That brings us to...

3. Big Thunder Mountain Railroad

The granddaddy of the Magic Kingdom mountains, Big Thunder Mountain soars 197 feet above Frontierland, dwarfing nearby Splash Mountain. This beloved attraction makes use of 2,780 feet of railroad track (over half a mile) and covers nearly two acres of land. As impressive as that is, Big Thunder Mountain is only the second highest mountain in Walt Disney World, but we'll get back to that in a minute.

2. The Twilight Zone Tower of Terror

In the meantime, we'll journey over to Disney's Hollywood Studios for the once-reigning height champion, the Twilight Zone Tower of Terror. The frightful facade of the Hollywood Hotel rises 199 feet in the air, and one might wonder why it came up just shy of the 200-foot barrier. In another example of Disney's attention to detail, it was noted that, per Florida law, the hotel would have required a red light to be affixed atop of it if it had been higher than 200 feet. Realizing that the light would ruin the theming of the attraction, the building was designed to come up just short, thus preserving the 1930s time-line and helping to reinforce the attraction's back story.

1. Expedition Everest

The tallest attraction at Walt Disney World beats out the Tower of Terror by a mere six inches, topping out at 199½ feet. Even more frightening is the 80-foot drop that you'll encounter, not to mention the 22-foot tall Yeti lurking within. And don't forget that Expedition Everest came in second in terms of speed at 60 mph, which certainly makes it the most thrilling attraction at Walt Disney World.

Top Ten Longest Attractions at Walt Disney World

Walt Disney World certainly has its share of thrilling attractions, but sometimes you just want a nice, relaxing ride – no loops, no high-speed drops, just a tranquil journey where you can enjoy the scenery, rest your weary feet, and (especially in the summer) get a break from the sweltering Florida sun. Fortunately, the "slow ride" is a Disney specialty, and you'll find no shortage of attractions that will meet your need for not-a-lot-of-speed. We'll take a look at the ten longest attractions, with a few honorable mentions along the way. For the purposes of our list, theatrical shows don't count (that's another subject!), nor do walk-through attractions, such as the Maharajah Jungle Trek. So sit back, put your feet up (but keep them in your ride vehicle please), and let's begin!

10. Jungle Cruise

Our first entry clocks in at just over nine minutes, and what better way to get started than with a leisurely cruise through the untamed wilderness of Adventureland. One of the best things about the Jungle Cruise is how it totally transforms at night. Somehow the journey seems much longer – and a lot spookier! Just watch out for those elephants; they look like they've packed their trunks. (Yep, it's jokes like that that'll make your trip seem much longer.)

9. Tomorrowland Transit Authority PeopleMover

We break the 10-minute barrier on our next journey, as the Tomorrowland Transit Authority PeopleMover (or TTA for short) takes you on a futuristic tour through Tomorrowland. The TTA is one of the few attractions where you can sometimes ride as long as you want. Assuming the station isn't busy (and it usually isn't), just ask the Cast Member at the unloading area if you can ride again. (A quick circular "go around again?" spin of your finger should be sufficient.) That will give you even more time to take in the sights of Buzz Lightyear's Space Ranger Spin, the Tomorrowland Speedway, and Space Mountain. Speaking of Space Mountain, keep an eye out for the "Starport Seven-Five" logo as you enter the dome. That's a clever reference to the year 1975, when Space Mountain and the Tomorrowland Transit Authority first opened.

8. Splash Mountain

Next up, also coming in at just a bit over 10 minutes, is the one thrill ride to make our list. The final drop might be wet and wild, but the majority of your tour is a whimsical journey through the world of Br'er Rabbit, Br'er Fox, and the rest of the gang from *Song of the South*. Particularly memorable is the double drop that leads to the Laughing Place, but don't get too relaxed, there's trouble brewin' ahead. Splash Mountain holds the unique distinction of appearing on the longest, tallest, and fastest attraction lists in Walt Disney World. No wonder it's often mentioned as a favorite!

7. "it's a small world"

Our next attraction also holds the distinction of being one of the oldest in Walt Disney World, originally developed for the 1964-1965 New York World's Fair. Part of the fun is in trying to figure out all the countries that you see throughout your 11-minute boat ride. Be sure to listen for the French dancers chanting "ooh la la" as they do the can-can. C'est magnifique!

6. The Haunted Mansion

At 12 minutes long, this true Disney classic is a veritable treasure trove of special effects and ghoulish delights. You might wonder how the tour can take so long, considering the smallish size of the mansion itself. As it turns out, the actual attraction building is hidden out of sight behind the trees. The structure you see is merely a clever facade. In fact, the purpose of the stretching rooms in the original Disneyland version is to transport Guests to an underground tunnel that leads to the actual show building, which is located outside the park's berm due to lack of space. Even though there were no such space restrictions at the Magic Kingdom, the stretching room effect was retained due to its popularity.

5. Living with the Land

Also coming in at 12 minutes (and our first entry outside of the Magic Kingdom), Living with the Land was the former centerpiece of The Land Pavilion before the introduction of Soarin'. Soarin' itself could be considered for this list, clocking in at 10 minutes in length, but it joins several other attractions (including such former attractions as the Great Movie Ride at 19 minutes, the Backlot Tour at 35 minutes, and Ellen's Energy Adventure at an impressive 45 minutes) as ones that could arguably be described as shows, even though they each featured moving ride vehicles. (Okay, one of those "vehicles" in the case of the Backlot Tour was your feet, but you get the idea.) Rather than trying to decide in which category these attractions properly fit, we decided to take the easy way out and place them in the "honorable mention" group. As far as Living with the Land goes, be sure to keep an eye out for the ladybugs – and Mickey-shaped pumpkins!

4. Liberty Square Riverboat

Let's go back to the Magic Kingdom and a leisurely 16-minute ride down the Rivers of America. The Liberty Square Riverboat is a wonderfully relaxing ride, and it also affords you some unique views of the Haunted Mansion, Tom Sawyer Island, Big Thunder Mountain Railroad, and Splash Mountain. Be sure to bring your camera!

3. Spaceship Earth

Spaceship Earth is the longest of the indoor attractions on our list, and it's a favorite of many. The 16-minute journey is filled with memorable moments and fantastic details. For example, look for the WDI logo on the microphone in the radio scene, that's a reference to Walt Disney Imagineering. For an extra bit of fun, once you've ridden a few times, try selecting a different language on your ride vehicle. You might be surprised at how much you understand.

2. Walt Disney World Railroad

Some people think of the railroad as a mere form of transportation, but don't be fooled. The Walt Disney World Railroad is a classic attraction unto itself, and it was near and dear to Walt Disney's heart. Like the Liberty Square Riverboat, it'll give you some unique views of Big Thunder Mountain Railroad. Be sure to look closely; you might be surprised at the details you discover, especially because they're usually a giant blur as you race through the town on your runaway train. Thunder Mountain's race through the rocky wilderness might take only three minutes, but the Walt Disney World Railroad provides a more relaxing train ride at 20 minutes in length – and it's a lot slower too.

1. Kilimanjaro Safaris

The granddaddy of long rides is also the only attraction on the list located in Disney's Animal Kingdom. (In case you were wondering, the Na'vi River Journey, one of the newest attractions in the park, clocks in at a mere 4 1/2 minutes.) Kilimanjaro Safaris also holds the distinction of being the largest attraction ever created at Walt Disney World. At well over 100 acres, the entire Magic Kingdom could fit inside. No wonder it takes you more than 20 minutes to make your way through as you ride in style in your expertly-driven Jeep. Curiously, Guests aren't the only ones who's comfort is a concern. The rocks in the lion area are actually climate-controlled. They're heated in the winter and cooled in the summer to encourage the lions to lie in good viewing areas. Hopefully you remembered your camera!

Top Ten Largest Attractions at Walt Disney World

As Walt Disney was formulating his plans for what would eventually become Walt Disney World, one of the things that most excited him was the sheer enormity of the project, and the endless possibilities that the Florida location afforded him. As Walt famously said, "Here in Florida, we have something special we never enjoyed at Disneyland...the blessing of size. There's enough land here to hold all the ideas and plans we can possibly imagine." Not only did the 42,000 acres of land acquired by Disney provide plenty of room for all the parks and resorts that we enjoy today, it also allowed each park to feature larger-than-life attractions that weren't constrained by the size limitations of their California cousins.

And some of these attractions are huge indeed! "Large" in this case doesn't mean tall, it means the actual area that the attraction takes up, or in other words, how much space it would occupy on a map. Unlike statistics for height or speed, these numbers are often hard to come by, so in order to create this list we had to set up a few rules. Rule number one was that the attraction needed to be self-contained; in other words, it couldn't "enclose" another attraction or land. That leaves out the Walt Disney World Railroad, even though the track forms a complete circuit around the Magic Kingdom, and the TTA, whose path circles throughout Tomorrowland. Additionally, for indoor attractions we're only counting the building itself and the immediate attraction-related areas (such as outdoor queues), and not the surrounding grounds, as it's sometimes hard to say where one attraction ends and the next one begins. Finally, there was admittedly a little guess work and a few judgment calls that went into compiling this list, but hey, that's half the fun! So, with the preliminaries out of the way, let's get our list started with Number 10:

10. Seven Dwarfs Mine Train

The Magic Kingdom's newest attraction kicks off our list in grand style, with an all-new twisty-turvy roller coaster that is easily the largest attraction in all of Fantasyland, both old and new. Nearly five times bigger than its Fantasyland cousin, The Barnstormer Starring the Great Goofini, Seven Dwarfs Mine Train even noses out the wildest outdoor coaster in Walt Disney World, Expedition Everest. (Though what Everest lacks in square footage it certainly makes up for in screams!) The sprawling track layout takes you on a family-friendly trek through rocky outcroppings, mountainous passages, and over babbling streams on your way to a glittering jewel mine that features everyone's favorite band of mine workers.

9. DINOSAUR

Our first entry from Disney's Animal Kingdom might also be the scariest on the list. More than three times larger than its prehistoric time-traveling rival, Primeval Whirl, the DINOSAUR attraction takes Guests on a thrilling journey back in time to retrieve a special Iguanodon. The Time Rover vehicles were based on the same innovative ride mechanism used in Disneyland's Indiana Jones Adventure attraction, the Enhanced Motion Vehicle. The passenger seating area is attached to the chassis by three hydraulic rams, which allow the passenger car to move independently of the frame. This allowed the Imagineers to combine the speed of a roller coaster with the pitching and tilting movements of a simulator. Throw in the ferocious roar of an angry Carnotaurus (in the dark, no less!), and you have the makings of a thrill ride that's sure to make even the bravest explorer scream in terror.

8. Universe of Energy/Ellen's Energy Pavilion

This is the first entry from Epcot, and even though this pavilion is now closed, we thought we'd include it on our list anyway. Even when you approached the building from ground level it seemed massive, and it certainly had to be to contain all those dinosaurs, not to mention the huge moving theater. The sheer size of the roof allowed room for the placement of 80,000 photo-voltaic solar cells that provided some of the power for the attraction. In addition to placing number eight on our list, Ellen's Energy Adventure also held the distinction of being the longest theatrical show at Walt Disney World in terms of duration, clocking in at 45 minutes. (Incidentally, if the Wonders of Life pavilion were still open, it would have fallen between the Seas and the Energy pavilion in terms of size. How we miss that DNA molecule!)

7. The Seas with Nemo & Friends

The Seas with Nemo & Friends is next on our list and is actually the largest entirely enclosed attraction in all of Walt Disney World. The bulk of that space is occupied by a massive 5.7 million-gallon saltwater tank, but that's just part of the story. In addition to the ride-though attraction itself, the pavilion features numerous interactive exhibits scattered throughout two floors, formerly known as Sea Base Alpha (and accessible via the infamous Hydrolators) but now referred to simply as the Sea Base. The pavilion is also home to the Turtle Talk with Crush theater, which may beg the question of whether the pavilion should be considered one attraction or two (or three, depending on how you're counting). But in the spirit of "fish are friends, not food," we'll consider everyone to be one, big happy family. The pavilion is also notable for its distinctive shape. All the Future World pavilions have their own unique shapes, and the Seas with Nemo & Friends pavilion features numerous swirls and curves that mirror the aquatic wonders found within.

6. Big Thunder Mountain Railroad

As we previously mentioned, the largest roller coaster in Walt Disney World also holds the distinction of being the tallest attraction in the Magic Kingdom, soaring eight feet higher than Cinderella Castle. And we've also discovered that, despite its size, Big Thunder Mountain Railroad isn't the fastest roller coaster in Walt Disney World, nor even in the Magic Kingdom. But Big Thunder Mountain does feature dizzying drops and wickedly tight turns, making it much scarier than its tamer counterpart in Fantasyland, so don't forget to "hang onto them hats and glasses, 'cause this here's the wildest ride in the wilderness!" The railroad twists and turns through a vast expanse of untamed wilderness, so vast that it would fill up the entirety of Main Street, U.S.A.

Let's Go For a Walk

We're going to take a break from our list to talk about a few attractions upon which we'll bestow some "honorable mentions." While they are all proper attractions, they are distinguished from the other entries on this list due to their manner of conveyance. In these attractions, your journey is undertaken not in a car, train, or boat, but with your feet! Similar to Main Street, U.S.A., the first two we'll discuss serve as your introduction to Disney's Animal Kingdom: The Oasis Exhibits and Discovery Island Trails. The Oasis is the smaller of the two, while Discovery Island Trails encompasses the entirety of the island that serves as the hub for Disney's Animal Kingdom. The Trails also surround two Animal Kingdom attractions, the Tree of Life and It's Tough to be A Bug, which, according to our self-imposed rules, disqualifies it from being an official entry on our list. However, both areas are well worth exploring, and while they aren't "attractions" along the lines of a dark ride or roller coaster, their sheer size certainly merits a mention when talking about the largest attractions in Walt Disney World. (In case you're wondering, the similar walking-trail Animal Kingdom attractions, Maharajah Jungle Trek and Gorilla Falls Exploration Trail, aren't big enough to crack the Top Ten.) The other walking-style attraction that gets an honorable mention can be found at the Magic Kingdom. Tom Sawyer Island actually falls somewhere between The Oasis Exhibits and Discovery Island Trails in terms of size, and though there are plenty of surprises to be found here, this is also an area that's much more about exploring than an actual ride experience.

5. Test Track

Back to the list now, and back over to Epcot for our next entry. This one is a bit debatable, because if you only counted the show building itself (which some sources seem to do when listing its square footage), it would barely crack the Top Ten, narrowly edging out the Seven Dwarfs Mine Train. But how can you discount the part of the attraction that makes it the fastest in all of Walt Disney World? You can't, of course, and when you factor in the outdoor straightaway and the first loop that sends you back toward the steeply banked 65 mph race around the building, Test Track vaults all the way up to number five, making it the largest self-contained attraction in all of Epcot. Wait, you might be saying, what about The Land Pavilion? While it's true that The Land Pavilion is nearly 50% larger than Test Track, even including the outside track section, the pavilion is home to several smaller attractions (including Soarin' Around the World and Living with the Land, none of which would make the Top Ten), so it doesn't qualify for the list. But it's still a great place to get a snack!

4. Lights, Motors, Action! Extreme Stunt Show / Backlot Tour

These are the only entries on the list from Disney's Hollywood Studios, and even though both closed a while back to make room for the new additions coming to the Studios, we thought they were still worth an honorable mention. While much of the space at the Stunt Show was devoted to the seating area, there was still plenty of room for the stunt cars and motorcycles, including a guest appearance by Lightning McQueen himself. (Visitors to earlier versions of the show will recall that Lightning took over the role formerly held by Herbie the Lovebug). The setting of the massive show arena was inspired by Villefranche-sur-Mer; a Mediterranean village in the south of France. Because of the vast area required for such an expansive show, a good chunk of space was taken away from the former Backlot Tour, the walking "behind the scenes" attraction that gave you a sneak peek at how movies were made. (We'll never forget Catastrophe Canyon and all that water!) The Backlot Tour was massive, and would definitely have made the top five of this list, but since the tour was constantly changing throughout the years to accommodate other additions to the park, and because the tour included glimpses into places that you could see but not enter, determining its exact size was a rather inexact science. The solution? We decided to give it an honorable mention near the top of the list, along with the Lights, Motors, Action! Extreme Stunt Show, after a careful evaluation process that involved many contributing factors. (In other words, we cheated!)

3. Tomorrowland Speedway

OK, no more asterisks, caveats, or honorable mentions. It's time to get back to the real list! In the spirit of fast cars and epic driving stunts, our next entry also involves racing cars (and no, it's not the Rock 'n' Roller Coaster, which barely cracks the Top 20 for those of you keeping score at home). These cars are of a tamer variety, and can be found in the Magic Kingdom at the Tomorrowland Speedway. Even though the track was slightly shortened to make way for Mickey's Birthdayland (which would eventually become Mickey's Toontown Fair), the attraction still comes in at number three on our list. The twisting serpentine course winds its way between Tomorrowland and Fantasyland, taking would-be racers up near the double Dumbo attraction and down underneath the overhead rails of the TTA. Formerly known as the Grand Prix Speedway, the attraction was later renamed the Tomorrowland Indy Speedway, and in 1999 added show elements inspired by the Indianapolis Motor Speedway (home of the Indy 500). In 2008 the name was changed to the current Tomorrowland Speedway, but for young (and young-at-heart) would-be race car drivers, this is one attraction that's not to be missed. Even though the cars are a bit slow, the scenery is remarkable!

2. Jungle Cruise

We'll stay in the Magic Kingdom for our next entry; a classic favorite in which Walt Disney took a personal interest. The Jungle Cruise in Adventureland carves out a huge area in the southwest corner of the Magic Kingdom, and it needs to be big in order to facilitate your journey along the Congo, Nile, Mekong, and Amazon Rivers. This attraction is so expansive that you could fit all of Space Mountain inside, with enough room left over to squeeze in the Carousel of Progress for good measure. Good thing your boat comes with a trusty guide! As large as the Jungle Cruise is, however, it's not the largest outdoor nature excursion to be found at Walt Disney World. That honor goes to...

1. Kilimanjaro Safaris

Kilimanjaro Safaris is by far the largest attraction in all of Walt Disney World, so large that the entire Magic Kingdom would fit inside. Or, if you prefer, all of World Showcase. In fact, if you were able to pick up Epcot and place it on top of Kilimanjaro Safaris (rotating it so the back of World Showcase lined up with the back of the safari grounds), Spaceship Earth would land approximately on the site of the Tree of Life. The fictional back story has you taking a jeep-tour through 800-square-miles (or 512,000 acres) of the rugged savanna (though in actuality the grounds are "only" slightly less than a fifth of a square mile, or 110 acres, which is 0.3% of the entire grounds of Walt Disney World). As you ride, you can see 34 different species of wild animals, including antelope, black rhinos, crocodiles, elephants, lions, giraffes, and even a warthog. That's a lot of animals, and a lot of driving around! This would be a good time to take a refreshing spin on one of the smallest attractions in all of Disney, the Magic Carpets of Aladdin...but that's a list for another time.

Parks & Lands

Ten Things You May Not Know About
Magic Kingdom

1. Bigger and Better

After the success of Disneyland in California, Walt Disney set his sights on bigger projects. The lessons learned in the construction and operation of Disneyland made Walt realize that he needed lots of space to overcome the logistical obstacles that he encountered in California. For example, he had no control over the area immediately surrounding Disneyland, and the park was soon surrounded by cheap motels and other opportunistic businesses attempting to cash in on the success of Disneyland. Walt wanted to create a Utopian environment; one where he could provide Guests with a complete fantasy escape from the real world. To do so he needed to have control over all aspects of a Guest's experience – everything from their arrival and where they stayed to their recreation and dining. (In addition, Walt had plans to build a city of the future called EPCOT, but that's a whole other story!)

2. Finding a Home

But where could he go to fulfill his dream? Many locations were considered but, in the end, Florida was selected due to its favorable climate, growing population, and availability of land. And so in the mid 1960s, Disney started to quietly acquire large parcels of land in central Florida. The mystery buyer was unveiled to the public in October of 1965, and construction of the Walt Disney World Resort was underway.

3. Water, Water Everywhere

During the construction of the Magic Kingdom, Bay Lake was drained and millions of cubic yards of earth were excavated to provide the foundation for the Magic Kingdom.

The area next to Bay Lake was found to be unsuitable for construction, so a lagoon was created to extend the natural boundaries of Bay Lake to the front of the Magic Kingdom. This lagoon (named Seven Seas Lagoon) was refilled, along with Bay Lake, and both were lined with thousands of tons of pure white sand that was found during the course of excavation. With the area fully prepared, the Magic Kingdom began construction, opening its doors to an eagerly awaiting public in 1971.

4. Opening Day Attractions

There were 23 attractions at the Magic Kingdom when it first opened. (Today that number has more than doubled.) Three of them were unique to Florida (apart from a few similarly-themed restaurants with new names). These were the Mickey Mouse Revue, the Country Bear Jamboree (whose Disneyland counterpart would open a few months later), and the Hall of Presidents.

5. A Small Problem...

The depth of the water table in Central Florida is a mere two feet. So how did they build the Utilidors beneath the Magic Kingdom without having them flood? Simple! Don't build under the ground, build over it! Wait, does that mean...? Yep!

6. The Utilidors

The Utilidors and maintenance areas were actually built on top of the park's foundation (not underground). The buildings were then backfilled and construction of the Magic Kingdom took place on top of that. This means that the Magic Kingdom that Guests see above-pavement is actually the second and third stories of a larger building (Fantasyland is at a higher elevation than the rest of the Magic Kingdom and is thus on the third story). That's also why you'll find a sign stating that the elevation of the Magic Kingdom is 108 feet.

7. How Big Is It?

The Magic Kingdom encompasses 142 acres. That may seem like a lot, but it's less than half the size of Epcot.

8. Saying Goodbye to Mickey's House

Though new attractions and lands have been added over the years, there was only one land that was permanently closed. That was Mickey's Toontown Fair, which was closed to make way for the New Fantasyland.

9. That's A Lot of Mickey Ice Cream Bars!

Today, the Magic Kingdom welcomes nearly 20 million Guests every year. In 1976, the 50 millionth Guest was welcomed to the most Magical Place on Earth.

10. So Magical, It's Happy

Wait, don't you mean the Happiest Place on Earth? It's a common mistake, but no. Disneyland's official tagline is "The Happiest Place on Earth," while the tagline for the Magic Kingdom is (naturally enough) "The Most Magical Place on Earth." But to be fair, they're both happy AND magical.

Ten Things You May Not Know About
Main Street U.S.A.

1. Walt and Mickey

The "Partners" statue and the statue of Roy Disney with Minnie Mouse were both created by Blaine Gibson, with lots of conceptual assistance from the many people who worked with them. Blaine Gibson also sculpted nearly all the presidents featured in the Hall of Presidents.

2. Tony Who?

The "Tony" in Tony's Town Square Restaurant is none other than Tony from *Lady and the Tramp*, the Italian chef who serves them their infamous spaghetti dinner.

3. Inside the Firehouse

In the Firehouse you may notice a display case filled with patches from firehouses across the country. These aren't props, they were actually donated by firefighters visiting the Magic Kingdom.

4. Anyone Home?

Many of the windows in the shops are lit from behind with flickering lamps. Some of those lamps cast shadows of "people," giving the illusion that the buildings are occupied, even at night.

5. The Windows of Main Street U.S.A.

You'll notice that many of the windows in the Main Street shops have names of companies on them. These are actually tributes to important people in Disney history. Walt Disney himself has two windows; one over the Walt Disney Railroad Station (Walter E. Disney – Graduate School of Design & Master Planning), and another above the Plaza Restaurant (Walt Disney World Railroad Office – Keeping Dreams on Track – Walter E. Disney, Chief Engineer).

See if you can find the window for Frank Wells as you walk along Main Street. Wells was the former CEO of Disney, and he loved mountain climbing. This is reflected in the name of the company in the window, "Seven Summits Expeditions, Frank G. Wells President," and fittingly, the window is the highest of all the windows on Main Street.

6. Just for the Kids

When designing Disneyland's Main Street, Walt Disney ordered that all the windows be lower than normal so that children would be able to easily look through them.

7. More Characters

The Partners Statue in front of Cinderella Castle is a favorite photo spot, but don't forget to look around Main Street for the smaller statues of many of your favorite Disney characters, including Minnie Mouse, Dumbo, Donald, Duck, Br'er Rabbit, Goofy, Pluto, Pinocchio, and Chip 'n' Dale.

8. The Walt Disney Story

Visitors to Walt Disney World could once tour an exhibit called The Walt Disney Story, which opened in Town Square two years after the park's opening. The out-of-the-way attraction (which rarely saw large crowds as most people toured the headliner attractions) showcased a variety of Disney memorabilia, including historical photos and Cinderella's glass slipper. Guests could also see a documentary film about Walt Disney, shown in two 300-seat theaters. The attraction closed in 1992, but many of the artifacts remained on display until the area was transformed into a meet-and-greet area for Mickey Mouse and friends.

9. That's A Lot of Shops, Or Is It?

Main Street U.S.A. is actually comprised of just four buildings (or blocks), bisected in the middle by a crossroad called Center Street. On the right side of Center Street (as you approach the Castle), you can hear the sounds of voice lessons emanating from a second story window. But fair warning, those voice lessons don't seem to be going so well!

10. Listening In

Another hidden secret that you can hear can be found in The Chapeau shop (where you can get your customized Mickey ears!). You'll see an old-fashioned phone hanging on the wall; if you pick up the receiver you'll find that you can listen in on an old-time party line call!

Ten Things You May Not Know About
Adventureland

1. More Adventures

The first major expansion of the Magic Kingdom occurred in December of 1973, when the Caribbean Plaza was added to Adventureland. In addition to providing an appropriate home for the Pirates of the Caribbean attraction, the Caribbean Plaza also helped to smooth the transition between Adventureland and the Spanish-influenced styles of the 1850s American Southwest architecture of Frontierland.

2. Dig, Dig, Dig

Landscapers needed to bore through 14 inches of impervious clay to make the pits necessary to accommodate the root structures of the various trees. This is because the Adventureland area of the Magic Kingdom was constructed over an extensive landfill (created to raise and level the grade of the site).

3. Creating a Jungle

Great care was taken in the landscaping of Adventureland. Imagineer Morgan ("Bill") Evans was primarily responsible for the design. The variety of exotic plants in Adventureland includes the cape honeysuckle, the Chinese hibiscus, Mexican flame vines, Brazilian bougain-villea, sword ferns, spider plants, and Australian tree ferns.

4. Up on the Roof

The rooftop of the Tiki Room building is also visible from Frontierland. In an amazing example of Disney's attention to detail, figures of Asian Water Buffaloes were placed there so that the structure would look equally at home in both Adventureland and Frontierland.

5. Pirate Ships

When Pirates of the Caribbean was being conceptualized for Disneyland, it was originally going to be a walk-through attraction with wax figures. Partly out of concern for crowding and traffic flow, it was later decided to incorporate boats as the means of conveyance through the attraction.

6. Murky Waters

The river in the Jungle Cruise is actually dyed brown to give it an authentic look. If it wasn't dyed, Guests would be able to clearly see the bottom of the river, which is only 3 1/2 feet deep.

7. From Film to Fantasy

One of the inspirations for Adventureland came from the *True-Life Adventure* series of documentary films created by Walt Disney.

8. Watch Out!

The camels that occasionally "spit" on riders of The Magic Carpets of Aladdin were first used in the Aladdin's Royal Caravan Parade at the Disney-MGM Studios. When that parade ended, they were relocated to the Soundstage Restaurant at the Studios.

9. A Spanish Fortress

The building in which Pirates of the Caribbean is housed is a fortress known as the Castillo del Morro, which stands in the shadows of the clock tower known as Torre del Cielo, which means "tower of the sun." It was inspired by one of the oldest of the Spanish citadels in the Caribbean, known as the "Castillo de San Felipe del Morro" in San Juan, Puerto Rico. The Roman numerals that were placed at the entrance to the building read 1643, which placed it squarely around the time of the real fortress, which was designed in 1637. It's therefore appropriate to the story of Caribbean Plaza, which represents an island seaport from the Spanish and British colonies of the West Indies from the 17th and 18th centuries.

10. Keeping Watch

Speaking of Pirates, as you make your way toward Frontierland from the Caribbean Plaza, you'll find the Crow's Nest. As part of the story of this portion of Adventureland, it stands as a lookout point to warn the town of possible invaders. If you approach the Castillo del Morro from the opposite side, you'll see a tattered Pirates of the Caribbean flag atop a ship's mast and a pirate skeleton keeping a watchful eye with his telescope from his lookout point. These two crow's nests serve as bookends to Caribbean Plaza. They ensure that no invaders to El Castillo can arrive unseen from either direction.

Ten Things You May Not Know About
Frontierland

1. What Do Those Numbers Mean?

Look for the address numbers on all of the buildings. They actually indicate the year that is represented by that particular style of architecture. (If you see a two-digit number, just add an "18" to the front to get the proper year.)

2. The "Mighty" Mississippi

You may notice a metal strip slicing across the walkway halfway through Frontierland. This is the "Little Mississippi," symbolically dividing Frontierland into the east and the west. This symbolism is not only figurative but literal – beneath the metal plate is a channel that carries water to the Rivers of America.

3. Mark Twain and Walt

In an interesting coincidence, Mark Twain (of Tom Sawyer fame) grew up in Hannibal, Missouri, just a mere 90 miles away from Marceline, the town were Walt Disney spent much of his youth. (Marceline provided Walt with the inspiration for Main Street.)

4. The Trail Boss...

"Texas" John Slaughter is the name of the Frontierland Trail Boss, as seen on the sign hanging over the entrance to his store.

5. ...And His TV Show

"Texas John Slaughter" was also the name of a TV Western series starring Tom Tryon that was produced by Disney in the 50s and 60s. It ran on the "Disneyland" show, which aired on ABC before it moved to NBC and was renamed "Walt Disney's Wonderful World of Color."

6. Keepin' An Eye on the Town

You could once find the Marshall keepin' the peace daily in Frontierland, as well as Prospector "Gold Dust Gus" appearing at various times throughout the day. These character actors seamlessly blended into the theme of the land, and gladly interacted with Guests.

7. Rollin' On the River

The Rivers of America surrounds Tom Sawyer Island and is home to the Liberty Bell Riverboat. Until the mid-1990s, Guests could travel the river on small boats called the Gullywhumper or the Bertha Mae, courtesy of Mike Fink's Keelboats.

8. Where's Main Street?

You can only reach Frontierland by passing through Liberty Square or Adventureland. Frontierland is the only land in the Magic Kingdom without its own "spoke" off the central hub.

9. Paddling Along

From 1971 until 1994, the Davy Crockett Explorer Canoes allowed Guests to paddle a real canoe around the Rivers of America.

10. Ready, Aim...

When the Frontierland Shootin' Arcade first opened, real lead pellets were fired from the rifles at the targets. However, the rifles soon had to be refitted to no longer shoot these projectiles. There were of course obvious safety concerns, but the real reason they were modified was paint. Paint? Yup! Because the pellets chipped the paint off the props in the attraction, it was necessary for Disney maintenance personnel to repaint the attraction every night. Over the course of a year, that amounted to over 2,000 gallons of paint!

Ten Things You May Not Know About
Liberty Square

1. Presidential Inspirations

The concept of a colonial town actually began as Walt Disney's vision for an attraction that would be a tribute to the presidents of the United States. The attraction would house Audio-Animatronic figures of the leaders of America and was to be called One Nation Under God. Plans for the show were made, but the task of building 36 Audio-Animatronics (a technology that was still in its infancy) proved to be a daunting task. Instead, Walt focused on creating a single figure of Abraham Lincoln, leading to the Great Moments with Mr. Lincoln attraction that was featured at the 1964-65 New York World's Fair.

2. A Unique Land

Liberty Square is the only Magic Kingdom land that doesn't appear in any other Disney theme park.

3. Numerical Tributes

You'll notice that each door has a number on it, which was designed to look like a street address. The number on the Hall of Presidents? It's the year that the United States Constitution was written, 1787.

4. The Court of Flags

The Court of Flags, located in the center of Liberty Square, showcases three symbolic pieces of American history. First are the fourteen flags that stand proudly in the center: the flags of the thirteen original colonies, and the American flag. You might notice, however, that these flags look a little different from the ones we know today. That's because these flags, hoisted on poles that feature plaques with the state name and the date of ratification, are styled to look as they did when the state became a part of the United States. Even the American flag features the original design of thirteen stars.

5. The Liberty Square Tree

Another prominent feature of Liberty Square is the Liberty Square Tree. The tree was inspired by the Liberty Tree, a famous elm tree that stood in Boston in the days before the American Revolution. Used as a meeting place for the Sons of Liberty, the tree was the site of protests against the hated Stamp Act of 1765 as well as a gathering place where many plots for freedom were discussed.

The Liberty Square Tree at Walt Disney World (actually an oak because it's native to the area) is usually overlooked as just another tree, but you can find a plaque honoring the tree on the side facing the Hall of Presidents. Take note of the 13 lanterns hanging from its limbs. They're a reference to the 13 original colonies.

6. The Liberty Bell

Finally, you will also find a replica of the famous Liberty Bell in Liberty Square. The Liberty Bell replica was cast from the same mold that was used for the original Liberty Bell (which is on display in Philadelphia). It was installed in 1987 to commemorate the Bicentennial of the U.S. Constitution.

7. Pennsylvania, er, Pensylvania

You may notice that the name 'Pennsylvania" is apparently misspelled ('Pensylvania) on the Liberty Bell. As it turns out, that's not a mistake, that was an acceptable alternative spelling for the Keystone State in use at the time. The state's name is spelled the same way on the U.S. Constitution.

8. Those Crooked Shutters

You may also notice that some of the shutters are hanging crookedly. And as you've probably figured out by now, that's not a mistake either. In Colonial times, homeowners would use leather straps at the tops of the shutters instead of hinges to conserve metal. This often resulted in the shutters hanging at an angle. In another example of Disney's attention to detail, this subtlety is faithfully reproduced on the Liberty Square store fronts.

9. Home on the Hudson

A variety of eras are represented in Liberty Square, and each area is defined by the architecture of the buildings within it. For example, the look of Liberty Square's most popular attraction, the Haunted Mansion, was inspired by New York's Hudson River Valley area.

10. The Heritage House

Surrounded as you are by America's history, if you find yourself curious about your own origins, make a stop at the Heritage House, which is the historical research center located next door to the Hall of Presidents. Here, Cast Members with a passion for history can aid you on your quest for knowledge. There's information on the origin and meaning of first names, as well as databases that contain a plethora of knowledge on surnames as well, possibly providing a detailed history on how your last name came about.

Ten Things You May Not Know About
Fantasyland

1. Creating a World of Fantasy

One of the challenges in creating Fantasyland was in the architectural design of the buildings. Imagineers needed to stylistically represent many of the classic Disney films in the attraction facades without creating a disorienting mish-mash of opposing styles. The solution was to create an eclectic European Gothic village. A wide variety of influences creates an enchanted storybook setting; everything from an Alpine Village and English Tudor Houses to a Medieval Tournament and even a mystical seaside land.

2. Carrousel...?

You may notice that the word "carrousel" in Prince Charming Regal Carrousel has two "r"s. Is that a mistake? No...that's the old-fashioned spelling, and it's spelled that way to keep in line with the "once upon a time" theming of Fantasyland.

3. Rapunzel's Tower

You may not remember, but the Tower that soars over Fantasyland was actually not the first to appear at Walt Disney World. As part of the 2011 Epcot International Flower and Garden Festival, a replica of Rapunzel's Tower was temporarily added to the Germany pavilion.

4. A Special Crown for a Special Princess

Look for the Cinderella Fountain on your way to Liberty Square. If you stand in just the right spot (slightly to the right and below eye level), the crown in the background mural will be placed perfectly over Cinderella's head!

5. From Days of Old

New Fantasyland is home to the longest running character in Disney animation history. Which character is it? It has to be Mickey Mouse, right? Nope! That distinction belongs to the mischievous Pete, who made his debut in 1925, three years before Mickey Mouse would arrive.

6. No Water for Dumbo

The versions of Dumbo the Flying Elephant in Disneyland and Disneyland Paris feature water elements in the center. The reason there weren't any in the original Magic Kingdom version (before it moved to its present home in Storybook Circus) was due to the Utilidors that ran directly underneath the attraction, which prevented the installation of any water piping.

7. A New Land

In preparation for the arrival of New Fantasyland, Mickey's Toontown Fair permanently closed in 2011. Ariel's Grotto, a princess meet-and-greet location, also closed in 2010, but has since been relocated to Under the Sea – Journey of the Little Mermaid. Another classic dark-ride attraction, Snow White's Scary Adventures, also closed to make way for Princess Fairytale Hall.

8. Try the Gray Stuff, It's Delicious!

Fantasyland is home to the Be Our Guest Restaurant, located beneath the distant spires of the Beast's Castle. Inside, you'll find a giant chandelier that serves as the restaurant's centerpiece. The chandelier features 84 candles and contains more than 100 jewels.

9. Colorful Gems

Speaking of jewels, you'll find a gem matching game in the queue of the Seven Dwarfs Mine Train. Matching up the different colored gems is hard enough, but can you remember what those colors are? No? They are six of them: red, green, amber, purple, blue, and clear. OK, "clear" isn't really a color, but since that's the "color" of a diamond, I don't think anyone will complain.

10. Riding the Rails

And now that we're on the subject of the Seven Dwarfs, each of the mine cars that took you through the former Fantasyland attraction Snow White's Scary Adventures was named after each of the Seven Dwarfs. Good luck to you if you got Grumpy!

Ten Things You May Not Know About
Tomorrowland

1. Where is Everything?

When Disneyland first opened in 1955, Guests were mystified as they walked through Tomorrowland and the pathway abruptly stopped at a dirt field! This wasn't a bleak vision of the future; Walt Disney simply ran out of time and funds to complete that area of the park before the grand opening.

2. Astronauts in Tomorrowland

On January 15, 1975, Space Mountain officially blasted off. Appropriately enough, the first mission pilot was astronaut Colonel James Irwin, who was the Lunar Module pilot on Apollo 15, which had landed on the Moon less than five years earlier. Irwin, along with Commander David Scott, were the first astronauts to use the Lunar Rover to drive across the Moon's surface. You can see a replica of a Lunar Rover on display at Mission: SPACE in Epcot.

3. Adventures in Space

Walt Disney always had a fascination with the future, and he even hosted a series of three television shows about space travel that aired as part of the "Disneyland" TV series. The first of these, "Man in Space," was a lighthearted look at the then-new world of space flight. Airing in May 1955, guests included Dr. Wernher von Braun, the preeminent rocket engineer of the 20th century, and Dick Tufeld, perhaps best known as the voice of the Robot in the TV adventure series "Lost in Space."

4. See If You Can Move It...

As you approach Rockettower Plaza, you'll see a large sphere perched on a marble stand. The sphere is supported by a thin film of water, allowing you to spin the sphere in its base. The sphere itself is so heavy that the fountain of water supporting it would shoot 210 feet in the air if the sphere were removed.

5. Look Down!

The paving in Tomorrowland is marked with a distinctive design of orbital paths and planetary shapes, sort of like a road map to the Galaxy!

6. A Show For the Ages

With its continuous showings from 1964 to today, the Carousel of Progress has become the most performed show in the history of American theater, as well as the most-seen stage show in America. Incidentally, if the narrator sound familiar, that's because it's Jean Shepherd, who also narrated the classic holiday film, *A Christmas Story*.

7. The Dumbbell Nebula

At the entrance to Tomorrowland, see if you can find the sign for the Space Collectibles Convention. Items on display include "The Latest M27 Sports Equipment." M27 is the astronomical designation of the Dumbbell Nebula. (Get it?)

8. Sonny Eclipse

If you grab a bite at Cosmic Ray's Starlight Cafe, you just might be treated to an out-of-this-world show, courtesy of Sonny Eclipse and his invisible back-up singers, the Space Angels. The show, which runs approximately 25 minutes and includes 8 songs, features a mix of musical numbers performed by Sonny on his "astro organ."

9. What Kind of Tree Was That?

Palm trees are ubiquitous to Florida of course, but in Tomorrowland there are a few that are a bit out of the ordinary. See if you find the metallic palm trees scattered throughout the area, particularly near Space Mountain.

10. A World of Color

Tomorrowland is filled with vibrant, neon colors, especially at night when all the attractions are lit up in brilliant hues of blue, green, purple, and more. Oddly enough, Tomorrowland can lay claim as the most colorful land in the Magic Kingdom. Odd because in its early days, it largely consisted of drab, gray buildings, in fitting with what the perceived vision of the future was at that time. However, it didn't make for the most exciting backdrop. When the entire land was refurbished in 1994, Imagineers opted to reimagine it as a depiction of the future as seen by past visionaries such as Jules Verne and H. G. Wells. Tomorrowland was completely re-built and altered to resemble a galactic spaceport as it would have been envisioned by the science-fiction comic strips of the early 20th century, like Flash Gordon and Buck Rogers. The result is the sci-fi retro-futuristic land you see today.

Ten Things You May Not Know About
Epcot

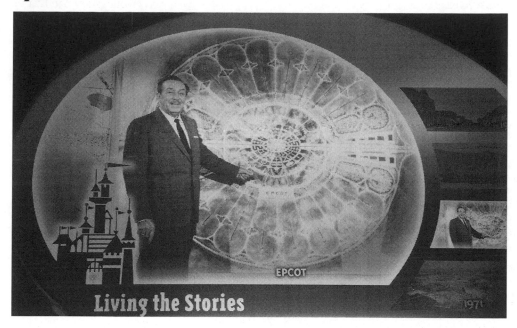

Living the Stories

1. The City of the Future

Epcot's origins go all the way back to Walt Disney's dream of building a city of the future. He wanted to create an environment where people could work, live and play, utilizing the newest technological advances of the day. When the Florida Project was being developed, this new city was always a vital component of the conceptual plans. The city project was named the Experimental Prototype Community Of Tomorrow, or EPCOT for short.

2. Planning a Community

In 1966, Walt was intently focused on researching and planning for EPCOT. The spring of that year saw him undertake research trips to a six-acre mall in Rochester, a shopping mall in Philadelphia, the Nieman-Marcus department store in Dallas, and the model city of Reston, Virginia, which was an actual planned community. He ended this trip with a visit to the Florida site itself, in order to envision how such concepts would take shape in this newly-developing area.

3. The Progress City Model

The city may have given way to the theme park we all know and love today, but you can still see remnants of Walt's original vision. At the Tomorrowland Transit Authority People-Mover in the Magic Kingdom, keep an eye out for the model of the original city concept. Constructed in 1967, the model was first installed as part of a fifth scene for Disneyland's Carousel of Progress, located on the second floor of the attraction building.

4. The EPCOT Film

Walt even had a short film produced in 1966 in which he unveiled his plans for the new city. The film was rarely seen until recently; you can view part of it in the Walt Disney Presents exhibit at Disney's Hollywood Studios. After Walt passed away, Epcot was eventually reconceptualized as an ongoing showcase of the latest technology and the various cultures of the world's nations – basically a permanent World's Fair.

5. Original Plans

The original design of Epcot (the park) was vastly different from the final version. For one thing, Future World and World Showcase were reversed, with World Showcase serving as the entrance to the park. Additionally, Epcot was at one time intended to be built across from the Magic Kingdom on Seven Seas Lagoon.

6. Building a City...in Miniature

When the park was still in its design phase, a 1/8th inch scale model of EPCOT was built. How big is that? The model actually covered an area of 1,428 square feet, about the size of an average home!

7. A Big Park for Big Dreams

That may seem big, but the park itself ended up being more than 300 acres in size, nearly three times as large as the Magic Kingdom. Even allowing for the 41 acres occupied by World Showcase Lagoon, that still makes the touring section of Epcot more than double that of the Magic Kingdom. Hope you brought your walking shoes!

8. What's That Name Again?

The name of the park has gone through several subtle changes. When it opened, the park was known as EPCOT Center (EPCOT was always printed in capital letters, signifying its use as an acronym for the Experimental Prototype Community Of Tomorrow). By 1994, it was thought that the name EPCOT was sufficiently recognized as a word unto itself (rather than just an acronym), so the name of the park was changed to simply Epcot.

9. 94, 95, 96...

Additionally, in keeping with the World's Fair concept, it was decided that the park would be reexamined and updated every year to keep it current and vital. Thus, EPCOT Center became Epcot '94, with Epcot '95 and Epcot '96 following in subsequent years. After 1996 that idea was abandoned, and the park has been known simply as Epcot ever since.

10. A Covered City?

Walt Disney originally envisioned a dome over the entire Epcot city in order to have complete control over the weather. That would sure come in handy during your typical Florida thunderstorm!

Ten Things You May Not Know About
Future World

1. The Wonders of Life

Future World East's original attractions included the Universe of Energy, Horizons, the World of Motion, and Communicore East. In 1989, the Wonders of Life pavilion opened between the Universe of Energy and Horizons. The 100,000 square foot golden geodesic dome contained a variety of exhibits that dealt with health-related themes. The dome still exists but is now only used for special events such as the International Flower & Garden Festival.

2. Shake Shake Shake

The entire seating area in the theater used for Honey, I Shrunk the Audience, Captain EO, and the current screening of Pixar film shorts is actually on a platform that can be raised four inches to simulate the lifting of the theater.

3. Angular Architecture

In contrast to the curved landscaping and architecture of Future World West, Future World East features angular designs, sculpted plantings, and metallic colors, in keeping with the more technological theme of its pavilions.

4. Power from the Sun

The Universe of Energy pavilion was a modern example of the capabilities of alternate energy sources. The roof was covered with two acres of photo-voltaic cells, which converted sunlight to electrical energy. These cells provided 15% of the power required to run the attraction inside.

5. What Are Those Odd-looking Benches?

As you wander around Future World, you may notice a purple bench with solar panels. This isn't a mere decoration, the solar panels actually provide energy for the fans and lighting on the bench, creating a futuristic resting spot for the weary Guest!

6. What's in That Building?

Behind Test Track you'll find the former restaurant, the Odyssey Center. The eatery has long been closed (today it's only used for private functions and Epcot's Festivals), but you can take the walkway for a peaceful shortcut to World Showcase. During the holiday season, the walkway is also a tranquil place to view the Christmas Tree lighting ceremony.

7. Something Doesn't Look Right...

When you're looking at a park map of Epcot, you may wonder why Future World East and West are on the "wrong" sides of the map. The answer is actually quite simple, the map is upside down...geographically speaking. World Showcase is actually to the south of Future World.

8. Kramer!

Ellen's Energy Adventure featured performances from Ellen DeGeneres, Bill Nye the Science Guy, and Jamie Lee Curtis, among others. But our vote for favorite cameo goes to Michael Richards ("Seinfeld"'s Kramer), who appeared briefly on screen as the caveman who discovers fire...in a way that only Kramer could do.

9. Let Your Imagination Soar

The Imagination pavilion was once home to The ImageWorks, an interactive play area located on the second floor that Guests could visit upon exiting the attraction. The area was home to a walk-through rainbow tunnel, Figment's coloring book, massive kaleidoscopes, and a giant pin table. This is where those mysterious stairs in the gift shop lead, if you were ever wondering. The area was partially dismantled during the 1998 renovation of the pavilion and was closed to Guests, though a few years later it was utilized as part of a temporary Kim Possible attraction. Some attractions like the Electric Philharmonic and the Stepping Tones can now be found in the current ImageWorks section in the post-show area, while the Rainbow Tunnel made a brief reappearance in Innoventions. Today, the area is used as a DVC Lounge.

10. A Hidden Treasure

As you exit Innoventions (heading out the back towards The Land Pavilion), you'll see a small courtyard with the names of some of the greatest innovators in history inscribed in the stone tiles. Most people tend to overlook this area, but it's a wonderful place to explore. (For more information on this interesting area of Epcot, see our Disney Myths list later in the book!)

Eleven Things You May Not Know About
World Showcase

1. Mexico

The landscaping in the Mexico pavilion is designed to make you feel as if you are in a Yucatan jungle! You'll find a variety of exotic plants, including Moreton bay figs, silver trumpet trees, Mexican fan palms, and orchid trees.

2. Norway

As you wander through the Norway pavilion, you'll be able to marvel at four classic Norwegian architectural styles. The Puffin's Roost and Kringla Bakeri og Kafe are designed in the Setesdal style, which features grassy roofs and logs that create a rustic appearance. The Bergen style is evident in the Fjording Shop with its gabled windows and wood construction. Akershus Castle reflects the architectural distinctiveness of Oslo (Restaurant Akershus is named for a 14th century fortress that stands in Oslo Harbor), while the entrance to Frozen Ever After (formerly Maelstrom) is modeled in the tradition of the Alesund style, which features white stucco and stone trim.

3. China

The Hall of Prayer for Good Harvest in the China pavilion contains a great many details of important significance. The 12 outer columns represent the 12 months of the year and the

12-year cycle of the Chinese calendar. Four columns in the interior signify the four seasons, which in turn support a beam that represents Earth. On top of this is a final, rounded beam, which symbolizes Heaven.

4. Germany

Look for the pickle Christmas tree ornament inside Die Weihnachtsecke (The Christmas Corner) in the Germany pavilion. You can also learn about the legend of the pickle ornament. (Which actually didn't originate in Germany, but that's a tale for another time!)

5. Italy

As you enter the Italy pavilion, you'll pass underneath a detailed recreation of St. Mark's Campanile, located in Venice. Rising high over the surrounding landscape, the tower is certainly tall, but it pales in comparison to the original, which soars 323 feet into the sky. (That's nearly twice as high as Spaceship Earth!)

6. The American Adventure

The American Adventure building needed to be five stories tall in order to accommodate the attractions, galleries, and work areas that would be inside. But traditionally, Colonial buildings were never constructed more than two or three stories high. The Imagineers wanted to maintain that historical accuracy (no detail is ever overlooked), but what could they do? Somehow they needed to make the pavilion look smaller than it actually was.

To solve this dilemma, they turned to a tried-and-true Imagineering technique – forced perspective. In the past, Disney Imagineers had used forced perspective to make buildings look bigger than they actually were. (You can see this technique put to use on Main Street U.S.A., where the second story windows are actually smaller than they typically would be; giving you the impression that they're further away, and thus making the buildings appear taller.) But this time they had to reverse things a bit.

In order to make the American Adventure building look smaller than it actually is, they enlarged the upper story windows proportionally so that the five-story building would look like a three-story building, thus keeping things looking historically accurate to the naked eye.

7. Japan

The Goju-no-to Pagoda is comprised of five stories representing the five elements that, according to Buddhists, produced everything in the world. The first story represents earth, the second water, then fire, wind, and sky. Mounted atop the pagoda is a *sorin*, a spire composed of nine rings each with its own wind chimes, and topped by a water flame, carefully masking a lightning rod.

Originally, the pavilion was going to be home an attraction called "Meet the World," which would have provided an overview of Japanese history through the use of Audio-Animatronics, live action film, and animation. The audience would have been seated in a carousel theater that revolved around four stages, with each stage depicting an historic moment in Japanese history.

8. Morocco

The King of Morocco sent a group of 19 maalems (royal artisans) to create the pavilion's extensive mosaic artwork during its construction. The centerpiece of the Morocco pavilion is a replica of the Koutoubia Minaret prayer tower, originally built as part of a 12th century mosque in Marrakesh. Because of the religious significance of the buildings, the Morocco pavilion remains unlit throughout the entire showing of IllumiNations.

9. France

The picturesque park near the lagoon was inspired by "A Sunday Afternoon on the Island of La Grande Jatte," painted in 1884 by the French artist Georges Seurat. The original painting is on display at the Art Institute of Chicago. Incidentally, the replica of the Eiffel Tower may look big, but it's actually only 1/10 the size of the real thing!

10. The United Kingdom

The Toy Soldier shop in the United Kingdom Pavilion is located inside a replica of Henry VIII's Hampton Court Palace. The nearby garden maze was inspired by the Somerleyton Hall Maze, which was built in 1846.

11. Canada

To create the sensation of height in the Rocky Mountains found in the Canada Pavilion, Imagineers once again employed the use of forced perspective. By using smaller and smaller plantings as they went up the mountainside, the illusion of greater height was achieved.

Ten Things You May Not Know About

Disney's Hollywood Studios

1. Epcot Origins

When Disney's Imagineers began planning EPCOT Center, one of the ideas was for a movie-themed pavilion to be located between the Land and Imagination pavilions. As the ideas flowed, it quickly became apparent that this concept was burgeoning with potential. It was so good in fact, that within a few weeks the idea of a movie pavilion was scratched from Epcot planning, and a third gated park devoted to the magic of Hollywood was on Disney's drawing board.

2. Studio Tours of Years Gone By

The origins of this concept actually go way back to the early years of Disney. Back then, Walt Disney's friends and celebrities would often stop by to see how the cartoons were made. Gradually, the tours became longer and more complex. Walt had even discussed bringing his scale model railroad around for visitors to ride. That studio tour morphed and evolved, and it's considered to be the foundation for Disneyland in California.

3. A Working Studio

It was decided early on that Walt Disney World's studio would not be just an amusement park. It was also to act as a true working film studio. At one time, Guests could take a behind-the-scenes tour at the Magic of Disney Animation and see real animators and other artisans at work. Several animated films were actually made at the new park, notably *Mulan*, *Lilo & Stitch*, and *Brother Bear*.

4. Making Movie Magic

A number of live-action feature films have also been shot at Disney's Hollywood Studios, including: *Passenger 57*, *Oscar*, *Quick Change*, *Ernest Saves Christmas*, *Splash Too*, and *Instinct*.

5. MGM

Originally, the park was called Disney-MGM Studios. Why? Because although the Disney Studio name is synonymous with wonderful animated features, its live-action film base wasn't as rich. To fill that void, contracts were signed with MGM Studios so that many of their films could be part of the new park. Unfortunately, those contracts included many restrictions, and over time a lengthy legal battle ensued over studio rights. The fact that Disney itself was amassing an ever-growing catalog of live-action films and franchises (lessening the need to rely on external film properties) resulted in the severing of the relationship, with Disney dropping "MGM" from the park's name and changing it to Disney's Hollywood Studios.

6. Surprises at Every Turn

Not everything at the Disney's Hollywood Studios is what it appears to be. Remember, movies are filled with special effects and clever tricks to make the unbelievable believable. That same movie magic was brought to the new park. Lampposts, wells, and other innocuous objects may actually conceal a clever surprise (for instance, if a sign warns you not to pull on a rope, try pulling it anyway!).

7. A Nod to a Hollywood Classic

The main gate at Disney's Hollywood Studios is a reproduction of the facade of the Pan-Pacific Auditorium in Los Angeles built in 1935. Considered to be one of America's finest examples of Streamline Moderne architecture, the green and white facade featured four stylized towers and flagpoles meant to represent upswept aircraft fins above the entrance. While the original was destroyed by fire in 1989, this faithful recreation continues to pay tribute to the structure that symbolized classic Hollywood.

8. The Stars Shine

Disney's Hollywood Studios has played host to a virtual who's-who of Hollywood and the entertainment industry throughout the years. Among the performers who've appeared at the studios are: Charlton Heston, Dustin Hoffman, Bette Midler, Warren Beatty, Sylvester Stallone, Tom Hanks, Liza Minnelli, Billy Joel, Christie Brinkley, Michael J. Fox, Samuel L. Jackson, Lou Gossett Jr., Drew Carey, Oprah Winfrey, and Susan Lucci.

9. A Galaxy Far, Far Away

In addition, Echo Lake and Star Tours have hosted special Star Wars weekends over the years, with many of the Star Wars cast and crew (including Mark Hamill, Carrie Fisher, and George Lucas) making guest appearances.

10. New Lands and New Stories

The park is currently going through one of the most extensive renovations ever undertaken at Walt Disney World, with two entirely new lands themed after *Star Wars* and *Toy Story* set to open in the next few years.

Ten Things You May Not Know About
Disney's Animal Kingdom

1. That's A Lot of Critters!

There are approximately 300 species of wildlife at the Animal Kingdom, with a population of more than 1,700 animals. Additionally, you'll find over 4 million trees, plants, shrubs, ground-covers, vines, epiphytes and grasses from every continent on Earth (except Antarctica), representing more than 4,000 species.

2. And They Need Lots of Room!

The Animal Kingdom covers more than 500 acres, making it by far the largest of the Disney theme parks. It's so big in fact that the Magic Kingdom, Epcot, and Disney's Hollywood Studios could all fit inside with room to spare.

3. Animal Kingdom Origins

The original concept for Disney's Animal Kingdom was presented on January 1990 by Imagineering Concept Designer Joe Rohde (who would later head up the project's worldwide research efforts). Disney's Wild Animal Kingdom Project (as it was then called) was going to be home to hundreds and hundreds of animals – some familiar, some exotic. But unlike a traditional zoo, the animals would live in large open areas specially designed to recreate their natural habitats. And unlike other drive-through safari parks, Guests would be able to wander through lush trails and authentically detailed villages to fully experience the wonder and beauty of the natural world. One of the highlights of the new park would be the opportunity for Guests to experience an actual safari through the exotic African savanna.

4. Traveling the World

A team of seven Imagineers (led by executive designer Joe Rohde), traveled all around the world doing research for the conceptualization and construction of the Animal Kingdom. The team logged an amazing 500,000 miles during their travels.

5. Grab a Shovel!

During construction of the Animal Kingdom, 4.4 million cubic yards of dirt were delivered by 60 dump trucks that continuously arrived on the construction site every day for two full years.

6. Where Are the Balloons?

You may notice that there are no plastic straws, balloon, or cup lids to be found at the Animal Kingdom. This is to protect the animals from potential choking hazards.

7. Conservation

The Disney Wildlife Conservation Fund has devoted more than $6 million to conservation efforts, lending their support to some 230 projects across the globe.

8. No, It's Not a Zoo!

When the Animal Kingdom plan was in its early stages, the term "nahtazu" was dreamed up to go along with the new park. Pronounced "not a zoo," the word punningly helped to emphasize that the park was more than the typical animal displays found in your everyday city zoo. As of January 2006, "nahtazu" started to be phased out of the Animal Kingdom's promotional material.

9. Did That Plant Just Move...?

As you wander about Disney's Animal Kingdom, you notice an unusual plant that seems to be moving. Are your eyes playing tricks on you? No that's DiVine, the stealthy "plant" that appears mysteriously throughout the Animal Kingdom, and she is brought to life by performance artist Priscilla Bright.

10. An Appropriate Opening Day

Disney's Animal Kingdom opened on April 22, 1998, a date that was particularly significant. Why? April 22 is (not-so-coincidentally) Earth Day!

Ten Things You May Not Know About
Pandora

1. Bringing the World of Avatar to Life

More than five years in the making since the 2011 reveal of the concept, Pandora forced Imagineering to dig deep into its bag of technical tricks. Joe Rohde, the man responsible for spearheading Animal Kingdom's design from its inception, once again stepped up to the plate to translate the cinematic brilliance of *Avatar* into a physical experience worthy of the Disney name. While elaborate steel structures and advanced Audio-Animatronics would help bring Pandora to life, Rohde built the true foundation of Pandora on that oldest of Disney principles: storytelling. As such, the immersive experiences – the sights, sounds, and sensations – are what bring this mythical land to life.

2. Setting the Stage

The time-line in which the new land's backstory takes place is a generation after the warring conflict between the indigenous Na'vi and the Resources Development Administration (RDA) that sought to exploit Pandora for its Unobtanium, as seen in the film.

3. It's All In the Story

According to the backstory, the Na'vi and humans have achieved peace, and Alpha Centauri Expeditions (ACE) – a fictional tourism company – has partnered with the Na'vi to present Pandora as a new destination for ecotourism and scientific research. Here in the Valley of

Mo'ara, an entire generation has passed since the conflicts of Avatar. This land now speaks to the importance of working in harmony – humans and Na'vi – to build a better future together and preserve nature's many gifts.

4. Floating Mountains

The visual focal point of Pandora is the Valley of Mo'ara and its jaw-dropping floating mountain ranges. The 156-foot tall mountains employ forced perspective to appear larger than they physically are.

5. But How Do They Float?

The mountains are indeed impressive and are a true engineering masterpiece. The immense steel foundations for the floating mountains alone required a year to complete. The mountains are held aloft by steel beams concealed by rockwork and vinery.

6. Research Trips

For the look of the mountains, Imagineers went to Zhangjiajie National Forest Park to study the jagged pillar peaks of the Wulingyuan region for inspiration, and also studied the foliage in Hawaii.

7. Beastly Kingdom

A mythical land of creatures was always part of the original plans for the Animal Kingdom, first known as Beastly Kingdom. (You can see an image of a dragon in the Animal Kingdom logo representing this planned-for but never-built land). Conceptual plans for the land began with Guests confronting a most consequential fork in the road. One way would have led to Dragon Tower, a headliner roller coaster that would heavily inspire the eventual design for Expedition Everest. The opposite choice sent Guests to The Quest for the Unicorn, an attraction housed within an elaborate hedge maze. Participants would have had to band together to find five golden idols scattered throughout the flowered labyrinth, ultimately revealing the unicorn's hiding spot. Beastly Kingdom never came to pass of course, and instead the torch was passed to Pandora and its uplifting message of man's harmony with nature.

8. Ecological Preservation

Disney takes its role in ecological stewardship very seriously and has pledged to back up this talk with action. Pandora offers a unique mobile adventure – available through the My Disney Experience app – that promises to both entertain and educate Guests. "Connect to Protect" assigns numerous missions to solve while traversing the Valley of Mo'ara, at the same time offering rewards that go far beyond mere pride in a job well done. Completed tasks trigger an automatic $10 donation to the Disney Conservation Fund, even allowing the donor to designate a particular animal group as beneficiary.

9. "Kaltxi!"

Pandora may stand apart from the typical Disney park experience, but it does share one very important similarity – amazing Cast Members. And, in the Animal Kingdom's newest land, they play a most vital role, starting with the first "hello." Don't be surprised to hear "Kaltxi!," the traditional Na'vi greeting, ring out as you enter Pandora. Additional surprises wait around each turn, as Cast Members have learned several Na'vi phrases for use in Guest interactions.

10. Everyone Has a Story

It goes far beyond language, as each Cast Member has also internalized a specific backstory for his or her character. Strike up some conversations and see for yourself how diverse these origin stories can be. Some describe themselves as employees of Alpha Centauri Expeditions, others are studious researchers, while more than a few simply fell in love with Pandora's beauty and decided to make this their new home.

Ten Things You May Not Know About
Africa

1. Creating a Village

Africa was home to one of the early headliner attractions at the Animal Kingdom, Kilimanjaro Safaris. In keeping with the safari theme, Imagineers created an entire African village named Harambe. In keeping with the idea of creating a self-contained, all-inclusive African environment, the Imagineers spent countless hours in the planning and construction of Harambe. The authentic buildings, exotic landscaping and attention to detail immerse Guests in the safari experience long before they arrive at Kilimanjaro Safaris.

2. Harambe

Harambe is actually a Swahili word meaning "coming together."

3. No More Gold

The fictional village of Harambe is based on the ancient Kenyan town of Lamu. Harambe (so the legend goes) was once a hub for the gold and ivory trade but is now a bustling tourist village.

4. Authentic Details

Zulu craftsman from Kwazulu-Natal, South Africa, were brought in to make the thatched roofs located on the buildings throughout Africa.

5. That's a Big Tree!

The largest tree replanted in Disney's Animal Kingdom (weighing in at 90 tons!) can be found right here in Africa.

6. Simba On the Move

The Festival of the Lion King was relocated to Africa from its original home in Camp Minnie Mickey to make way for Pandora – The World of Avatar.

7. Kilimanjaro

Kilimanjaro Safaris is named for Mount Kilimanjaro, which holds the notable distinction of being the tallest mountain in Africa. Admittedly though, it comes nowhere close to the lofty heights of Mount Everest, whose Disney namesake, Expedition Everest, can be found a short walk away in Asia.

8. Yep, Mickey's Here Too!

As you approach Tamu Tamu Refreshments, look on the ground to the right to find some pebbles around a manhole cover forming a Hidden Mickey.

9. But It Seems Like Such a Long Journey...

The Gorilla Falls Exploration Trail is about 3/8 of a mile, and while that may seem like a long way (especially on a hot day), it's actually less than a third of the length of the promenade that circles World Showcase in Epcot.

10. The Baobab Trees

Have you ever wondered if those upside-down trees in Harambe and Kilimanjaro Safaris are real? Well, they're actually not, but they are inspired by the real-life Baobab tree. As you probably suspected, the trees aren't actually upside-down, they just like that way due to their unique arrangement of branches. They may look dried out and barren, but the real Baobab tree can store up to 32,000 gallons of water in its trunk!

Ten Things You May Not Know About
Asia

1. A New Land...

Asia was the first land to be added to Disney's Animal Kingdom, and started welcoming Guests in 1999 (a year after the park opened).

2. ...and a New Show

Pandora may be the most recent land to open at the Animal Kingdom, but Asia is home to the park's newest nighttime show, The Rivers of Light. The new show consists of five acts and features eleven barges, with a new seating area that can accommodate 5,000 Guests.

3. The Villages of Asia

Asia actually consists of two villages; Anandapur and Serka Zong. Serka Zong is home to Expedition Everest and nestled in the foothills of the Himalayas.

4. Anandapur

The mythical land called Anandapur was created to provide a mysterious setting and backdrop for Asia. Legend has it that this mythical village was established in 1544 as a royal hunting reserve. The reserve has long since been transformed into a conservation area, but the mystery surrounding the village survives to this day.

5. But What Does It Mean?

"Anandapur" means "City of Delights" (or "place of delights") in Sanskrit, one of the oldest Indo-European languages in the world.

6. Art is Everywhere

You'll find portraits of Anandapur's Royal Family throughout the area, as well as several detailed murals that were created by more than 120 artists working for more than five months.

7. Architectural Inspirations

The buildings here are inspired by the architecture of India Nepal, Thailand and Indonesia.

8. Mickey in Asia

When you enter the village of Anandapur from the bridge to Africa, look for the "Welcome to Anandapur" sign. One of the carved flowers in the border is missing some petals, forming a Hidden Mickey.

9. Hiding Amongst the Gibbons

Also, look for the white-cheeked gibbon habitat on your right as you enter Asia. On the island there is a gourd hanging from a tree with a hole forming a Hidden Mickey. You'll have to squint. It's fairly obscure!

10. Building a Bridge

Asia welcomed the Animal Kingdom's first roller coaster, Expedition Everest, on April 7, 2006. As part of the expansion, a new bridge was constructed connecting Asia directly with Dinoland U.S.A.

Ten Things You May Not Know About
Dinoland U.S.A.

1. That's No Bridge...

As you enter Dinoland, U.S.A. from Discovery Island, you'll pass under the Olden Gate Bridge, which is actually a replica of a 40-foot tall Brachiosaurus skeleton.

2. Prehistoric Plants

The cycad collection along the Cretaceous Trail is the third-largest such collection in North America. Though cycads are a minor part of the plant kingdom today, during the Jurassic period they were extremely common.

3. Digging for Fossils

The dinosaur bones scattered throughout the Boneyard are casts taken from actual fossils found in such places as Utah's Dinosaur National Park.

4. What's That Sign?

Even the Boneyard sign itself is an archaeological find. It's a replica of a Stegosaurus's shoulder blade. That's one big shoulder!

5. Dinosaurs and...France?

Primeval Whirl was built by Reverchon, a French company specializing in smaller roller coasters and other thrill rides. The company was founded in 1927 by Gaston Reverchon, a young coach builder who created his own workshop in the suburbs of Paris.

6. DinoSue

Keep an eye out for DinoSue! She is an exact replica of Sue, a Tyrannosaurus rex that was discovered in South Dakota and whose skeleton is on display at the Field Museum of Natural History in Chicago. But even though "she" is named Sue, no one is sure if Sue was a boy or a girl. It turns out that she wasn't named Sue because she was a girl; she was named Sue in honor of her discoverer, Susan Hendrickson. It's only for convenience sake that Sue is referred to as a "she."

7. Building a Dinosaur

Scientists working at the Animal Kingdom worked with scientists at the Field Museum to clean and study the bones that were removed from the dig site. The bones were carefully transported and meticulously cleaned at the workshops in Chicago and Florida. (Florida scientists worked mostly on bones from Sue's tail.) When the bones were all cleaned and prepared, they were reconstructed and put on display in the Field Museum, where they can be seen today. Once Sue's skeleton was completed, several casts were made of each bone, allowing scientists to create three full-size replicas. One skeleton was sent to Disney's Animal Kingdom where it stands today, and the other two travel around the country.

8. Diggs County

The fictional backstory for Dinoland U.S.A. takes place in Diggs County, a sleepy little community for much of its early years. Back in the 1930s, it was said that the town was made up of nothing more than a gas station and fishing lodge. For almost two decades, anglers came to Diggs County looking for the biggest catch of their lives in the deep cool waters of nearby Discovery River or, at least, the story of the one that got away. Things were quiet for many years as Diggs County maintained a tranquil existence. But that was to change forever in 1947. The legend goes that this was the year a monstrous Tyrannosaurus rex skeleton was discovered, putting in motion a series of events that would transform this small corner of the world into a paleontologist's delight. By 1950, the dig site had grown considerably, and the Dino Institute was founded, taking up residence in the one-time fishing lodge to act as a workplace and a makeshift museum.

9. Fossil Finding in the Boneyard

The site of the original Tyrannosaurus rex discovery, dubbed the Boneyard, immediately became a hotbed for paleontologists. As it turned out, the T. rex was only the tip of the iceberg. In the days following the discovery, paleontologists and amateur fossil hunters turned the once-quiet area into a flurry of exploration and excavation. Since that time, the operation has taken on a more formal approach with the graduate students and professors of the Dino Institute taking the lead. Today, the maze of scaffolding, chutes, tools, and fossils seems like a hopeless jumble. As fossils were discovered, the excavation set-up had to accommodate the needs of the specimens, including chutes to transport them to the ground level and proper clearances to make sure none of the outlying bones were damaged. Among the various remains discovered in the Boneyard were a Hadrosaur, Triceratops, Sauropod, Theropod, and even a mammoth. Even now, case notes accompany many of the active dig areas, and they offer information about the species as well as observations about the potential life and death of the creature. Hand-scribbled notes from professors to students, and vice versa, can be found throughout the quarry.

10. Chester and Hester's Backstory

Back in the 1930s, when Diggs County was known only for its clear water and abundance of fish, the only other establishment was a gas station named after its owners, Chester and Hester. The small service station did a slow business until the discovery of the first fossils in 1947. Sensing an opportunity, Chester and Hester's turned into a roadside attraction for Dinoland's newfound tourist population. The first changes were made to the inside of the station, where dinosaurs of every shape, size, and material began filling the crevices throughout the establishment. Comics and movie posters depicting dinosaurs lined the walls, toy dinos were hung from the rafters, and a plethora of other dinosaur figures created the roadside attraction that came to be known as Chester and Hester's Dinosaur Treasures. Even though the automotive services of Chester and Hester's were no longer needed, many items were left about as reminders of the slower days before the dinosaurs came to Diggs County. The remnants of its service station days haven't gone to waste; today you'll find license plates turned into hedge planters, gas pump nozzles crafted into dinosaur art, and old tires transformed into planters. As Diggs County grew and thrived, so did the roadside dreams of Chester and Hester's, and a fair sprang up overnight in the Dinosaur Treasures parking lot. Complete with carnival games, snack trucks, and wild rides, the fair was named Chester and Hester's Dino-Rama.

Attractions

Ten Things You May Not Know About
The Monorail

1. The Monorail's Origins

The forerunner of the modern monorail system was tested in Germany in the 1950s, and two of Walt Disney's Imagineers introduced him to a monorail system created by the Alweg Corporation in Germany in 1958. This system allowed Walt to see the potential for bringing a monorail to his park. Rather than a traditional suspended-track design, the Alweg Corporation had created a unique straddle-beam track with a slender design that would allow the beam to blend perfectly with the surrounding landscape in Walt's world of "tomorrow." Walt also loved the combination of electric propulsion and rubber wheels on the beam that produced an almost noiseless operation – preventing distraction for Guests either on the attraction or who were passing nearby. Walt Disney asked Alweg to design the original 8/10-mile beamway around Tomorrowland and enlisted a young designer, Bob Gurr, to design the train. Through the efforts of this collaborative effort, the Disneyland Alweg Monorail System opened on June 14, 1959 as the first, new-style daily operating monorail system in the Western Hemisphere.

2. Colors!

Each of the 12 monorail trains in Walt Disney World is identified by its own colored stripe: Peach, Teal, Red, Coral, Orange, Gold, Yellow, Lime, Green, Blue, Silver, and Black.

3. That's a Long Way Around...

The entire monorail system contains 14.7 miles of track. Over half that is devoted to the Epcot loop alone.

4. I Mean REALLY Long

Just how long is that? Well, since the monorail began operation, it's made the equivalent of more than 17 trips to the Moon!

5. Up Up and Away

At its highest point, the monorail track is 65 feet above the ground. Coincidentally, that's the same height as the highest section of Space Mountain. (The track we mean, not the building; that's nearly three times higher!)

6. The Monorail Trains

Each monorail train is 203 feet long. If you were to string all of the monorails end to end, they would stretch out to more than seven and a half football fields!

7. Don't Forget the Beams!

Each beam is 110 feet long, 26 inches wide, and weighs an astonishing 55 tons!

8. The Wheels on the Monorail Go Round and Round...

While the Tomorrowland Transit Authority PeopleMover uses a series of powerful magnets to propel the trains forward, the monorail uses tires as you might expect. But just how many? Well, there are 12 load bearing tires, 52 steering/guide tires, and 60 nylon safety wheels per monorail. That's 124 all together!

9. All Aboard!

Each monorail can accommodate up to 360 Guests, which breaks down to 60 people per car. That's on a busy day of course. Speaking of busy, roughly 50 million Guests travel on the monorail each year. That's more than two-and-a-half times the entire population of Florida!

10. Up to Speed

The monorail reaches a maximum speed of 40 mph during normal operations. That's just as fast as the drop in Splash Mountain, though the monorail is much drier, of course.

Ten Things You May Not Know About
The Walt Disney World Railroad

1. Carolwood

It's well known that Walt had a great love of steam engines and railroads. In fact, he loved them so much that he had a working miniature steam engine railroad in his backyard. Walt named it the Carolwood Pacific Railroad, and he delighted in taking his family and friends out for journeys around his property. So when work began on Disneyland in California, it was no surprise that plans included the building of a railroad track that would transport Guests around the park.

2. Finding the Locomotives...

In 1968, a group headed by Roger E. Broggie traveled to Mexico to look at possible steam engines for the Walt Disney World Railroad. They ended up purchasing five locomotives, all of which were made between 1916 and 1928. However, it was later determined that one of the five steam engines was unfit for use, and that's why there are only four today.

3. ...And Then Buying Them

And how much did those trains cost? $32,000. For comparison, that's roughly the same as the cost of two tickets on the Golden Eagle Trans-Siberian train that takes you on a luxurious two week trip from Moscow to Vladivostok. And keep in mind we said tickets, not the cost of the train itself!

4. The Trains of the Walt Disney World Railroad

There are three main distinctions between the four steam engines used at the Magic Kingdom: name, number, and color. The Walter E. Disney is Steam Engine #1 and is red. The Lilly Belle is Steam Engine #2, and it's mostly green. The Roger E. Broggie is Steam Engine #3, and it's primarily green, with a touch of red. Lastly, the Roy O. Disney is Steam Engine #4, and it's primarily red with a bit of green. The Roy O. Disney is the oldest of the locomotives, having been built in 1916. The youngest locomotive is the Lilly Belle, which was built in 1928.

5. Fill 'Er Up!

Each train can hold up to 1,837 gallons of water. That might seem like a lot, but each train needs to replenish its water supply every three or four trips around the park via the water tower by the Fantasyland Station.

6. Car Capacity

Each passenger car is 40 feet in length, each containing 15 benches. Each train can accommodate up to 75 passengers.

7. A Year in the Life of the Railroad

But just how many people ride the railroad each year? 10,000? 100,000? How about 1.5 million! That sure saves a lot of foot steps!

8. Backstage

As the Walt Disney World Railroad circles around the rear of the Magic Kingdom, it actually comes within 100 yards of the backstage staging area for the park's nightly fireworks show. Now you know why railroad transportation is suspended during the show.

9. The Twins

The "Walter E. Disney" and "Roger E. Broggie" trains are often referred to as "the twins," because they were actually built simultaneously by United Railways in 1925. They even sport sequential serial numbers: 58444 and 58445.

10. Three is the Magic Number

The maximum number of trains that can be in operation at the same time is three. Walt Disney World's safety regulations prohibit the operation of all four locomotives together due to the length of the track. That's just as well; since the "Lilly Belle" is currently out of general service, save for its appearance in the morning as it brings a cast of Disney characters into Main Street Station to welcome Guests to the Magic Kingdom.

Ten Things You May Not Know About
Jungle Cruise

1. Creating a Jungle...in Florida
The lush jungle foliage was designed by landscape architect Bill Evans, who carefully selected a variety of plants that would be hardy enough to withstand the hot Florida climate (and more surprisingly, its relatively cool winters), while maintaining the look and feel of a tropical equatorial jungle.

2. All Aboard!
There are 16 boats in all, each named for an Imagineer that worked on the original attraction: Amazon Annie, Bomokandi Bertha, Congo Connie, Ganges Gertie, Irrawaddy Irma, Kwango Kate, Mongala Millie, Nile Nelly, Orinoco Ida, Rutshuru Ruby, Sankuru Sadie, Senegal Sal, Ucyali Lolly, Volta Val, Wamba Wanda, and Zambesi Zelda.

3. They're Corny, But You Know You Love Them
Here are some of the jokes you might hear on your journey:

"Here in the rain forest it sometimes rains 365 days per year...some years it even rains every day."

"And look at all the elephants out here today! If you want to take pictures go ahead – all the elephants have their trunks on."

"Over there is Schweitzer Falls, named after the famous Dr. Albert [pause] Falls."

"There's old Trader Sam, head salesman of the area. Business has been shrinking lately, so this week only, Sam's offering a two-for-one special: two of his, for one of yours!"

4. Hidden Tributes...

As you approach the Jungle Cruise, check out the planter boxes that contain the large trees. You'll see that they're tagged "Evans Exotic Plant Exporters," a tribute to landscape designer Bill Evans. You'll also find an animal cage in the queue area with a tag bearing the name of Wathel Rogers. He was a key designer of the mechanisms that bring the Jungle Cruise animals to life. Additionally, look for the crate labeled "crocodile-resistant pants," which are labeled as Goff-brand. This is a nod to famed Disney Imagineer Harper Goff. Goff served as art director for the 1954 Disney live-action film, *20,000 Leagues Under the Sea* starring Kirk Douglas and James Mason, and contributed many early sketches for what would become known as Disneyland (Main Street, U.S.A. in particular).

5. ...And Hidden Jokes

The queuing area is filled with visual jokes and puns. Look for the Jungle Navigation Co. Ltd. Employee of the Month board near the boarding area. One of the names is E. L. O'Fevre. (Say the name a few times fast to discover one thing you don't want to find on your cruise!) A chalkboard on the exit path for the Jungle Cruise lists several Skippers who have apparently gone missing, including "Ilene Dover"/"Ann Fellen." You'll also spot the Crew Mess Lunch Menu, which lists a number of exotic dishes such as "Fricassee of Giant Stag Beetle," "Barbecued Three-Toed Skink," "Consommé of River Basin Slug," and "Filet of Rock Python." However, the menu notes that all these items taste like chicken. Fortunately, on Fridays, chicken is actually served!

6. Listen Close

When traveling through the Jungle Cruise queue, be sure to listen carefully, as you may just hear Albert Awol, the "Voice of the Jungle," who provides humorous news updates.

7. Amazing Animatronics...Or Are They?

Walt Disney had originally wanted real animals in the Jungle Cruise attraction, but quickly realized that they might often be asleep or hiding away where Guests wouldn't be able to see them. So instead, the decision was made to use Animatronic animals instead. Or so it seems. In actual fact, none of the animals or figures you see on the Cruise are Animatronics, because the sophisticated mechanisms used in these life-like creations wouldn't be able to withstand the weather elements. The animals on the Jungle Cruise are more simplistic machines that use a combination of pneumatics and air pressure.

8. Around the World

The first part of your journey takes you to the Amazon River. You'll next enter the Congo River, where you'll come across war canoes on a nearby beach, with the sound of tribal drums playing in the background. Next up is the Nile River, where you'll see lots of wild animals, including elephants, giraffes, and zebras, as well as vultures in the distance. The Jungle Cruise boats also pass by a pack of lions and an unfortunate zebra that they've "welcomed" to dinner (don't worry, the scene is family-friendly and the Skippers usually joke that the animals are "playing"). The Mekong River leads you through a series of ancient ruins, including a crumbling temple that houses a tiger, pythons, and spiders, all of which are more than enough to scare away adventurous explorers from plundering the treasure that is hidden inside the temple. Keep your eyes peeled as you exit and you just may spot a Hidden Mickey in the crumbling remains of one of the walls!

9. Where's the Other Half?

One of the scenes in the Jungle Cruise features the remains of a crashed plane, buried deep in the jungle undergrowth. The other half of the plane used to be seen in the *Casablanca* scene in the now-closed Great Movie Ride in Disney's Hollywood Studios.

10. The Jingle Cruise

In recent years, the Christmas season has brought on a whimsical change to the Jungle Cruise, transforming it into the festive Jingle Cruise. According to the Jingle Cruise storyline, the Skippers have grown homesick for the holidays, so they decided to add some holiday cheer to the Jungle Cruise with decorations and new holiday-inspired jokes. The Jingle Cruise overlay includes numerous fun details: The Jungle Cruise boats are renamed with a holiday theme, including "Icicle Irma," "Fruitcake Zelda," "Reindeer Ruby," and "Mistletoe Mille." Tropical wreaths with reindeer heads are scattered throughout the queue. A can of ethanol is changed to eggnog...but I would encourage you not to drink it! Be sure to look for the chalkboard with "New Year's Resolutions for Skippers" near the exit, which include a "75% passenger return rate." Hmm...let's hope they keep that one!

Ten Things You May Not Know About
Walt Disney's Enchanted Tiki Room

1. A Tiny Bird Leads to Big Dreams

The story of Walt Disney's Enchanted Tiki Room actually begins with a shopping trip taken by Walt Disney decades prior to the Magic Kingdom's opening. The accounts of this trip vary greatly depending upon the particular source; some say that Walt took his famous shopping excursion while in Europe, while others swear that Walt was visiting unique gift shops while strolling through the streets of New Orleans. Regardless of the actual location, the end result was that Walt purchased a mechanical toy bird. While this may sound like a non-monumental occurrence, Walt became fascinated with this toy, which could move its head, wings, and other features in an almost magical manner. Being amazed by this mechanical bird, Walt handed it off to his creative team (who would eventually become known as Imagineers) to examine, dissect, and improve upon it.

2. Dining with Confucius

Walt eventually came up with an idea for a Chinese restaurant that would be located on Main Street, U.S.A. in Disneyland, which would have been unlike any other restaurant on the planet. What would make this restaurant unique was that it would include a character based on Confucius, the famous Chinese philosopher. Walt envisioned a dining experience where Confucius would interact with Guests, answer questions, and generally provide words of wisdom to fascinated observers while they enjoyed their meals. But Walt did not want a human actor portraying Confucius, he wanted a lifelike mechanical representation to do it! To say that this idea was revolutionary would be a vast understatement.

3. Enter the Tiki Birds...

Walt eventually revisited his plans for a restaurant concept. However, instead of a Chinese philosopher entertaining Guests, Walt decided to tap into the Polynesian craze that permeated American culture during the late 1950s. But after researching the logistics of having a dinner show, including the average amount of time spent by diners eating, Walt decided to scrap the restaurant concept in favor of a standalone show starring a wide variety of Audio-Animatronic birds, flowers, and Tiki statues.

4. ...And a Catchy Tune

Walt assigned his Imagineers the massive project of creating hundreds of Audio-Animatronic birds, flowers, and Tikis of all shapes and sizes that would move and sway in conjunction with a variety of musical tunes. He also tasked the famous Sherman Brothers with creating a catchy tune for the attraction, which resulted in the famous theme song "The Tiki Tiki Tiki Room." Walt and his team also developed the storyline of the attraction, which centered around four hilarious birds, each of a different nationality: José (Mexico), Michael (Ireland), Pierre (France), and Fritz (Germany).

5. New Hosts

The show made its Disneyland debut on June 23, 1963, with the Magic Kingdom version (known as Tropical Serenade) being an opening day attraction. Although the Tropical Serenade continued to entertain Guests over the coming decades, its popularity significantly declined in the 1990s. Because of this, the show closed on September 1, 1997 for an extensive renovation. When the attraction reopened in April of 1998, it had both a new name, The Enchanted Tiki Room: Under New Management, and two new hosts, Zazu, the hornbill from *The Lion King*, and Iago, the villainous parrot from *Aladdin*.

6. A Classic Returns

Unfortunately, The Enchanted Tiki Room: Under New Management never developed into the fan favorite that Disney hoped it would. Many Guests felt that the classic touch of Walt that was represented in both the original Disneyland and Walt Disney World versions had been lost. Under New Management did enjoy a thirteen-year run in the Magic Kingdom until a small fire occurred in the attraction show building in 2011. The damage caused by the fire and the resulting water damage from the sprinkler system gave Disney the opportunity to once again make a change, and the attraction reverted back to a version of the show closer to the Disneyland original, with the name being changed to Walt Disney's Enchanted Tiki Room.

7. The Grinch in the Tiki Room?

Fritz is voiced by famed voice actor Thurl Ravenscroft, whose numerous credits include Tony the Tiger from Kellogg's Frosted Flakes commercials, and as the singer of "You're a Mean One, Mr. Grinch" from the famous television special "Dr. Seuss' How the Grinch Stole Christmas."

8. Bird Calls

Purvis Pullen provided the birdcalls and whistles for the attraction. Pullen also provided "bird voices" in the classic Disney animated films *Snow White and the Seven Dwarfs* and *Sleeping Beauty*.

9. A Puff of Air

Air valves are utilized to create movements in the Tiki Room Audio-Animatronics, as opposed to oil-filled valves that are used in many other attractions.

10. WED Enterprises

When Walt Disney's Enchanted Tiki Room first opened in Disneyland, it was actually owned by Walt's private company WED Enterprises, not by The Walt Disney Company (known then as Walt Disney Productions).

Ten Things You May Not Know About
Pirates of the Caribbean

1. No Pirates in Florida?

It may surprise you to learn that Pirates of the Caribbean was never intended to be a part of Walt Disney World. When the original Pirates of the Caribbean attraction was unveiled at Disneyland in 1967, it was an instant hit. But the Imagineers didn't include it in the master plans for the Magic Kingdom in Florida. The reasoning was that because of Florida's proximity to the Caribbean Sea (where real pirates used to roam), the notion of an attraction based on local history wouldn't be interesting. (Also, and perhaps more realistically, the company's resources were already stretched so thin that, in the words of Walt Disney World's Operating Chief Dick Nunis, "To add that one attraction, we would have had to eliminate five others.") However, when the Magic Kingdom opened, Guests immediately noticed its absence and, to the surprise of the Cast Members and park managers, began demanding a similar Pirates of the Caribbean attraction be brought to Florida. Walt Disney management acquiesced, and less than six months later publicly announced that Pirates would be coming to Walt Disney World in time for Christmas 1973.

2. Walt's Final Attraction

Walt himself directed the development and production of the original Pirates of the Caribbean at Disneyland. It was the last park attraction he supervised before his untimely passing.

3. A Walking Tour?

Interestingly, the initial concept for the attraction bears little resemblance to the final version. Pirates was originally going to be a walk-through "Rogues' Gallery" wax museum, depicting various scenes in pirate history. However, the success of the Audio-Animatronic Abraham Lincoln and "it's a small world" at the 1964-65 World's Fair led Walt to re-imagine Pirates as a boat ride featuring animated pirates.

4. A True Collaboration of Disney Legends

In addition to Walt Disney, no less than eleven Disney Legends had a hand in the creation of Pirates of the Caribbean. These included Marc Davis, whose sketches of various pirates in action were translated into the instantly recognizable sight gags that would become the centerpieces of the show. Claude Coats developed the three dimensional scenes and employed the well-used trick of forced perspective to create extra height and depth in the limited spaces. Blaine Gibson created sculptures of the pirates based on Marc's sketches, which became the prototypes for the sophisticated Audio-Animatronic figures that would inhabit Claude's scenes. Marc Davis' wife, Alice, costumed the buccaneers, and had the foresight to create duplicate wardrobes for each character. This helped the original attraction immediately get back on its feet when a small fire – in the burning town scene, of all places – caused significant damage to several costumes. Alice's secondary costumes, whose existence was previously unknown to Disney management at the time, saved the day and the attraction was back up and running in short order.

5. Creating "Fire"

Yale Gracey, a name well known to fans of the Haunted Mansion, played a key part in the development of the special effects for Pirates. The Burning Town scene, as the name implies, needed to appear to be on fire, but in a safe manner. Yale's technique is a simple as it is elegant. To produce the illusion of flickering flames, Yale used fans to blow strips of Mylar (a strong polyester film) up in the air, lit with orange-filtered lights.

6. Torre Del Sol

Pirates of the Caribbean eventually found its way to the Caribbean Plaza in Adventureland, an elegant recreation of a British- and Spanish-influenced seaport in the West Indies, circa 17th and 18th centuries. The buildings all have traditional terra cotta roof tiles, and there are plenty of merchants and vendors in the Caribbean town. Attention is drawn first to a prominent clock tower, Torre Del Sol ("tower of the sun"), which looms over the entrance to Pirates. Next to the tower is a replica of a pirate ship mast and sail, with the attraction namesake written in red across the black sail.

7. The Eternal Game of Chess

As the queue winds around a particular dungeon cell, two deceased pirates can be seen sitting at a table, playing chess. They have been reduced to skeletons, but they steadfastly continue their game. As it turns out, the game is at a stalemate, with both pirates in eternal check and neither able to win. It seems that rather than admit defeat, they both remained locked in this epic duel, and eventually succumbed to their deaths. Marc Davis is responsible for this sight gag, which interestingly enough has another twist to the story. During a refurbishment of Pirates in 1999, the chessboard was temporarily removed from the dungeon to be cleaned. It wasn't until they went to set it back up that the Imagineers realized they had no idea of the precise layout of the chess pieces on the board. It was critical that it be restored to its original condition, since this is what caused the two buccaneers to be in a perpetual state of check. It was Marc Davis himself who came to the rescue. Imagineers referred to his original concept sketches, and there on the back was the specific layout of the chess pieces that would cause eternal frustration for the two pirates. (Well, that's the official tale anyway...for more on this tidbit of trivia, be sure to read our "Myths of Disney" list!)

8. Jack Sparrow

The attraction was updated in 2006 to incorporate characters from the Disney hit movie *Pirates of the Caribbean: The Curse of the Black Pearl* (including Captain Barbossa and Jack Sparrow). It reopened on July 7, 2006 to coincide with the premiere of the much-anticipated sequel, *Pirates of the Caribbean: Dead Man's Chest*. Apart from the additions of some new Audio-Animatronic figures (some of the best that Disney has produced), one of the more notable changes was a refurbishment of the large pirate ship. It now more closely resembles the Black Pearl and is under the command of Captain Barbossa.

9. Who's Chasing Who?

The addition of Jack Sparrow and his tyrannical counterparts from the Pirates of the Caribbean film franchise to the attraction wasn't the only update in its history. Another significant update occurred in 1999, most notable for its controversial changes to the show. Chief among these were the chase scenes that depicted randy pirates pursuing women throughout the town. These scenes were either removed, or in one case altered to show a woman brandishing a rolling pin, chasing a pirate instead. These changes prompted show writer X Atencio to wryly quip, "it's Pirates of the Caribbean, not Boy Scouts of the Caribbean!" In 2006, another notable change took place that was overshadowed by the arrival of Jack Sparrow; the removal of the barker bird. This pint-sized Audio-Animatronic parrot used to greet Guests outside the entrance, and he even had his own song, warbling "yo ho, yo ho, a parrot's life for me." He may be gone from Adventureland but he's not forgotten; you can find him at his new home at the World of Disney store at Disney Springs.

10. George

A tour of the Pirates of the Caribbean would not be complete without a brief discussion of...George.

Who's George?

No, he isn't a pirate featured in any of the elaborate scenes, nor was he one of the Imagineers who brought the attraction to life. Rather, George is the ghost that haunts Pirates. Born mostly from superstition, legend has it that a welder named George lost his life during the building's construction. Public records show that there were no deaths during the construction, but, as the expression goes, why let the facts get in the way of a good story. Cast Members can be a superstitious lot, and those who work at Pirates are exhorted to begin each day with a hearty "good morning, George" and offer a "good night, George" at closing. Failure to do so will apparently lead to mechanical breakdowns of various lengths. Yo ho indeed!

Ten Things You May Not Know About
Splash Mountain

1. Into the Briar Patch

The final plunge into the briar patch is 52 1/2 feet high and is pitched at an angle of 45°. During the drop you hit a top speed of 40 mph (that's faster than Space Mountain!).

2. A Long Journey

The flume itself is 2600 feet long, nearly half a mile!

3. Coloring a Mountain

The coloring of Splash Mountain (originally based on that of the film *Song of the South* as designed by Claude Coats and Mary Blair), was shifted to a stronger magenta shade to tie in with Big Thunder Mountain Railroad.

4. So Where Does All That Water Go?

The runoff from Splash Mountain leads to the Rivers of America, further integrating Splash Mountain into Frontierland.

5. The Tree Stump

The twisted tree stump you see at the top of Splash Mountain isn't just any old stump, that's Br'er Rabbit's hilltop hideout!

6. Thurl Ravenscroft

If the singing bullfrog sounds familiar, you may have just visited Liberty Square. That's

Thurl Ravenscroft, who also sings "Grim Grinning Ghosts" in the graveyard scene at the Haunted Mansion.

7. Zip-A-Dee-Doo-Dah

The original name for the attraction (as it was being developed for Disneyland) was Zip-A-Dee-River Run. It was renamed Splash Mountain not because of the final plummet, but in recognition of the Disney film *Splash* starring Daryl Hannah, which was a current hit in the theaters. Coincidentally, Hannah's co-star Tom Hanks sang the famous theme song "Zip-A-Dee-Doo-Dah" during the film!

8. The Riverboat

The riverboat in the final scene (named the Zip-A-Dee Lady), is 36 feet wide and 22 feet high, and features 12 Audio-Animatronic figures singing "Zip-A-Dee-Doo-Dah."

9. Lots of Critters!

You'll find a total of 68 Audio-Animatronic figures in Splash Mountain. As impressive a figure as that is, it pales in comparison to the 105 figures found in the Disneyland version (many of those figures had been relocated from the America Sings attraction in Tomorrowland, which closed in April 1988).

10. Wait, Who Was That?

When you enter the Zip-A-Dee-Doo-Dah scene after the final plunge, look at the sky background to the right of the riverboat. If you look carefully, you'll see a cloud shaped like Mickey lying on his back.

Ten Things You May Not Know About
Big Thunder Mountain Railroad

1. Thunder Mesa

When the Magic Kingdom opened on October 1, 1971, Frontierland looked much different than it does today. The areas where the headliner attractions Splash Mountain and Big Thunder Mountain Railroad now reside were vacant lots. Disney's plan was to fill this space with a monumental project known as Thunder Mesa, the brainchild of Imagineer Marc Davis. Plans for Thunder Mesa called for two headliner attractions, along with numerous smaller offerings set inside, around, and on top of a massive mountainous landscape. However, as costs for the Magic Kingdom soared, Disney executives decided to place Thunder Mesa on the "Phase One" project list, which were experiences that would be completed within the first five years after the Magic Kingdom opened. As such, the large crop of land dedicated for Thunder Mesa lay empty in Frontierland when the Magic Kingdom first opened.

2. Resurrecting a Dream

With construction of Pirates of the Caribbean complete, and Marc Davis' hopes of salvaging some portion of Thunder Mesa quickly dwindling, another legendary Disney Imagineer, Tony Baxter, started developing plans for a mine train style attraction in Disneyland that was almost identical to the runaway railroad concept for Thunder Mesa. The Baxter project was green-lit, including a version of the attraction for Walt Disney World.

3. A Mountain Comes to Florida

Groundbreaking for Big Thunder Mountain Railroad in Walt Disney World took place in 1979 while the Disneyland version was still under construction. The massive project took 22 months to complete and cost approximately $17 million dollars.

4. Now That's BIG!

The main spire of Big Thunder Mountain stands 197 feet tall, towering over the landscape of Frontierland on a 2.5-acre plot of land.

5. Naming the Trains

The coaster track itself is 2,780 feet long (longer than the Disneyland version), with six trains named U.B. Bold, U.R. Darling, U.R. Courageous, I.M. Brave, I.B. Hearty, and I.M. Fearless.

6. Racing Through the Mountains

The maximum speed of the attraction is approximately 30 miles per hour. As temperatures rise throughout the day and the grease on the tracks melts, the speed of the attraction gradually increases.

7. A New Backstory...

In 2012, Disney announced an entirely new backstory for Big Thunder Mountain: *"Barnabas T. Bullion is the founder and president of the Big Thunder Mining Company. The longtime mining magnate comes from a very powerful East Coast family and considers gold to be his very birthright by virtue of his oddly appropriate name; in fact, he considers the ultimate gold strike to be his destiny. And that is why he is having so much trouble with Big Thunder Mountain. According to superstitious locals, Big Thunder Mountain is very protective of the gold it holds within, and the unfortunate soul who attempts to mine its riches is destined to fail. And so far that prophecy is coming to pass. The mine has been plagued by mysterious forces and natural disasters ever since. And yet the Big Thunder Mountain Co. is still in operation. In fact, Bullion is discovering new veins of gold and digging new shafts every day, offering a closer look at the Big Thunder mining operation than ever before. But a word to the wise from anyone attempting to visit the mountain: watch out for the runaway trains."*

8. ...And a New Queue

A substantial renovation in 2013 brought with it a completely reimagined interior queue. The building is constructed of worn and aged timbers reflecting the frontier time period, with rafters housing a variety of barrels, crates, and boxes. The periodic flickering of lamps helps to emphasize the idea that this is a working mine operation.

9. Hidden Secrets

There are lots of fun finds in the indoor portion of the queue, including a sign informing Guests and workers that there will be "No Drinking, Fighting or Whistling. No Kidding!"

10. Southwest Realism

Look around the ghost town to find an ore crusher, a mining flume, and an ore-hauling wagon. These are no mere props; they're actual artifacts that were acquired on trips by Disney Imagineers through the American Southwest at a cost of more than $300,000.

Ten Things You May Not Know About
Tom Sawyer Island

1. Mark Twain and the "Mighty Mississip"

Tom Sawyer Island may have made its Florida debut in 1973, but its roots go back much further. Walt Disney was always fascinated with Americana. This passion was sparked at a young age during his years living in Marceline, Missouri. Coincidentally, just 90 miles east of Marceline is the town of Hannibal, the childhood stomping grounds of another American legend, Samuel Langhorne Clemens, better known by his pen name, Mark Twain. Twain is responsible for creating two of the most beloved characters in American Literature, Tom Sawyer and Huckleberry Finn. Their adventures along the "Mighty Mississip" have excited the imaginations of readers since the novels were first published in 1876 and 1885 respectively. When you think "Americana," Mark Twain and his thrilling adventures of Tom and Huck certainly come to mind. As Disneyland undertook its first expansion, Tom Sawyer Island was added to the mix, officially opening on June 16, 1956.

2. Jumpin' On a Raft

The four rafts that transport Guests to the island each have a normal capacity of around 60 people. The four rafts are all named after characters from the novels: "Tom Sawyer," "Huck Finn," "Becky Thatcher," and "Injun Joe."

3. Where's the Track?

Contrary to popular belief (and unlike many other boat attractions at Walt Disney World), the rafts don't run along an underwater track. That's right. The human captains are actually piloting the rafts back and forth along the Rivers of America without the aid of a motorized track!

4. Gettin' Around

Helping to guide you on your journey around Tom Sawyer Island are large Explorer Maps. You'll find the maps posted up at various spots around the island, including one just as you exit the landing area. At first glance, you may see some names or places you recognize from the books. This is certainly no coincidence. In order to make you feel as if you've been transported into Tom and Huck's world, the Imagineers have named each and every area after a character or location from the Twain novels.

5. Harper's Mill

Harper's Mill can be seen from the mainland and boasts a working water wheel. The name "Harper" refers to another character from the Twain novels, Joe Harper. Joe was one of Tom's best friends, and the Mill was named after his father. Many people assume that Harper's Mill is named after Joe, but a sign in front of the Mill (written by Tom) states that the Mill was named after his friend Joe Harper's "Old Man." Disney buffs may also know that the Mill's name also pays homage to legendary Imagineer Harper Goff, who created many pieces of concept art for Disneyland.

6. Singing Gears

As soon as you step foot inside the Mill, you'll notice the gigantic wooden gears all moving in unison. If you listen closely, you may also notice that the gears appear to be "singing." This is not your imagination! The gears really are creaking along to the tune of the 1910 classic "Down by the Old Mill Stream," which was written by Tell Taylor in 1908.

7. The Old Mill

In addition, the 1937 Academy Award winning Disney cartoon *The Old Mill* is honored inside Harper's Mill. The cartoon (from the Walt Disney Silly Symphonies series) depicts a violent thunderstorm ravaging a rundown, decrepit old mill, while the inhabitants of the mill (various country critters such as mice, birds, bats, and owls) try to hunker down and make it through the storm. Next time you're inside Harper's Mill, try to look and listen for the different animals.

8. Whitewashing Mischief

On the path between Harper's Mill and Aunt Polly's, you'll find a wooden fence that has been partially whitewashed. On the part that has yet to be completed, you'll see the names of Tom, Huck, and Becky. If you're not familiar with the story behind the fence, here's a quick refresher. Aunt Polly gave Tom the task of whitewashing a fence (a punishment which came as a result of Tom skipping school the day before and getting his clothes filthy in a minor scuffle). But what young boy wants to waste his entire Saturday whitewashing a fence? Tom didn't want to paint a fence all day; he wanted to go exploring. So after beginning the chore, Tom uses his smarts to trick a few kids into thinking that whitewashing is fun. Long story short, he ends up recruiting several of the kids into continuing the task in his absence.

9. Paint Brushes

At one time, you could search the island for a paint brush of your own! Each day, six brushes were hidden in various spots around the island. If you happened to discover one of the hidden brushes, you could return it to a Cast Member and be rewarded with a prize (usually a special FastPass for you and your entire family that could be used at Splash Mountain or Big Thunder Mountain Railroad). Sadly, the paintbrush scavenger hunt ended several years back.

10. Fort Langhorn

Superstition Bridge takes you to Fort Langhorn, which gets its name from Mark Twain... aka Samuel Langhorne Clemens (though the Fort's spelling of Langhorne omits the "e" at the end). When Tom Sawyer Island first opened in 1973, the Fort was known as "Fort Sam Clemens." In 1996, the name was changed to "Fort Langhorn" to coincide with the release of the Disney movie *Tom and Huck*. The movie had a Fort Langhorn in it, so the name was changed to keep the island's theme up to date.

Ten Things You May Not Know About
Liberty Square Riverboat

1. One of Walt's Earliest Attraction Concepts

Even though it wasn't an opening day attraction, the origins of the riverboat go all the way back to Disneyland...and beyond. When Walt Disney first conceived of a park to be built near the Disney Studio in Burbank, California, one of the attractions he had in mind was a "Mississippi Steamboat." The idea of a family park soon grew into Disneyland, complete with the working riverboat, which was renamed the Mark Twain Steamboat.

2. The Mark Twain Steamboat

The Mark Twain Steamboat was unique at the time, as it was the first fully-functional paddlewheel boat built in fifty years. In order to faithfully recreate all the details of the famed ships of yore, the WED designers studied the steam powered ships of the past so that they could accurately replicate the functionality and ornamentation of the old-style riverboats. The ship itself was assembled in two locations. The decks were manufactured at the nearby Disney Studios at Burbank, while the 105-foot hull was constructed in San Pedro, California. The project was supervised by former navy admiral Joe Fowler, and on his insistence a dry-dock was built alongside the site of what was to become the Rivers of America. The project briefly ran into some financial trouble, but was saved when Walt Disney himself stepped in to fund the rest of the construction out of his own pocket. The Mark Twain Steamboat set off on her maiden voyage on July 13, 1955, four days before the park officially opened. The occasion was a private party celebrating the 30th wedding anniversary of Walt and Lillian.

3. Magic Kingdom Riverboats

When plans were being put together for what would become Walt Disney World, the inclusion of a riverboat was only natural, right down to the idea of recreating the Rivers of America in Florida. When the Magic Kingdom opened, the riverboat was named the Admiral Joe Fowler in honor of the man who oversaw the construction of the original attraction. A second boat, the Richard F. Irvine (named for Richard Irvine, a senior figure at Walt Disney Imagineering who was instrumental in the design of many Disneyland attractions) set sail on May 20, 1973. Though largely identical, the two ships differed in one major respect; the Admiral Joe Fowler had two smokestacks, while the Richard F. Irvine only had one. The two ships continued to ply the waters of the Rivers of America until the fall of 1980, when the Admiral Joe Fowler was retired, having been damaged when being moved into drydock. The riverboat was subsequently dismantled, although its bell was reused on the Walt Disney World Railroad, specifically the No. 4 train known as the Roy O. Disney.

4. A New Name

In 1996, the Richard F. Irvine was renamed the Liberty Belle to better tie in to nearby Liberty Square. In addition to the new name, the boat itself was heavily renovated. A new superstructure was manufactured from aluminum and vinyl, with the hull, boiler, and engines being the only original components to be retained during the refurbishment. (In 1999, one of the ferries that transports Guests across Seven Seas Lagoon was renamed the Richard F. Irvine in his honor.)

5. The Burning Cabin

Prior to 2005, Guests could see a burning cabin at this location on the river. Early versions of the scene included an unlucky setter who had fallen victim to an Indian attack. Over time the narration was changed to alter the fate of the unfortunate settler, instead telling Guests that the frontiersman was simply sleeping, having drunk too much moonshine. In 2005 the entire scene was removed, due to corrosion in the pipes that created the fire. Today Guests simply see a deserted cabin.

6. Tell City

You may spot some crates on the banks of Frontierland marked "Tell City Tool Co." Tell City is an actual town on the Mississippi River in Indiana, and was one of the country's first "planned cities." During Tell City's early years, the steamship was the only mode of transportation available.

7. Hidden Secrets

Another crate on the Frontierland side of the river says "71," a reference to the year that Walt Disney World opened.

8. Crockett's Sidekick

See if you can spot another crate marked "Russel's Falls." This is a reference to Davy Crockett's sidekick, George E. Russel.

9. Did You See That Dog?

If you look closely, you might be able to spot an Audio-Animatronic dog near Beaker Joe's, who turns his head as a fish jumps by.

10. Sam Clemens

During your journey, you'll hear several clever sayings spoken by Sam Clemens. Though these nuggets of wisdom weren't actually penned by Mark Twain, they humorously reflect the famous writer's unique sense of humor. Some of the phrases include:

"It seems to me that when I was younger, I could remember everything whether it happened or not. But as I grow older I seem to remember only the things that never happened at all,"

"Believe me when I tell you, truth is the most valuable thing we have, so I make sure I only use it with economy," and

"My feeling is these days there's a lot less frontier and a lot more civilization than is truly necessarily."

Ten Things You May Not Know About
Haunted Mansion

1. Ghoulish Beginnings

The Haunted Mansion was originally intended to reside on Disneyland's Main Street U.S.A., at the end of a small, winding path that would lead Guests to a mysterious old house on a hill. The location was soon changed to the New Orleans Square section of the park, and the original design was retooled to make it fit in with the early 19th-century plantation style of the haunted house's new home. Though Imagineers envisioned the house as being run-down and decrepit, Walt Disney disagreed. He wanted the exterior of the mansion to look nice, to match the pristine look of the park. He didn't want people to think that Disneyland wasn't taking care of its attractions. Walt famously said, "We'll take care of the outside, and let the ghosts take care of the inside."

2. Oh, We Didn't Mean to Frighten You...

Imagineer Rolly Crump once told a story about how they knew they were on the right track with the effects they were developing when they received a call from personnel saying the janitors requested that they leave the lights on at night, due to how creeped out they were getting every time they went into the building to clean. The Imagineers agreed, but they decided to have a little fun, and they outfitted the building with motion sensors. When the janitors tripped the sensors, the lights turned off, and all of the ghostly effects came to life! The next morning, the Imagineers came in to find all the effects still running and a janitor's broom in the middle of the floor. The janitors said they wouldn't be back to clean anytime soon.

3. The Raven

It was originally thought that a black cat would be our guide through the mansion, popping up at various times to show us the way. After that, a raven was proposed to do the job. This idea actually got so far along in the process that the raven does show up in the mansion in a few scenes. Be on the lookout for him in the conservatory (near the skeleton trying to claw his way out of the coffin), perched on Madame Leota's chair, and toward the end of the ride, just before you meet up with the Hitchhiking Ghosts. Eventually it was decided that an unseen presence would work best for the mansion's theme, and X Atencio created the memorable character of the Ghost Host to help us find our way.

4. Breathing New, um, "Life" Into the Mansion

In 2007, the Walt Disney World version closed for a major refurbishment. Aside from general maintenance and upkeep for the attraction, several new effects were added to liven up the place (so to speak). The gigantic spiders and their webs were replaced with an M.C. Escher-esque staircase, where ghostly footsteps could be seen going up, down, sideways, and upside down. The creepy wallpaper that looked as if it was staring at you can now be seen blinking its eyes as you pass. The attic received the most drastic changes in order to flesh out the ghostly Bride's backstory (whose name is now known to be Constance Hatchaway) and to show that she is truly a "black widow."

5. The Hatbox Ghost

The holy grail for most Mansion fans is the Hatbox Ghost, a long-lost citizen of the Disneyland attraction. This effect, intended to be located in the attic, had the Hatbox Ghost's head disappear from his shoulders and reappear in the hatbox he was holding. This illusion proved to not work as well as the Imagineers wanted, and it was quietly removed shortly after opening day.

6. The Stretching Room

But back to the attraction of today...and the answer to a long-standing question. Is the stretching room stretching up or down? Well, it depends on the park. In Disneyland, you're actually going down, the reason being that Guests need to make their way down and through a tunnel leading underneath the railroad and to the attraction building. When building the Walt Disney World version, there was no need for such shuttling about since there weren't' any space constrictions on the new park. However, the effect was so well known that it was decided to replicate it in the Florida version. However, since Guests didn't have to travel down, in the Florida version the ceiling is actually rising.

7. From the Jungle to the Mansion

The frightened caretaker, who greets you speechlessly just before you enter the graveyard, looks very familiar, doesn't he? He should! His face also appears on the Jungle Cruise as the low man on the totem pole getting chased by the rhino. I guess he didn't get the point... in the end.

8. Chess Pieces?

A popular story is that you can see various chess pieces scattered amongst the architecture on the roof. And indeed, there are some features that resemble the classic bishop and rook from your standard chess board. The only missing piece is the knight. Why? Because it's night INSIDE the mansion! (Get it?) It's a cute story, but in reality that's all it is...a story. The resemblance of the architectural ornaments to chess pieces was purely happenstance.

9. Servant's Quarters

On your way out of the mansion, there's a door to your right marked "Servant's Quarters." Despite rarely being seen by Guests, this short hallway contains a large key rack, with hooks labeling every room within the Mansion. Unfortunately, the keys that once hung from these hooks were lost over the years. Or perhaps someone - or something - borrowed them to get around the mansion.

10. Someone's In There...

When standing in line for the attraction at night, look at the windows. You can sometimes see a ghostly image going from room to room, holding a flickering candle.

Ten Things You May Not Know About
The Hall of Presidents

1. Ambitious Origins

The Hall of Presidents was originally conceived as part of the Main Street expansion in Disneyland that was announced in 1958, which was to feature two new areas including Edison Square and Liberty Street. The original concept of The Hall of Presidents was a presentation that told the story of the American Revolution. The centerpiece of the show was to be a theater presentation introducing all the United States presidents depicted as life-size Audio-Animatronic figures. Unfortunately, the available technology was simply not good enough to bring this vision to life.

2. Mr. Lincoln

Instead, Imagineers concentrated on building a prototype figure, that of Abraham Lincoln, for the 1964-1965 New York World's Fair. The fair presented an opportunity to showcase this new technology, and the attraction entitled Great Moments with Mr. Lincoln proved to be a resounding success. The attraction was recreated in 1965 for Disneyland, and with renewed confidence the Hall of Presidents was put back on the drawing board as one of the opening day Magic Kingdom attractions.

3. Historical Inspiration

The building itself is an homage to the Federal-style civic buildings of Philadelphia.

4. A Presidential Museum

Inside the lobby, you'll find a large display of presidential memorabilia – from the likes of Gerald Ford, Franklin Roosevelt, Herbert Hoover, and George Washington. You'll also find a display case filled with dresses and personal objects worn by several first ladies, including Edith Roosevelt (wife of Theodore Roosevelt), Elizabeth Monroe, and Nancy Reagan.

5. The Presidential Roll Call

The show takes place in a beautifully appointed sit-down theater, and it begins with a stirring movie presentation tracing the growth of the United States from the Revolutionary War to the present day. When the film is over, the screen lifts to reveal the presidents of the United States past and present, represented by amazingly realistic Audio-Animatronic figures. As the narrator announces each president in turn, a spotlight falls on each one. They acknowledge the audience with a dignified nod. (Half of the fun is in trying to quickly locate the president being introduced.) After the presidential role call is completed, the focus is on the current president as he delivers a patriotic speech. When he's finished, the attention shifts to Abraham Lincoln at center stage for a few final words of inspiration.

6. The President Speaks

The first serving president to deliver a speech was Bill Clinton. Subsequent presidents would also record their own speeches for the show after each election.

7. Did You See That?

The Hall of Presidents is renowned for its attention to detail, from the period clothes of each president to the amazing likenesses. Take special note of all the presidents who aren't speaking. You might catch them fidgeting in their chairs or shuffling their feet!

8. A New Script, a New Speech...

In 1993, the Hall of Presidents received a major upgrade when Columbia history professor Eric Foner persuaded Disney that an update was needed. The new show featured a completely rewritten script, a new narration by poet Maya Angelou, and a new Audio-Animatronic figure of then-President Bill Clinton.

9. ...And a New Narration

In July of 2001, the narration was rerecorded by actor J.D. Hall, who had originally provided the voice of Frederick Douglass in Great Moments with Mr. Lincoln. Another major renovation followed in 2009, with a new narration read by Morgan Freeman and the addition of a new speaking part by George Washington. The voice of Washington was provided by actor David Morse, who also portrayed the first President in the HBO mini-series "John Adams."

10. Two If By Sea

On the Haunted Mansion side of the Hall of Presidents, you'll find a second story window with two lanterns. That's a reference to the Henry Wadsworth Longfellow poem "Paul Revere's Ride," which includes the famous stanza, *"He said to his friend, 'If the British march / By land or sea from the town to-night, / Hang a lantern aloft in the belfry-arch / Of the North-Church-tower, as a signal-light, / One if by land, and two if by sea; / And I on the opposite shore will be, / Ready to ride and spread the alarm / Through every Middlesex village and farm, / For the country-folk to be up and to arm."*

Ten Things You May Not Know About
Peter Pan's Flight

1. Bringing Pixie Dust to Florida

Peter Pan's Flight was one of the opening day attractions in Disneyland (and one of the few to still exist!). Years later, the Magic Kingdom version opened on October 3rd, 1971, two days after the opening of the park itself. This version saw the inclusion of Peter Pan (no, he wasn't in the Disneyland version), as well as the addition of several new scenes, such as the Mermaid Lagoon and the Lost Boys camp. Captain Hook's 48-foot pirate ship was now fully realized and served as the setting for Captain Hook and Peter Pan's climactic duel. The Florida version introduced the moving walkway load/unload system, similar to the setup at the Haunted Mansion. This allowed the queue to move faster, thus increasing the attraction's capacity.

2. The Flight to Neverland

The experience of flying above London is one you'll never forget, and the attraction is home to one of the simplest special effects in the Magic Kingdom; that of the cars driving through the streets below. The cars are actually small black-lit dots that are painted on chains (similar to bicycle chains). Simple? Yes. Unforgettable? Definitely. (Pay close attention and you can even hear the faint honking of the horns!) There are no fancy holograms here, no complex CGI effects, just some classic Disney cleverness and cinematic know-how. Continuing on, you'll soar past the full Moon, where you can see the silhouettes of Peter Pan, Wendy, Michael, and John. Everyone has their favorite scene, whether it's the Mermaid Lagoon, the thump-thump-thump of the Indian drumbeats, the final battle between Peter Pan and Captain Hook, or the humorous encounter between Hook and his nemesis, the crocodile. And who among us hasn't peered into the volcano, trying to see how far down you can see!

3. Wendy's Outfit

The Wendy figure on the gangplank is the only character wearing real clothing on the whole ride. The rest are made of plastic.

4. What Could Have Been

In August 1954, while working on the attraction, Imagineers wanted to build other scenes that never made it to the ride. These included a giant rainbow, scenes from Crocodile Creek, and Hangman's Tree. They also wanted the boats to be flying in a clockwise-direction at Skull Rock, which is the opposite of how it turned out.

5. No Building? No Problem!

During the construction of the Disneyland version of the attraction, Imagineer Bob Mattey and others built a testing track right inside the Disney Studio. This had to be done since the buildings for the dark rides in Fantasyland had not been finished yet.

6. Down to the Wire

Imagineers Claude Coats and Ken Anderson worked tirelessly in an attempt to complete Peter Pan's Flight in time for the opening day of Disneyland. Under the pressure of such an extreme time restriction, they painted straight onto the wood inside the building, making up a lot of it as they went along. Normally, a great amount of time and consideration would go into the planning and painting of an attraction. Templates would be made, and care would be taken to perfectly match the concept drawings done in pre-production. Unfortunately, the time constraints imposed by the tight deadline didn't allow for such preplanning. The results, however, were still spectacular!

7. Building Blocks

If you look closely at the toy blocks in the Darling nursery at the beginning of the attraction, you'll notice they spell out "Disney." Others spell out "P Pan."

8. Hey, Those Aren't Real Clouds...

The clouds above London are actually plastic bags.

9. Flying High...Well, Not Really

Despite the use of forced perspective to make you seem farther up than you already are, the highest you'll ever be is a mere 17 feet.

10. Landmarks You Didn't Notice

Famous scenes in the attraction include the Thames River, St. Paul's Cathedral, the Tower Bridge, and the Parliament Building.

Ten Things You May Not Know About
"it's a small world"

1. Getting the Name Right

We'll start this list off by talking about the name, as it's a name that's commonly misspelled. The proper spelling of the name is with all lower case letters, and the name is always enclosed in quotation marks. Why is that? It was a stylistic decision to convey the notion that you are on an innocent, care-free voyage around the world, joined by children from all nations coming together to sing in harmony.

2. That Famous Song

Speaking of singing, the famous song was of course written by the Sherman Brothers. But that wasn't the original plan for the soundtrack. Walt Disney's first concept was for all of the children to be singing their respective national anthems, but he soon realized that his would create a cacophony of sound that would be hard to decipher. So instead, he asked the Sherman Brother to come up with a simple song that could be sung in a round, and that's how they came up with the song that we know and love today. By the way, if you're referring to the song itself, that indeed is spelled with capital letters as you would expect.

3. Ooh La La

The song can actually be heard in five different languages throughout your voyage, and if you pay attention, you can hear the French dolls add an "ooh-la-la" after each chorus.

4. it's a small world...world....world...world...

Incidentally, the word "world" is used 14 times through the course of song.

5. Mary Blair and Alice Davis

The colorful designs seen throughout the attraction are the work of famed Disney artist Mary Blair, who also designed the mural in the Contemporary's Grand Concourse and created concept art for films such as *Alice in Wonderland*, But while her unmistakable style can be seen in every scene, she didn't actually design the dolls themselves, as most people believe. That was the work of Disney Legend Alice Davis, who created the designs for ever outfit for every doll in the attraction. Though certainly inspired by Mary Blair's work, the dolls were a pure Alice Davis creation.

6. The Happiest Cruise That Ever Sailed Around the World

The attraction takes you through seven different rooms. The first room takes you to Europe, where you'll find the children of Sweden, France, England, Scotland, Ireland, Holland, Germany, Spain, Italy, and Switzerland. You then travel into the second room, which starts in the Middle East and then sails over to Asia for stops in China, Russia, India, and Japan. You then make your way into the third room, which takes you on a journey to the continent of Africa, starting with Egypt. The fourth room begins in chilly Antarctica, and then quickly whisks you over to South America before finishing up in North America with a stop in Mexico. The adventure continues as you head into the fifth room, which starts in Hawaii for a trip through the Pacific Islands. (Incidentally, this is the only room in which the song isn't sung). The room then concludes with a visit to Australia. The sixth room is the Grand Finale, and it includes singing and dancing children from most of the nations that have been represented in the previous five rooms. The seventh and final room wraps up the attraction with goodbye greetings, which are written in many different languages.

7. Water Water Everywhere

The waterway that you sail upon is known as the Seven Seaways, and contains more than 500,000 gallons of water in its 1,085-foot-long canal.

8. The Original Name

When originally conceived for the 1964-65 New York World's Fair, the attraction's original name was "Children of the World."

9. Disney Characters

The attraction contains 289 Animatronic dolls, but unlike the Disneyland version, there are no Disney characters in the Magic Kingdom version of the attraction. Or are there? In the final scene, you'll find a carousel filled with children each holding a memento from their respective country. At one point, one of those items was a marionette, and on closer inspection you could see that it was none other than Pinocchio! The figure seems to come and go over time, but if you're lucky, you just might be able to spot that one elusive Disney character in Florida's "it's a small world"!

10. Don Quixote

If you look closely, you'll also see a stylized version of Don Quixote aboard his horse Rocinante, accompanied by his faithful sidekick Sancho Panza. These were the characters from "The Ingenious Nobleman Sir Quixote of La Mancha," written by Miguel de Cervantes and published in 1615.

Ten Things You May Not Know About
Mickey's PhilharMagic

1. A Rich History

The building that is currently home to Mickey's PhilharMagic has seen many changes over the years. It was originally known as the Fantasyland Theater and hosted an opening day attraction, the Mickey Mouse Revue, which was an Audio-Animatronic stage show, featuring Mickey Mouse and friends performing a selection of favorite Disney tunes, including "Zip-a-Dee-Doo-Dah" and "Who's Afraid of the Big Bad Wolf?" The attraction closed to make way for the 3D film Magic Journeys (itself relocated from Epcot to make way for Captain EO). In 1993, Magic Journeys was closed in preparation for the opening of the live-action puppet show, Legend of the Lion King. The show ran until 2003, when it was closed, and the theater was renamed the PhilharMagic Concert Hall, in preparation for Mickey's PhilharMagic, which made its debut on October 3, 2003.

2. Mickey in 3D

Mickey's PhilharMagic represents the first time that Mickey Mouse has been rendered in Computer Generated Imagery (CGI). Glen Keane, the original animator of Ariel in *The Little Mermaid*, returned to re-render Ariel in 3D especially for Mickey's PhilharMagic. Animator

Nik Ranieri, who brought Lumière to life for Disney's animated classic *Beauty and the Beast*, returned to render him in 3D.

3. A Magical Partnership

Mickey's PhilharMagic was the result of an unprecedented joint effort between the Disney Imagineers and Walt Disney Feature Animation. What they came up with is a unique show that combines 3D visuals, a memorable soundtrack, interactive scents, and special effects to create a breathtaking presentation that's overflowing with Disney magic.

4. Hidden Mickeys? Of Course!

Look on the wall in the queuing area to find several white Hidden Mickeys among the specks surrounding the musical instruments. You can also spot a Hidden Mickey in the French horn on the right-hand pillar of the movie screen.

5. Another Hidden Secret

There's another hidden gem to be found here, but it's not a Hidden Mickey! During the Flying Carpet sequence, keep an eye out for the cloud that forms the shape of Genie's lamp.

6. Cinematic Tributes

The long mural that spans the lobby is a composite of imagery from animated classic Disney movies with musical themes: *Toot, Whistle, Plunk & Boom*, *Melody Time*, and *Fantasia*.

7. A Giant Canvas

When it opened, Mickey's PhilharMagic featured the world's largest seamless projection screen. The opening screen measures 40' by 16', and it gradually expands to an impressive 150' long and 24' high.

8. Astounding Sound

The theater features a state-of-the-art audio system, with nine full behind-the-screen audio clusters. Note the use of "traveling sound," particularly before the curtain rises, as Goofy's footsteps move throughout the theater as he runs from back to front.

9. Cyber Lights

The interactive lighting system features a series of "cyber lights," which are precisely synchronized with the on-screen action via computerization. Smoke effects enable Guests to see the lights, casting shadow elements that are integrated into the performance.

10. Donald's Voice

The voice of Donald Duck was created from classic performances of the past by Clarence "Ducky" Nash, the original voice of Donald. Tony Anselmo, the current voice of Donald, added a few lines that were not recorded by Ducky in the past, such as the humming of the melody to "Be Our Guest."

Ten Things You May Not Know About
Under the Sea — Journey of the Little Mermaid

1. From California to Florida

Under the Sea – Journey of the Little Mermaid resides in Eric's castle, surrounded by water-falls and geysers. The attraction first appeared in Disney California Adventure on June 3, 2011, as part of the grand Disney California Adventure renovation (which would go on to include the new Cars Land as well as other attractions). It proved so popular that Disney decided to include it as part of the New Fantasyland.

2. Gadgets and Gizmos Aplenty

As part of Disney's growing "interactive queues" initiative, you'll find plenty of magic the moment you get in line, namely Scuttle's Scavenger Hunt. This fun-filled diversion features the comical and famous seagull, Scuttle. As you walk along the queue, little animated blue crabs scamper around collecting whatchamacallits, gizmos, and gadgets. These crabs show up in multiple locations. If they're carrying something that doesn't belong with the items in that area, just point at them and they'll take that item away and come back with something else. Soon you'll come upon an Audio-Animatronic version of Scuttle, who proceeds to show off all the crabs and all the items you've chosen for them to collect.

3. Under the Sea

Once you board your clamshell, you'll proceed backward down a small ramp. Using innovative technology, you'll see a projection of water rising on the back of the clam in front of you, as well as on the ceiling, complete with sound effects. This is an astounding effect that makes you feel as if you're actually going underwater!

4. That Unforgettable Hair

A new skin technology had to be used for all the Audio-Animatronics to make them look more realistic, since they show more skin than usual. Look closely and you'll even see Ariel's hair moving as if it were being pushed by the ocean currents. (Remember, you're under the sea!)

5. Animatronic Magic

There are about 200 Audio-Animatronics throughout the attraction, including 128 alone in the "Under the Sea" room.

6. Now THAT'S Scary!

Ursula is one of the largest Audio-Animatronic figures ever created by the Imagineers, standing a staggering 7 ½-feet tall and 12-feet wide! She has special flexibility built into her torso so that she can move freely.

7. Miniature Models

Imagineers created a one-quarter-inch scale model, and then a one-inch version, in order to better work out how the attraction would run and what the Guest experience would be like.

8. 20,000 Leagues Under the Sea

Near the entrance to the attraction, look around the rocks near the shipwreck. You'll find a few carvings that are in the shape of the *20,000 Leagues Under the Sea* submarine. This is a tribute to the area's original attraction located in that section of the park.

9. And Those Portholes...

Look for other tributes to that attraction throughout the queue. For example, there are some portholes that may look familiar!

10. A Dress for a Princess

If you look closely, you'll see that Ariel's wedding dress is embroidered with seahorses and starfish.

Ten Things You May Not Know About
Cinderella Castle

1. Smile!

Both Cinderella Castle in Florida and Sleeping Beauty Castle in Disneyland face south. Why is that? Walt Disney specified that the castles be oriented in that fashion so that amateur photographers would have ideal shooting conditions when taking their souvenir photos.

2. Coloring the Castle

Though the Castle has gone through some temporary make-overs throughout the years, the structure of the Castle has remained largely intact. But that hasn't been the case for the paint color. In 2006 the Castle received a new palette, with the walls and towers becoming a pinkish off-white, and the turrets becoming a darker, royal blue.

3. An Aerial Landmark

In 2001, the Federal Aviation Administration implemented a Temporary Flight Restriction (TFR) over Walt Disney World. The restricted zone was a circle six nautical miles across, and the only planes permitted to fly in that space are WDW Cessna 172 and law enforcement aircraft. (Don't be alarmed if you see a plane flying high overhead though, the TFR zone only extends to 3,000 feet.) In order for pilots to visualize the location of the circle, a suitable landmark was needed to mark the center. What landmark? Why, Cinderella Castle of course! (In case you're curious, Tinker Bell has special permission to take her evening flight from the top of the castle.)

4. The Castle Suite

The Castle Suite is a dream destination for every Walt Disney World Guest, though as of now this privilege is restricted to specially chosen Guests and Cast Members who are occasionally awarded with a night in the Castle. But where is the Suite exactly? If you're looking at the side of the Castle from the Liberty Square bridge, look for a grouping of three tall stained-glass windows; those are the windows to the Castle Suite. If you look closely you may be able to make out the three designs in the windows which are, from left to right, a clock, an invitation, and a smaller castle.

5. Gus and Jacques

If you have eagle eyes, another set of three windows can be seen around the corner toward the rear of the castle, though these are somewhat obscured and harder to make out. From left to right, this set of windows depicts a grander castle, Gus and Jacques holding a key, and the glass slipper.

6. The View from the Suite

You would think that the Suite would offer spectacular views of the Magic Kingdom, but such is not the case. This is largely due to the fact that much of the park maintenance is done at night, and it was felt that that wouldn't make for a very magical view. You can get a blurry glimpse of Fantasyland through the glass slipper on one of the rear windows, but it's a limited view. (That's OK though, there's enough magic in the Suite itself to keep you more than occupied!)

7. A Castle for Tokyo

The Cinderella Castle in Tokyo Disneyland had a walkthrough attraction that operated through 2006. The Cinderella Castle Mystery Tour took Guests on a walking tour through the Gallery, the Ball Room, the Dining Room, the Guest Room, and the Tower. The attraction focused on Disney Villains, and featured a Magic Mirror (even though this was Cinderella's castle and not Snow White's).

8. Coat of Arms

In addition to the Disney family coat of arms that hangs over the entrances to the castle, you can find an additional 40 or so hanging in the restaurant. Each one pays tribute to a key Disney individual, similar to the windows on Main Street U.S.A.

9. Yes, the Castle Has Elevators!

The Castle includes three elevators; one that takes Guests to Cinderella's Royal Table, one that goes to the Suite, and one reserved for Cast Member use only.

10. Just a Reminder...

While the Castle was being constructed, a makeshift banner was hung above the entrance that read "Remember, Opening Oct. 1971." Just in case anyone forgot!

Ten Things You May Not Know About
The Many Adventures of Winnie the Pooh

1. Winnie the Pooh Comes to the Magic Kingdom

On June 5, 1999, the attraction The Many Adventures of Winnie the Pooh was added to Fantasyland where it famously (or infamously, depending on one's point of view!) replaced the much-loved Mr. Toad's Wild Ride. A tribute to the former attraction can be found in the early portion of the ride, where you might be able to spot a picture of Mr. Toad handing the property deed for the space over to Owl.

2. Winnie the Pooh in Critter Country

Disneyland's version of the attraction contains a similar homage to its predecessor. There, the Pooh attraction replaced the Country Bear Jamboree in the park's Critter Country section on September 4, 2000, and the heads of the Max the stag, Buff the buffalo, and Melvyn the moose are mounted on the back of the entrance to the "hunny" scene, following the "heffalumps and woozles" segment. (This tribute, however, is not as obvious to Guests, who must turn around in order to see it.)

3. Pooh's Playful Spot

As a means of allowing younger Guests to further experience the Hundred Acre Wood, "Pooh's Playful Spot," a small playground, opened across from the attraction in 2005. The centerpiece of Pooh's Playful Spot was Mr. Sanders' tree: Piglet's smiling face greeted Guests from the top of the tree while children could explore Pooh's house in the tree's base. The ceiling inside the door featured an image of a submarine; this was the Nautilus and served as a nod to the area's previous attraction, 20,000 Leagues Under the Sea. Pooh's Playful Spot closed in April 2010 to make room for the Fantasyland expansion.

4. A New Interactive Queue

In its place, the attraction received an all-new interactive queue. Here you'll find Eeyore's Gloomy Place, a crawl-through log tent identical to Eeyore's home in the stories. In Rabbit's Garden, you'll find a walk through over-sized collection of "cabege" and "kerits" leading to a brightly-colored play area, featuring a tug-of-war, vegetable-shaped drums, and a delightful garden where young ones can make piles of pumpkins and carrots. Even pesky gophers pop up out of the ground. Sunflowers can be spun to make the sound of tinkling bells, and a variety of games will keep younger Guests from getting impatient if the line is long. A feature enjoyed by Guests of all ages is the honey wall, where honey appears to be oozing from a beehive. Run your finger over the wall to see what happens!

5. A Very Blustery Day

It's always "Windsday" inside the attraction, and as Guests board their "Hunny Pot" vehicle they are taken through the pages of the classic A. A. Milne book, learning that they are joining Pooh on a "Very Blustery Day." Robert and Richard Sherman's melody of the same name accompanies Guests as a storm begins to brew: Piglet grasps his broom frantically among the swirling leaves...Eeyore watches incredulously as Pooh reaches for his beloved honey, grasping the end of a swaying blue balloon... Kanga worriedly hangs on to Roo, who is gleefully imagining that he is a kite at the end of his mother's scarf...a flabbergasted Rabbit surveys his wind-swept garden...and meanwhile an oblivious Owl drones on and on about... well, himself.

6. Bouncing with Tigger

The next scene of the ride introduces Guests to Tigger, just as Pooh makes his acquaintance in the film. Guests in their hunny pots bounce along to the tune "The Wonderful Thing about Tiggers," but look out: Tigger warns that Heffalumps and Woozles are ahead! Guests are carried along through Pooh's nightmare, as the colorful-but-dreaded creatures take over his beloved honey supply.

7. Rain, Rain, Rain

Pooh awakens to discover that while he was asleep, the "Rain Rain Rain Came Down Down Down," flooding the Hundred Acre Wood. A frightened Piglet floats on a chair alongside Pooh, who is stuck head-first in a bobbing pot of honey. Guests, too, become part of the adventure as their hunny pots roll over the waves. Christopher Robin, Tigger, and the rest rescue their stranded friends, and both the story and the attraction end in a celebration: everyone is safe and Pooh is happily immersed in a hive full of honey, as the films' title song carries Guests into the Hundred Acre Goods shop. A menagerie of plush pals from the Hundred Acre Wood, apparel, and an assortment of Pooh-related merchandise can be found here. (The store was originally called Pooh's Thotful Shop, but was re-named when the attraction was refurbished in 2010.)

8. Diane Disney and Winnie

Pooh fans have Diane Disney to thank for the addition of Pooh and pals to the Disney cast of characters. It was Walt's young daughter who first introduced her father to the stories, which Lillian Disney would read to Diane and her sister Sharon at bedtime.

9. Pooh's Blue Balloon

In the Many Adventures of Winnie the Pooh, Pooh is first seen holding on to a blue balloon, reaching for honey in a beehive. While most of the attraction is devoted to *Winnie the Pooh and the Blustery Day*, this scene is found in *Winnie the Pooh and the Honey Tree*, when Pooh sings "I'm Just a Little Black Raincloud." This is actually quite appropriate, for in the *Blustery Day* film, the same melody accompanies Pooh as he is pulled along to Owl's house by Piglet's unraveling scarf.

10. Smoke Rings

During the heffalumps and woozles portion of the attraction, keep an eye out for one of the heffalumps blowing smoke rings in the air!

Ten Things You May Not Know About
Carousel of Progress

1. Edison Square

Carousel of Progress was originally proposed as an attraction for a new area of Disneyland to be called "Edison Square." This area, which would be an offshoot of Main Street U.S.A., was intended to be a tribute to Thomas Edison and his contributions to society. The area would consist of 1920s-style houses surrounding a small park with a statue of Edison in the middle. The square was also going to feature an attraction called Harnessing the Lightning, which would show how we used electricity throughout past decades (sounds familiar, right?). Originally, Guests would walk from theater to theater to see each part of the show (that would change, of course). Unfortunately, the idea for Edison Square was eventually scrapped, but when Disney was approached to provide attractions for the upcoming 1964-65 World's Fair in New York, Harnessing the Lightning was given new life.

2. Progressland

The attraction was reimagined for the 1964-65 World's Fair in New York and became Progressland, with sponsorship provided by General Electric. One of the major changes was eliminating the need for Guests to walk from theater to theater; instead they would enter in one area to be seated, and they would stay in that section as the entire seating area revolved around the central stage. This allowed more Guests to watch the show simultaneously, and allowed for a smooth transition between scenes, since Guests would now remain seated. After viewing the show, Guests would walk upstairs where they could see a scaled model of Walt Disney's Progress City, the key component of Epcot, Walt's vision for a working community of the future. Another key component of the show was the theme song, "There's a Great Big Beautiful Tomorrow," written by Robert and Richard Sherman specifically for the new attraction. Throughout 1964 and 1965, the attraction was immensely popular. But even after the World's Fair had ended, Walt had future plans for his famed show.

3. Disneyland

Renovations for Tomorrowland at Disneyland were being planned for 1967, and Walt thought it would be the ideal setting for his incredibly popular attraction, which was all about progress and the promise of tomorrow. Unfortunately, Walt passed away in December 1966 and was not able to see the completion of the new Tomorrowland, but GE and the Walt Disney Company worked together to bring his plan to fruition. The new attraction had two levels, just like the World's Fair version, but now featured a built-in speed-ramp to transport Guests to the upper level and Progress City. The attraction's name was also changed from Progressland to the General Electric Carousel of Progress.

4. Moving to Florida

After six years in Disneyland, audiences were starting to dwindle, and GE was questioning their continued sponsorship of the attraction (surmising that the majority of the audience had seen the show multiple times and thus the message was losing its impact). It was decided that the show would move to the Magic Kingdom, and the show components were packed up and moved into the new theater built for the attraction. Unlike the Disneyland version, the new building was only one-story, though it did include a loft that was used for the Tomorrowland Transit Authority. The Progress City model was dismantled and partly reassembled in a special display area that can be seen from the TTA. With the newly revamped attraction, GE also wanted a new theme song to encourage people to buy their new GE appliances today, instead of looking ahead to tomorrow. The new song, "The Best Time of Your Life," was written by the Sherman Brothers as a new theme for the attraction. (In their hearts though, the Sherman Brothers much preferred the original, as to them it not only perfectly reflected the spirit of the attraction but was more or less Walt Disney's personal theme song, at least in their eyes.) A new cast was assembled for the show, and the Christmas scene was slightly updated. (This scene would undergo another update in 1981.)

5. Revamping the World of Progress

GE opted not to renew their contract when it expired on March 10, 1985, and the attraction closed briefly to remove most of the General Electric references (however, you can still see the occasional GE logo here and there, most notably on the refrigerator in the 1940s sequence). In August 1993, the attraction was refurbished to better reflect the new concept for Tomorrowland, "The Future That Never Was." A gear motif, prominent in the new Tomorrowland design, was added to the signage and show building, and the attraction was renamed Walt Disney's Carousel of Progress. To the delight of nostalgic fans, "It's a Great Big Beautiful Tomorrow" was brought back as the show's theme, and a new voice cast was brought in. The Christmas scene also underwent some changes, bringing it more in line with modern day technology. (This scene has always presented the same problem as Tomorrowland itself, how do you depict the future-or present day-without becoming out-of-date? Even today Disney fans debate the final scene, and while it is a favorite among many, there's always a murmur that the technology should be updated.)

6. An Instant Hit at the World's Fair...

Throughout the 1964-65 World's Fair, an average of 45,000 Guests saw the show every day (250 every four minutes!). Over the course of the entire event, about 16 million Guests saw the show.

7. ...And an Instant Hit in Disneyland

When brought to Disneyland, the theaters could sit 3,600 Guests per hour. During its run from 1967-1973 in Disneyland, over 31 million people saw the show.

8. Traveling Through Time

Astute viewers will note that as you progress through the years during the show, you also progress through the seasons. The first scene takes place around Valentine's Day, the second around the Fourth of July, the third around Halloween, and the last at Christmas.

9. Bringing Our Favorite Family to Life

Mel Blanc, the voice of Bugs Bunny, voiced Cousin Orville, one of the few occasions he did voice work for Disney. (He also did minor vocal effects for *Pinocchio*.) Rex Allen, who voiced the original father in the Disneyland version, was hired to voice the grandfather in the Christmas scene of the current version.

10. Iron Man

In the film, *Iron Man 2*, Tony Stark hosts a "Stark Expo," much in line with the New York World's Fair. The map of the Stark Expo shows the same building that Progressland was in (though here it is referred to as the Kodak pavilion). Richard Sherman also wrote the theme song for the Stark Expo, "Make Way for Tomorrow Today."

Ten Things You May Not Know About
Tomorrowland Transit Authority PeopleMover

1. The Ever-Evolving Name

Even though the attraction is popularly known as the TTA, its proper name is the Tomorrowland Transit Authority PeopleMover (and yes, that's quite a mouthful!). When the attraction first opened in 1975, it was known as the WEDWay PeopleMover. (WED standing for "Walter Elias Disney.") As part of the massive Tomorrowland renovation in 1994, the attraction was renamed the Tomorrowland Transit Authority (or TTA for short). In 2010 the name was once again changed to the Tomorrowland Transit Authority PeopleMover.

2. The Linear Synchronous Motor System

The attraction was based on the original PeopleMover at Disneyland, though unlike the California version, which used Goodyear tires as its propulsion system, the Magic Kingdom version is powered by a linear synchronous motor system. This system consists of a series of powerful electro-magnets embedded in the track that are switched on and off in sequence. As the car approaches, the magnet pulses on and the opposing magnetic field pushes the vehicle forward. Each motor is made up of a proximity sensor, speed sensor, and a motor unit. By turning on the magnets in sequence, the vehicles are propelled forward. (In fact, the merits of this innovative propulsion system were pointed out in the attraction's original narration. As the trains left Space Mountain, the narrator informed Guests that there were "no moving parts in [the PeopleMover's] clean, quiet motor.")

3. A Model of Efficiency

The system is so efficient that even if 20% of the magnets were to fail, the attraction would still run properly.

4. But How Fast Are We Going?

The PeopleMover travels at a speed of just under 7 mph (or about 10 feet per second), slowing down to 1.8 mph (or 2.7 feet per second) in the loading area.

5. Touring the World of Tomorrow

In 1985 the original narration was replaced by ORAC One - "The Commuter Computer," until its renovation in 1994. A new narration track was introduced at that time, recorded by Pete Renaday, which featured a fictional backstory of Tomorrowland. In the new backstory, the TTA vehicles were called "Metroliners," and the fictional transportation system consisted of three different lines; the Blue Line (or "local" line which wound throughout Tomorrowland – this was the line that you were traveling on), the Red Line, which could transport Tomorrowland residents anywhere in the galaxy, and the Green Line, which could take you to the outlying "Hover-Burbs," Tomorrowland's suburbs. Inside the Interplanetary Convention Center, Guests could see (and can still see today) a diorama showing the Red and Green lines, as well as some local residents boarding their vehicles.

6. Sightseeing in Tomorrowland

Sights along the way included the aforementioned Tomorrowland Interplanetary Convention Center, the Tomorrowland Metro Retro Historical Society (home to the Progress City model, described as "Walt Disney's Twentieth Century vision of the future"), the Tomorrowland Super Highway (the Tomorrowland Indy Speedway as it was then known), the League of Planets Astro Obelisk (the Astro Orbiter), the Transportarium, the Metropolis Science Center (then home to the Timekeeper attraction), and Rocket Tower Plaza Station.

7. Galaxy M31

The narration featured a number of memorable announcements or pages, including the tongue-in-cheek safety spiel, "all visitors from Galaxy M31, please keep forward facing tentacles clear of oncoming Metroliner vehicles." M31 is the actual astronomical designation for the Andromeda Galaxy. Other announcements included a description of the Astro Orbiter, "(a) symbol of universal harmony and inter-planetary fellowship," a brief description of the aforementioned TTA lines, "TTA services all of Tomorrowland's outlying areas, including the personal rocket ship docking lot, and of course Perfect Park Acres, the latest in Hover-Burb Communities," and of course the infamous "Paging Mr. Morrow, Mr. Tom Morrow, your party from Saturn has arrived. Please give them a ring."

8. If You Had Wings

The most notable structural change that has occurred over the years was in the section of the attraction that now passes by Buzz Lightyear's Space Ranger Spin. Originally, that section featured three windows, two on the right and the third on the left. When the PeopleMover opened, the attraction in that building was If You Had Wings, and the windows provided Guests with views of the Mexico, Jamaica, and Trinidad scenes.

9. Look for the Volcano!

When the attraction was replaced by Delta Dreamflight, the windows needed to be reconfigured as the scenes inside had been replaced. Consequently, the first window was replaced by a backlit panel that showed the new attraction's barnstormer scene, and the last window was completely covered. Today, those windows provide Guests with a sneak peek at Buzz Lightyear's Space Ranger Spin. (See that volcano? You might want to aim for that the next time you take part in your Space Ranger adventure!) During the latest refurbishment, LED lighting was added along the beamway that moves in time with the background music playing in Tomorrowland.

10. A New Narration

The attraction closed in 2009 as part of the renovation of Space Mountain, and when it reopened in 2010 it received another new narration, provided by Mike Brassell, which is the narration you can hear today with some slight modifications over the years...most notably the reintroduction of the "paging Mr. Morrow" announcement that had been retired in 2010. The new narration reverted back to the storyline of the original narration; that of taking you on a tour of Tomorrowland itself (foregoing the fictional backstory that was part of the 1994 refurbishment). Characters from the various attractions in Tomorrowland were added to the narration, including Stitch, Roz, and Buzz Lightyear.

Ten Things You May Not Know About
Space Mountain

1. Outer Space Origins

Space Mountain's origins actually go all the way back to the late 1950s. Disneyland's Matterhorn had proven to be a great success and had convinced Walt Disney that a new thrill ride could be the headline attraction in Tomorrowland, which was scheduled to be renovated by 1967. The attraction, originally called "Space Voyage," would be a roller coaster in the dark, complete with special effects and lighting to simulate a flight through space. The concept evolved over the next few years (being renamed "Space Mountain" in 1966), but technical and logistical roadblocks made the concept all but impossible to construct in its intended Disneyland location. The overwhelming success of the Magic Kingdom led to the necessity for Imagineers to come up with a thrill ride for the new park. A version of the Matterhorn was considered for Florida's Fantasyland, but it turned out there wasn't enough space. Ironically, the same problem that led to the stalling of Disneyland's Space Mountain (a lack of space in its intended home), opened the door for its arrival in the Magic Kingdom.

2. Relocation

Space Mountain was intended to be built in the southern section of Tomorrowland, the area now home to the Carousel of Progress. Instead, the mountain itself was eventually built outside the park's perimeter, with a tunnel called the "star corridor" built underneath the tracks of the Walt Disney World Railroad to serve as the entrance to the attraction.

3. Keeping Everything Running Smoothly

A computerized "zone system" was employed in the new coaster, which controlled the flow of the multiple trains that would be operating on the same track. The system automatically maintained the proper interval between trains, controlling their speed with individual brake zones that could make adjustments depending on the weight and speed of the trains. Unlike the Matterhorn, Space Mountain didn't utilize any boosters or retarders; instead relying solely on gravity to propel the trains after their initial climb.

4. Space is Big

The attraction building itself is a massive 300 feet in diameter. How big is that? If the building were centered over the Partners statue in front of Cinderella Castle, it would stretch from the end of Main Street, U.S.A. all the way up to the Castle Forecourt Stage! By comparison, the Disneyland version is only 200 feet in diameter.

5. Aventures Dans La Galaxie

Disneyland Paris features a more elaborate version of Space Mountain that is located in Discoveryland, the European park's version of Tomorrowland. Based on the novel 'From the Earth to the Moon' by Jules Verne, the attraction was originally named Space Mountain: De la Terre à la Lune. Of the five Space Mountain versions throughout the world, the one in Disneyland Paris is the fastest, reaching a top speed of 47 miles per hour, and is also the only one with inversions. These include a sidewinder, corkscrew, and a cutback.

6. Cookies!

Is that large meteor flying over your head really a photo of a chocolate chip cookie? Some people may try to convince you that it is, but alas, it's not true! (It makes a delicious story, however.)

7. Alpha and Omega

Space Mountain actually houses two tracks: Alpha, the left track, and Omega, the right track. The Alpha track is 10 feet (3.0 m) longer than the Omega track in order to permit the two tracks to cross each other.

8. The Astronaut Seal of Approval

When the attraction was given the green light, Mercury 9 and Gemini 5 astronaut Gordon Cooper joined the Space Mountain creative team as a consultant. He wanted to make sure that the attraction incorporated information learned during NASA's early space missions, and that the experience felt like actual space flight.

9. Horizons

One of the bags in the baggage claim (located to the left at the beginning of the exit moving sidewalk) has the words "Mesa Verde" written on it. Mesa Verde was the desert farm of the future shown in Horizons, the now-closed Epcot attraction.

10. 20,000 Leagues Under the Sea

The undersea post-show scene (the only new scene added to the post-show during the 2009 refurbishment) features a flat screen display that says "20,000 Light Years under the Sea," a pun on 20,000 Leagues Under the Sea.

Ten Things You May Not Know About
Buzz Lightyear's Space Ranger Spin

1. Attention Space Rangers!

After Buzz Lightyear completes his briefing, it's time to board your space cruiser, power up your laser blaster, and get ready to travel to infinity and beyond to take on the evil Emperor Zurg. And just what kind of space cruiser are you flying? An XP-37, the latest in space fighter technology, complete with twin ion cannons. How does it work? Crystallic fusion of course! (Well, that's code for batteries but don't tell Buzz!)

2. The Omnimover

Prior to the arrival of Buzz Lightyear and company, the show building had played host to a number of attractions over the years. The first was If You Had Wings, which opened in 1972. The attraction made use of the Omnimover system, a system that was subsequently used in every attraction to occupy the show building. The Omnimover system was developed by Roger E. Broggie and Bert Brundage in order to convey a cinematic experience to ride-through attractions. The key component to the Omnimover system is the ability to have the cars rotate independently of their forward motion. For you Junior Space Rangers, that provides the freedom to swing around and take aim at targets in any direction.

3. Putting the "Spin" in Space Ranger Spin

This added element of control differentiates the Omnimover system from similar designs, such as that used in The Seas with Nemo and Friends, where the vehicles always face sideways and don't rotate (much like the now-closed Horizons). Additionally, the Omnimover system used here, like the one used in the Haunted Mansion, makes use of a continually moving chain of vehicles that required the installation of a moving walkway to allow Guests to easily board and disembark the vehicles. While Journey Into Imagination uses an Omnimover type of system, the vehicles there aren't in constant motion. In fact, the only time the vehicles come to a stop in Space Ranger Spin is if a Guest needs additional time during the loading or unloading process. If this occurs, Guests on board the attraction can take advantage of the stoppage by racking up extra points, since the guns and targets remain active even though the vehicles aren't moving. Unlike the Haunted Mansion (and earlier attractions in the same building), the vehicles in Space Ranger Spin can be rotated by the occupants with full 360-degree freedom, allowing them to face in any direction in order to blast away at out-of-the-way targets. Because of this, the designers of Space Ranger Spin needed to ensure that every line of sight was filled with visual excitement, and that there would be no opportunity for Guests to get a peek at off-stage elements.

4. Galactic Hero

The top score, 999,999, earns you the rank of a Galactic Hero. The other ranks, from lowest to highest, are Star Cadet, Space Scout, Ranger 1st Class, Planetary Pilot, Space Ace, and Cosmic Commando.

5. Targeting Tips

There are several high-scoring targets located throughout the attraction. The secret to amassing 999,999 points is to find them and blast away! Two can be found in the first scene. One can be found on the large orange robot on your left. Blast the inside of his left hand and earn yourself a ton of points! Also, look for the structure that looks like a street lamp as you exit the area. The target underneath the "lamp" is also worth big points and is best targeted by swinging around once you pass it and shooting it from behind. In the next scene, look for the large volcano in the distance for another high scoring target.

6. Watch Out for Those Lasers!

Yes, the laser blasters do actually shoot real laser beams! They are completely harmless however, as they pack about the same punch as a barcode scanner.

7. The Superspeed Tunnel

If you were a fan of If You Had Wings or any of the other attractions that preceded Space Ranger Spin, then the Escape Tunnel scene may seem very familiar to you. This is because the tunnel used in this scene is the exact same superspeed tunnel that was featured in If You Had Wings and all other subsequent attractions housed in the building.

8. Bringing Buzz to Life

The Audio-Animatronic figure of Buzz Lightyear in the attraction's queue was the first of its kind. The figure features a computer-generated image of Buzz projected onto the face, creating a very lifelike (well, for a toy anyway) appearance.

9. The Voice of Buzz

Speaking of Buzz, the Audio-Animatronic figure is voiced not by Tim Allen (as he is in the films), but by Pat Fraley, who also played the part of 19 different characters in *Teenage Mutant Ninja Turtles*. Fraley also provided the voice of Buzz in early video games and other merchandise.

10. Pollost Prime

One of the cleverest Hidden Mickeys in the Magic Kingdom can be found here. In the queue, look on the giant map and see if you can find the planet called Pollost Prime. On it you'll see a continent in the shape of a profile Mickey!

Ten Things You May Not Know About
Spaceship Earth

1. A Unique Icon

When EPCOT was being developed as a new theme park, Disney Imagineers knew that it would require an iconic landmark similar to Cinderella Castle. Imagineers came up with the concept of a geodesic sphere, which was soon to be named Spaceship Earth, home to a dark ride that took Guests on a tour through the history (and future) of communication. To create the attraction, Disney Imagineers collaborated with noted author Ray Bradbury (who would later contribute to the conception of the Orbitron space ride at Disneyland Paris, then known as Euro-Disney), the Smithsonian Institution, the Huntington Library, the University of Southern California, and the University of Chicago.

2. Just How Big is That Giant Golf Ball?

The massive construction project took 26 months to complete, requiring a total of 40,800 labor hours to build. (That's more than 4½ years!) Spaceship Earth is 180 feet high and 165 feet in diameter, and it weighs nearly 16 million pounds. The foundations for the six massive support legs are buried from 120 to 185 feet into the ground. That's quite a lot of support, but it actually wasn't anywhere near enough to hold up the entire sphere. Not to fear, the imaginative Disney team came up with an ingenious solution. What was it? Split it apart! The sphere you see is actually comprised of two parts; the upper part sits on top of a "table" supported by the six legs, while the bottom half is suspended underneath.

3. All Those Triangles

The exterior of Spaceship Earth is made up of 11,324 silvered facets on 954 triangular panels. In theory, there should be 11,520 total isosceles triangles forming 3,840 points, but some of those triangles are partially or fully nonexistent due to supports and doors.

4. But What Are They Made Of?

The exterior panels went through a number of changes during the design phase, to determine their pattern and color. John Hench signed off on what is now the geometric design. An original idea was to have the triangular panels constructed from a reflective glass; the panels would produce unique daytime reflections from the sun and at night they would be backlit from long-lasting sodium light bulbs housed between the spheres. This approach, however, was scuttled after consideration of the costs, particularly the necessary maintenance that would be needed for the panels. Fiberglass or metal panels were next considered, with a specialized reflective coating. Imagineers considered coating the panels with satellite images of earth, so when completed it would appear as a general represen-tation of our planet. The final concept called for a machine-like metal look, and ALUCOBOND was the material of choice. ALUCOBOND is two layers of aluminum sandwiched around a layer of polyethylene plastic and chemically bonded. It's a space-age material, appropriately enough invented in 1969, the year man first walked on the Moon. A benefit of ALUCOBOND is its self-cleaning quality in the rain. With the material chosen, the next decision was the color. Metallic gold was the initial choice but dropped when Imagineers factored in the Florida heat and sunshine, which would retain heat inside the sphere and cause a blinding reflection to Guests below. Instead, silver was chosen, softened by opting for brushed ALUCOBOND panels. The triangles, attached to the inner sphere of Spaceship Earth via hidden rods, are one inch apart to allow for contraction with weather changes.

5. The Inner Sphere? Yep!

You may not know it by looking at it, but Spaceship Earth is actually composed of two spheres nested inside each other. The outer sphere is what we see from the, um, outside, while the inner sphere contains the tracks and maintenance rooms for the attraction itself.

6. The Millennium Mickey Hand

During the Millennium Celebration, a large Mickey Mouse hand was added to the exterior of Spaceship Earth. It originally included the year "2000" in large numbers, temporarily making it the tallest attraction at Walt Disney World. After the Millennium Celebration concluded, the "2000" was replaced with "Epcot." The entire structure was removed in 2007.

7. Renovation and Innovation

Spaceship Earth closed for a lengthy rehab at the end of 2007, reopening on February 18, 2008. Many of the Animatronic figures were updated (with stunning results), and a new interactive video feature was added to the latter half of the ride. A few scenes were removed, such as the Internet communication scene between two teenagers, as were all of the scenes after the planetarium segment (including the much beloved fiber-optic City of the Future).

New scenes included the birth of the personal computer and a retro-futuristic computer center. An updated narration was also recorded by Dame Judi Dench (who recently played the role of M, James Bond's boss, in the 007 films, and was the voice of Mrs. Caloway in the Disney animated film *Home on the Range*).

8. Geometry

To be mathematically precise, Spaceship Earth is not a sphere but a pentakis dodeca-hedron. A what? It's not as confusing as it sounds, the pentakis dodecahedron is a variation of a geodesic polyhedron. OK, that didn't actually make things any easier. All it really means is a shape made up of triangles that approximate a sphere. There, that makes much more sense!

9. Fleetwood Mac...a Mac...Hmmm...

In the scene showing the birth of the personal computer, look for the poster of Fleetwood Mac on the wall. Could the second part of the band's name give you any clue as to which computer is being developed?

10. Keeping Everyone Dry

A specially developed gutter system keeps rain from cascading off of the sphere and on to unsuspecting Guests below. Rainwater is instead channeled through underground drains that lead to World Showcase Lagoon.

Ten Things You May Not Know About
Mission: SPACE

1. Saying Farewell to Horizons, and Saying Hello to Mars

Mission: SPACE replaced the original Epcot attraction Horizons in 2003. This ultra-realistic space flight simulation has you boarding your space capsules with three other adventurers. The capsules themselves are attached to a multiple-arm centrifuge that spins the vehicles at 35 mph around a giant circle, subjecting you to forces up to 2.5 g, more than twice the force of gravity. The capsules can also tilt and rotate to further simulate the motion of space travel. Secured by an over-the-shoulder restraint, your view is of a high-resolution display that, when combined with the motions of the capsule itself, create an amazingly realistic simulation of space flight. How realistic? Mission: SPACE was designed with the help of actual NASA astronauts, who say it is the most accurate simulation of space flight that they've ever experienced.

2. Intense is an Understatement!

Unfortunately, it was so realistic that many Guests had trouble handling the intense forces created by the spinning of the centrifuge. (Motion sickness bags were in fact introduced to the attraction shortly after it's opening...just in case!). For those who wanted to experience the wonders of space travel but who didn't necessarily have the "right stuff," good news came in 2006 when a gentler version of the attraction was introduced. This version eliminated the spinning of the centrifuge, though still maintained the tilting simulator effects that would allow the capsule to mimic the forces of take-off, acceleration, and landing.

3. One Small Step for Man

The model of the Moon at the entrance to the building contains a number of markers. These represent the locations where manned and unmanned missions have landed on the Moon. See if you can find the special orange marker that indicates the landing site of Apollo 11, where Neil Armstrong took that historic first step on the Moon.

4. Opening Day

The grand opening of Mission: SPACE was marked by a special ceremony attended by then-CEO Michael Eisner, Hewlett-Packard CEO Carly Fiorina, and NASA Administrator Sean O'Keefe, as well as several NASA astronauts representing historic space programs of the past including Mercury, Gemini, Apollo, the space shuttle program, and the International Space Station.

5. Sponsoring Space Flight

Mission: SPACE was originally sponsored by Compaq, who worked with Disney Imagineers on the design. Hewlett-Packard assumed sponsorship for the attraction upon its merger with Compaq in 2002.

6. Don't Move!

If you join the Orange Team (the "intense" version), the most important tip for avoiding motion sickness is to stay focused on the screen, with your eyes facing straight ahead. If you turn your head, the spinning sensation will become much more apparent (and that could mean trouble!).

7. A Big Price Tag

It is estimated that the cost of developing the attraction was $100-150 million. For comparison, the cost to build the actual Saturn V rocket that carried Apollo 11 to the Moon was approximately $110 million.

8. Yep, Mickey's Here Too!

Before the launch doors open, look for a pair of Hidden Mickeys on the horizontal bar above the door.

9. Horizons Tribute

Look for the Horizons logo (the attraction that Mission: SPACE replaced) in the center of the rotating gravity wheel in the queue area.

10. ISTC

Your mission is overseen by the ISTC, which stands for International Space Training Center. Also, the officer overseeing your training is played by actor Gary Sinise, well known for his portrayal of astronaut Ken Mattingly in the film *Apollo 13*.

Ten Things You May Not Know About
Test Track

1. Thrill Rides Come to Epcot

Test Track was the first thrill ride built in Epcot (discounting the mild thrills of Maelstrom in the Norway pavilion of World Showcase), replacing the World of Motion, a slow-moving ride similar to Spaceship Earth that took Guests on a visual tour of the history of transportation. The attraction went through a long development process, with many delays resulting from changes to the attraction made in light of some performance issues revealed during testing. A few opening dates were announced but then missed (including May 1997 and August 1998), but after several years of waiting Test Track finally opened to an eagerly-anticipating public who soon made it one of the most popular attractions in all of Walt Disney World.

2. A New Look

In 2012, the attraction closed for a lengthy refurbishment. After more than ten months, the totally redesigned Test Track debuted on December 6, and Guests were greeted not by the colorful, frenetic testing facility of the original attraction, but by a sleek, futuristic neon facility reminiscent of the computerized world of *Tron*. The attraction was now sponsored by Chevrolet, a division of General Motors, the sponsor of the original version. While the ride experience itself was basically the same (in terms of the track layout and the different sections your vehicle went through), the concept of the attraction was totally reimagined, introducing a new level of interactivity that would provide Guests with a whole new experience. Instead of putting you through the rigors of a testing facility, Guests now had the opportunity to design their own cars and to see how they performed on the open road.

3. How Did You Do?

You can actually see how well your car design performed during your test. Once you exit your sim-car, you'll head to the Scoring Area, where you can also see how your vehicle performed compared to other Guests who've ridden throughout the day.

4. Don't Race Out Quite Yet!

The post-show area also features a number of interactive attractions, including Give It a Spin, a racing game where you can steer miniature digitized cars through a computerized track against your opponents. Finally, it's off to the show room, where you'll get to see some of the latest advances in automotive innovation, as well as Chevrolet's newest vehicles.

5. Speed Champ

At 65 mph, Test Track is the fastest attraction in Walt Disney World, even surpassing the speeds of the Tower of Terror, the Rock 'n' Roller Coaster and Expedition Everest.

6. But That Speed Comes with Complexity

Due to the lengthy start-up time and nightly maintenance required to keep Test Track operating smoothly, the attraction is usually kept running 20 or more hours every day.

7. Windy Day? No Problem!

The track has been engineered to withstand winds up to 200 miles per hour.

8. Putting NASA to Shame

Each car in Test Track has three times the computing power of the space shuttle.

9. Deceptively Lightweight

There is no steel between the front and rear wheels, the vehicle chassis is made of composite materials.

10. World of Motion

You can find the logo for the World of Motion, the attraction that Test Track replaced, in various places around the attraction building, including the trash cans.

Ten Things You May Not Know About
The Seas with Nemo & Friends

1. The Living Seas

The pavilion was originally known as The Living Seas and was one of the last of the original Future World pavilions to arrive, opening on January 15, 1986 (Wonders of Life would follow three years later, though that pavilion has since closed). At the time, it was the largest man-made underwater exhibit in the world, containing 5.7 million gallons of water and some 8,500 inhabitants, including more than 100 different species of marine life. (It has since been surpassed in size by the Georgia Aquarium, which holds an astonishing 8.5 million gallons of water).

2. Former Props

The original entryway included a 125-foot mural, photos of John Lethbridge's diving barrel, and Frederic de Drieberg's breathing device (dating back to 1809), an old-fashioned diving suit and a model of the Nautilus submarine that was used in the 1954 Disney film *20,000 Leagues Under the Sea*.

3. And It Rained...

The original pavilion also included a two-minute multimedia presentation honoring the pioneers of ocean research, and a seven-minute film demonstrating the role of the seas as a source of energy, minerals and protein.

4. Warm Caribbean Waters

In order to keep all the aquatic residents comfortable, the temperature of the tank is closely monitored to remain between 74 and 78 degrees Fahrenheit. The tank, which is 203 feet in diameter, is 27 feet deep and contains a man-made coral reef, similar to one that would be found in the Caribbean. The windows, which are made of a special acrylic that does not distort or magnify objects in the aquarium, are anywhere from 6 to 8 inches thick. Each of the 8-foot by 24-foot panels weighs about 9,000 pounds.

5. Keeping Those Aquarium Walls in Place

Believe it or not, the walls of the aquarium are actually held in place by the water itself. When the pavilion was being constructed, it was decided not to introduce anything into the aquarium that might harm the animals (including any materials that might have ordinarily been used to secure the walls), so instead the tank was simply filled with water, and the resultant pressure was used to hold the panels in place.

6. The VIP Lounge

The pavilion houses an 11,000 square foot VIP lounge on the second floor of the pavilion. Even though the lounge itself closed in December 1991, the impressive facility is still there, and includes a full working kitchen, meeting areas, a dining room looking into the aquarium, and more. It is still used for special occasions and can even be rented out for wedding receptions!

7. That's A Lot of Water!

One inch of water off the top of the aquarium tank can fill a regular-sized swimming pool. That's about 20,000 gallons!

8. What Could Have Been

The original plans for The Living Seas included a huge bubble-like dome for Guests to walk or ride through, all under a 5-million-gallon water tank.

9. The Coral Reef

As mentioned earlier, the "coral" in the Living Seas tank is actually man-made. If it were real, it would have taken over 100 years to grow to that size.

10. Keeping the Aquarium Clean

The aquarium uses what is known as a "reverse-flow filtration system," which forces impurities up to the top of the water. These impurities flow out with skimmed water which is then filtered, and the newly-cleaned water is returned to the tank through the floor.

Ten Things You May Not Know About
Living with the Land

1, Inspirational Words

The queue of Living with the Land contains numerous inspirational quotes from different world leaders, scientists, celebrities, and children painted on the walls. These include:

"I may only be one person, but I can be one person who makes a difference." (From a 10-year-old child from Kentucky)

"Let us remember as we chase our dreams into the stars that our first responsibility is to our earth, to our children, to ourselves." (From former United States President George Bush)

"The earth is like my mother. You get punished if you make a mess. Why do you think this planet's called Mother Earth?" (From a 10-year-old child from Hong Kong)

"If we don't save the animals, the air, and the sky, they will be gone in a blink of an eye." (From a 13-year-old child from Iowa)

2. A Curious Address

One of the scenes in the early portion of the attraction is the farmhouse scene, complete with a dog on the front porch. A large tree in the front yard holds a swing, and a rooster stands proudly atop a mailbox. Be sure to look closely at the house number on that mailbox; it's 82, a reference to the year that Epcot opened.

3. On to the Real Thing

The second half of the attraction takes place in the brightly lit greenhouses (well, at least it's brightly lit in the daytime). Here you'll find five unique "living laboratory" greenhouses where different food production techniques are being tested and expanded by Epcot's scientists. First up is the Tropics Greenhouse, featuring a variety of different agricultural crops from areas such as Africa, Latin America, and the Southwestern United States. Among the plants that are on display for Guests in the tropics greenhouse are bananas, cacaos, papayas, jackfruits, date palms, dragon fruits, fluted pumpkins, vanilla, cleomes, and pineapples.

4. Fish Farming

Next up is the aquacell area, one of the most popular areas of the entire attraction. This unique food growth area focuses on aquaculture (essentially, growing fish). Animals on display in different tanks and tubes include tilapia, sturgeon, bass, catfish, and shrimp. Guests will even see an area that houses American alligators. The Land Pavilion produces thousands of pounds of fish each year, much of which is served in the Coral Reef Restaurant in the adjacent Seas with Nemo and Friends Pavilion and in other Epcot restaurants.

5. Nine Pound Lemons and More

The Temperate Greenhouse features, not surprisingly, crops from temperate climates. This greenhouse includes some of the most popular specimens in the entire attraction, including the famous "nine-pound" lemons and giant pumpkins. Sunflowers, beets, and turnips are also displayed. The temperate greenhouse utilizes numerous innovative growing techniques like cross-breeding of plants to create those that are more resistant to diseases, and "drip irrigation" techniques that allow scientists to deliver specific amounts of water to crops.

6. Mickey Mouse Pumpkins and Other Agricultural Innovations

The next two areas showcase some of the great innovations happening in agriculture today. The String Greenhouse focuses on innovative growing techniques that produce higher volumes of foods, including "vertical growing," where plants are grown on specialized trellises. Perhaps the most popular sight in the string greenhouse is the "tomato tree," which at one point produced more than 32,000 tomatoes in a 16-month period. It's here you'll also find those famous pumpkins that are grown in the shape of Mickey Mouse, crafted through the use of special molds. The Creative Greenhouse features agricultural growing techniques that are...well...creative! Many of the plants in this greenhouse are grown using a technique known as Aeroponics, where a mist of water and nutrients is sprayed directly onto the roots of the plants. Rather than being buried in the soil, the roots of the plants hang freely in the air. Guests will also see an innovative aquaculture system where the environments of both fish and plants are combined to create a symbiotic food growth system. Also, be sure to give the good scientists of the United States of Department of Agriculture a wave. They work in the Biotechnology Lab attached to the creative greenhouse and can be seen through a series of windows. (You'll also find a great Hidden Mickey in the form of green-capped test tubes arranged in a familiar shape.)

7. What's in a Name

When the attraction first opened in 1982, it was known as "Listen to the Land."

8. Your Original Hosts

Cast Members previously provided the narration for Living with The Land as they rode with you. Their "role" has since been replaced with the recorded narration you hear today.

9. Thunder Mesa

The Audio-Animatronic buffalo and prairie dogs in the American prairie scene were not originally produced for Living with The Land. They were instead created for use in the greatest Walt Disney World attraction that never came to be: Thunder Mesa (which would have been a Wild West version of Pirates of the Caribbean).

10. A Word from Our Sponsors

Living with The Land (and its predecessor Listen to The Land) has been sponsored by numerous companies throughout its history, including Kraft, Nestle, and Chiquita.

Ten Things You May Not Know About
Soarin' Around the World

1. Soarin' Over California

The original version of Soarin' Around the World, known simply as Soarin', debuted at Epcot in 2005 and took Guests on a hang gliding excursion over the Golden State, complete with scents of pine trees and orange groves.

2. Traveling the World

Soarin' Around the World now takes you on a tour around the globe, with stops at the mighty Matterhorn on the Swiss-Italian border, the frozen fjords above Norway's Arctic Circle, Sydney Harbour in Australia, and the Neuschwanstein Castle in Bavaria, Germany. From there it's on to Tanzania and a herd of elephants, the Great Wall of China, the pyramids of Giza, the magnificent Taj Mahal, Utah's Monument Valley, the coast of Fiji in the south Pacific, and the Eiffel Tower in Paris.

3. Last Stop

The final destination is determined by which park you're in: Walt Disney World Guests are returned to Epcot and Spaceship Earth, while those in Anaheim see Disneyland (which means their trip is bookended by views of the Matterhorn!). At the newly-opened Shanghai Disney Resort, where Soarin' Around the World debuted a day before its American openings, Guests see a view of the city's sky at night.

4. A New Queue...

Not only is Epcot's film new, but as Guests cross the threshold into the attraction, they will discover an entirely overhauled queue as well. Gone are the neutral ecru and beige hues of the entrance corridor, and in their place are walls, floors, and ceilings of deep blue. A new interactive game also helps Guests while away their wait times: the Soarin' Challenge. While the former queue game involved four large screens enticing Guests to engage in virtual bird races and garden-building, the new competition is a trivia game testing Guests' knowledge of the globe, covering everything from history and culture to buildings and traditional foods. Guests are able to access the game on their mobile devices via soarinchallenge.com, or use the screens to compete against fellow riders, making the wait time go by in a flash.

5. ...And a New Theater

Actually, the shorter time in the queue is not an illusion at all! Wait times have been significantly reduced due to the addition of a third theater, thus allowing the attraction to process more Guests through Soarin' Around the World at one time.

6. Patrick

Even with the new film, some old favorites have stuck around. Chief Flight Attendant Patrick, played by Patrick Warburton ("Seinfeld" and "Rules of Engagement"), continues to welcome Guests to the updated attraction. The queue loop music still features melodies from the former attraction, such as selections from John Williams's score to *Far and Away* (1992), music from *The Rocketeer* (1991) and *Apollo 13* (1995) by James Horner, as well as the opening themes to *Steel Magnolias* (1989) by Georges Delarue and the 1978 television series "Battlestar Galactica,"composed by Stu Phillips.

7. A Vision...and an Erector Set

How was this unique attraction created? How do you hoist a theater full of Guests up into the air? It actually took a lot of trial and error, as Soarin' represented an entirely new type of attraction, with virtually no history or existing technology from which to draw. Eventually, after a few failed concepts, Mark Sumner, senior technical director and project/ride engineer at Walt Disney Imagineering, came up with the idea for the new ride vehicle while he was home one weekend. Sumner made a simple prototype out of an old Erector Set to demonstrate the sophisticated mechanism that would simulate a high-flying adventure on Soarin'. Sumner's concept – small enough to hold in his hands – grew into a ride structure containing one million pounds of steel that is able to lift 37 tons.

8. IMAX

The counterpart to the engineering complexity of the attraction was the cinematic challenge of creating the movie itself. Disney used an IMAX camera with a special lens mounted to a helicopter to capture everything a person would see, including peripheral vision. Shooting in a variety of locations around California proved to be a challenge, especially at Yosemite National Park where governmental restrictions usually prohibit flying inside the park's valley.

9. New Technologies

To create the new visuals for Soarin' Around the World, Disney Imagineers had to develop new innovative photographic technology. A new high-resolution camera system was created, with the cameras either being dangled from or attached to the front of aircraft, in order to get as close as possible to each setting. These vivid images are displayed on the 80-foot screens by laser-powered projection in the attraction theaters, drastically improving the quality of the visual image.

10. Princess Aurora?

At one point in your journey you'll see the Neuschwanstein Castle in Bavaria, Germany. If the castle seems oddly familiar, it's because this beautiful structure, visited by Walt and Lillian Disney, served as the inspiration for Sleeping Beauty Castle in Disneyland.

Ten Things You May Not Know About
Journey Into Imagination With Figment

1. Introducing Figment

When EPCOT Center first opened, the Kodak-sponsored pavilion had only one attraction, the film Magic Journeys which played in the Magic Eye Theater. At the time, our little purple friend was still being created, but the world met Figment soon enough when he joined Bryant Gumbel on "The Today Show" in the fall of 1982. Barry Braverman, senior vice-president and executive producer for Walt Disney Imagineering, was also on the show. Braverman explained the plans for the pavilion, which included Figment's ride, created by Imagineers Tony Baxter and Steve Kirk, as well as a showcase of futuristic play at Kodak's ImageWorks.

2. And Introducing the Dreamfinder

On March 5, 1983, the new attraction opened and Guests finally got a chance to meet Figment in person. After heading through the glass pyramid's doors, they boarded OmniMover-style vehicles that took them through clouds toward a strange blimp. This odd, vacuum-powered vessel held the Dreamfinder, voiced by character performer Chuck McCann as well as Ron Schneider. The red-bearded, top-hat-wearing old man used his flying blimp (commonly known as the Dream Catcher) to collect dreams, ideas, and inspiration. With the following words: "Two tiny wings, eyes big and yellow, horns of a steer, but a lovable fellow. From head to tail, he's royal purple pigment, and there...voilà! You've got a Figment!" he created Figment, a fun-loving, mischievous creature originally voiced by film actor Billy Barty. The Dreamfinder and Figment took riders through several rooms focusing on art, literature, performing arts, and science. Here Figment painted walls, avoided scary monsters in stories, tried on theater costumes, and gazed into space.

3. The Original ImageWorks

After an inspirational goodbye from the Dreamfinder and Figment, Guests would exit and climb the stairs to the ImageWorks, which was a creative playground of the future. The second floor featured interactive attractions that mixed imagination with computer technology. Large kaleidoscopes, pin-tables, and vibrating mirrors filled the floor. A popular feature was the Rainbow Corridor, a twisting tunnel with colored lights that followed Guests as they walked through. Families were able to electronically "paint" pictures of Figment by swiping their hands over a screen. Kids could also try their hands at acting. The Dreamfinder's School of Drama used bluescreen technology to transport Guests into Western, fantasy, and science fiction films.

4. Reimagining Imagination

In October 1999, the Dreamfinder – along with Figment's explorations into art, literature, performing arts, and science – were dropped to make way for a revamped attraction called Journey Into Your Imagination. The attraction featured Dr. Nigel Channing from the 3D film Honey, I Shrunk the Audience which was now playing next door. Even the name of the pavilion was changed to Imagination!, and the song 'One Little Spark' disappeared from the attraction. The attraction was much more science-based than fantasy, but many missed the whimsy of the former attraction.

5. Figment Returns

To the delight of many, Figment was brought back to the attraction during a 2001 renovation and is now a playful foil to Dr. Channing's imagination studies. This time, Figment and Dr. Channing take Guests through new labs based on the human senses. Figment causes chaos in three of the sense labs, forcing Dr. Channing to give up the tour and leave Figment in charge. (Persistent rumors swirl that the original incarnation of the attraction, or a variation of it, may soon be coming back...complete with the Dreamfinder himself!)

6. Hidden Jokes

Visual jokes and puns can be found throughout this whimsical attraction. For example, look for the name 'Dean Finder' on an office door in the initial showroom; this is a clever reference to the Dreamfinder. As you pass by the computer lab, see if you can spot a pair of red sneakers outside the door. This is a reference to the 1969 Disney film, *The Computer Wore Tennis Shoes*. The film takes place at the fictional Medfield College, home of Professor Brainard and his humorous invention, Flubber (as seen in the 1961 classic, *The Absent-Minded Professor*). And now you know why Professor Brainard's portrait is hanging alongside that of Dr. Channing and Professor Szalinski's in the queue.

7. The Dream Catcher

You can see a silhouette of the original Dream Catcher on the sheet music for 'One Little Spark' in the final scene. You can also spot a deconstructed Dream Catcher blimp on the west wall of Epcot's Mouse Gears store.

8. A Mystery Princess

In the Smell Lab, look closely at all the pipes and tanks running throughout the room. You'll find lots of puns and clever jokes! For instance, see if you can spot a (perhaps unintentional) reference to a Disney Princess...

9. The Figment Vase

In the Sight Lab, see if you can spot the variation of the famous vase/two faces optical illusion. Look closely and see if you can find Figment!

10. A Treasure Trove of Special Effect

78 out of the 200 special effects patents created for the original Epcot Center were used in the Journey Into Imagination attraction.

Ten Things You May Not Know About
Frozen Ever After

1. Bringing Frozen to the Parks

The attraction's origins actually go all the way back to September 12, 2014, when Chief Operating Officer Tom Staggs announced the new attraction on the Disney Blog. In the announcement, Staggs reflected back on Walt Disney's promise that Disneyland would never be completed, and that this idea still holds true today, inspired by the film that "...captured the hearts and minds of people around the world." The new attraction would replace the Maelstrom attraction in Epcot's Norway pavilion, and would immerse Guests in the world of Arendelle with the help of beloved scenes and songs from the film. (Maelstrom would close permanently on October 5, 2014.)

2. A Snowy Celebration

The backstory of the attraction is that you are invited to the Summer Snow Day Celebration, in honor of the day that Princess Anna saved her sister Queen Elsa with an unselfish act of true love. The royal reception takes place inside the ice palace.

3. Meet Anna and Elsa

In addition to the attraction itself, the pavilion also features the Royal Sommerhus, where you can meet Anna and Elsa. According to Portfolio Creative Executive Kathy Mangum, "...This cabin is based on an actual historic log cabin in Norway. In fact, in order to make sure we (got) the character and detailing right, we...sent our project team to Norway on a research trip to study the country and its cultural arts and crafts in person, just as the film team did."

4. Keeping True to the Spirit of Norway

And indeed, Walt Disney Imagineers did travel to Norway for architectural and design research, specifically visiting the Detli House in Sverresborg and the Open Air Museum of Cultural History in Trondheim.

5. Memorable Music

Composers Bobby and Kristen Lopez created new lyrics for the cherished *Frozen* film songs, and all of the original voice talent from the film returned and recorded dialogue and songs for the attraction.

6. Back and Forth

The attraction makes use of the same ride mechanism used for Maelstrom, which includes a 28-foot drop at the end, and conveyor belts underneath the water that propel the log boats backward on their way to the final plunge.

7. A New Village

However, there was a slight change in the location of the boarding area. The new boarding area is now located in what used to be the unloading area for Maelstrom (which also served as a waiting area for the Norway film). Maelstrom's unloading area was designed to evoke a Norwegian fishing village, and you can still see many of those details today. But you'll also find lots of new additions, such as a quick trip through Oaken's Tokens. Take a peek at the small window that leads to the sauna. You'll get on occasional glimpse of Oaken himself peering through the steam-covered window!

8. The Northern Lights

Also, be sure to keep your eyes open for the Northern Lights shimmering off in the distant sky, as well as the many lanterns hanging throughout the village, many of them sporting the distinctive Frozen snowflake. And yep, you're going to see that snowflake several more times in your journey ahead!

9. Oh Sven!

The Audio-Animatronic figures for the attraction feature the improvements in facial animation that were first used on the Seven Dwarfs Mine Train, which opened in 2014 at the Magic Kingdom. Speaking of facial expressions, keep an eye out for Sven's look of confusion when he gets his tongue frozen to a post!

10. Animatronic Advances

The Audio-Animatronics are also the first ever all-electric Audio-Animatronics, with previous Audio-Animatronics using either pneumatics or hydraulics.

Ten Things You May Not Know About
Star Tours – The Adventures Continue

1. Touring the Galaxy

Star Tours originally debuted at Disneyland in 1987 and came to Disney-MGM Studios on December 15, 1989, after the park opened in May of that year. According to the backstory, Star Tours is a galactic travel company with its own spaceport, offering sightseeing tours of celestial bodies throughout the galaxy. In the original attraction, Guests were on a typical spaceflight to Endor on the StarSpeeder 3000.

2. Captain Rex

Your inexperienced pilot (it was his first flight and he was still getting used to his programming), was RX-24, known as Captain Rex. Unfortunately (though predictably), Rex went the wrong way, getting the ship caught in a tractor beam, then took you "safely" through an asteroid field at light speed...right into a battle between the Rebellion and the Empire. Unwittingly, Rex gave the squadron of X-Wing fighters a hand and helped them to destroy the Death Star. The film for the attraction was produced by George Lucas and the team at Industrial Light & Magic.

3. A New Adventure

In September of 2010, Guests took one "Last Tour to Endor" as the attraction prepared for a major refurbishment. At Walt Disney World, Star Tours – The Adventures Continue opened on May 20, 2011, with a special midnight event and an Imagineer Q&A session. The next day, a grand opening celebration was held with several dignitaries from around the galaxy in attendance.

4. C-3PO and R2-D2

In the updated attraction queue, Guests walk into a bustling spaceport and are greeted by the famous droid duo, C-3PO and R2-D2. Guests are also introduced to AC-38, a hotshot droid pilot known simply as "Ace," and Aly San San (voiced by actress Allison Janney), the "spokesbot" for the spaceport. After winding through the spaceport, Guests board the StarSpeeder 1000 spacecraft for Star Tours Flight #1401. Through a series of mishaps, C-3PO finds himself in the pilot's seat instead of Ace, and it's up to him and R2-D2 to navigate you through the galaxy.

5. New Worlds

The newly renovated attraction gave Guests the chance to visit new destinations in the Star Wars universe, including the ice planet of Hoth, the underwater Gungan world of Naboo, the lush jungles of Kashyyyk, podracing on Tatooine, and more. Original movie favorites such as Boba Fett, Princess Leia, Admiral Ackbar, Darth Vader, Yoda, and others now made appearances aboard the StarSpeeder 1000 in the 3D attraction.

6. What's Up with Our StarSpeeder Number?

Why is the current StarSpeeder numbered 1000, when the previous version was numbered 3000? Shouldn't it be higher? Well, with the inclusion of many new scenes that established the timeline for this attraction as taking place before the events of the original Star Tours, the ship was "back-numbered" accordingly!

7. You Are Part of the Rebel Alliance and a Traitor!

Also, Guests just might find themselves being accused of being the "rebel spy" that the Empire is looking for while aboard the speeder. (If they pick you, just act casual...perhaps they won't notice!)

8. A Universe of Possibilities

The updated attraction randomly combines different scenes and characters, meaning Guests can ride the attraction multiple times without ever experiencing the same adventure twice. Indeed, much of the fun now is in seeing which characters and locations will pop up next, and many fans will ride numerous times in order to "collect" the experiences. Altogether, there are more than 50 possible ride scenarios. (How many have you seen?)

9. Your Flight Number

In case you were wondering, the 1401 flight number came from the number of the street address for Walt Disney Imagineering in Glendale, California.

10. Defective Rex

And for those nostalgic for the original Captain Rex, he can still be found in the attraction. Since the events of the new attraction predate those of the original, Rex is not yet a pilot, but he can be found in the pre-show security area called "Droid Customs," being "returned to sender" for defects, which actually explains a lot for those who enjoyed the original attraction.

Ten Things You May Not Know About
Rock 'n' Roller Coaster Starring Aerosmith

1. Hang On!

The Rock 'n' Roller Coaster propulsion system utilizes a series of electromagnets that engage in rapid-fire sequence to propel the attraction vehicles forward. As a result, the "stretch limos" go from 0 to 57 miles per hour in an astonishing 2.8 seconds.

2. A Rocking Soundtrack

Each attraction vehicle features its own unique soundtrack that was developed by Aerosmith, working in conjunction with Disney Imagineers. These soundtracks include numerous Aerosmith songs including "Nine Lives," "Love in an Elevator," "Walk This Way," "Young Lust," "F.I.N.E.," "Back in the Saddle," "Dude (Looks Like a Lady)," and "Sweet Emotion." Some of these songs have been slightly modified to tie in thematically with the attraction. For example, "Love in an Elevator" is changed to "Love in a Roller Coaster."

3. A LOUD Soundtrack

Given the significance of music to both the theming and actual experience of the attraction, it should come as no surprise that these soundtracks are blasted in Guests' ears by virtue of numerous speakers embedded inside each vehicle. How many? The attraction actually contains more than 900 speakers. Now that's loud!

4. Twisting and Turning

The attraction includes three inversions (a corkscrew and two roll-over loops). Notably, Guests experience a g-force between 4 and 5 Gs upon entering the first inversion on the track.

5. Is It Over Already?

After making their way through Los Angeles, the attraction ends with Guests arriving at the theater, just in time for the show. In total, the attraction's duration is approximately one minute and twenty-two seconds and includes more than 3,000 feet of track.

6. The License Plates

Pay close attention to the license plates on the Rock 'n' Roller Coaster limos, as they feature funny inscriptions, including: "1QKLIMO," "UGOBABE," "BUHBYE," "H8TRFFC," and "2FAST4U."

7. Hollywood Treatment

Guests exit the attraction by walking down – appropriately enough – a red carpet.

8. Where's Aerosmith?

When The Walt Disney Company decided to feature the band Aerosmith in the attraction, executives initially had a difficult time reaching the band's stars Stephen Tyler and Joe Perry. Disney executives were unaware that Tyler and Perry were actually vacationing at Walt Disney World at the time!

9. They Must Have Liked It...

Rumor has it that Tyler and Perry rode the attraction 12 times in a row shortly before it opened to the public.

10. The Rock 'n' Roller Coaster Featuring...the Stones?

Aerosmith was not the first band considered by The Walt Disney Company for inclusion in the Studios roller coaster. Disney had initially looked to partner with The Rolling Stones. Although the Stones were interested in participating in the project, their licensing fee demands were too large for Disney to accept. As such, Disney moved on to Aerosmith.

Ten Things You May Not Know About
The Twilight Zone Tower of Terror™

1. Elevating to a New Dimension

The heart and soul of the Tower of Terror are of course the "elevators," and there are eight elevators inside the Tower, each with a capacity of 21 Guests. However, in the tower's early days, this was not the case. When the Tower first opened, each elevator had room for 22. But in 2002, the lap bars in the elevators were replaced with seatbelts. As a result of the change, each elevator lost one seat.

2. Faster Than Gravity

So are you really falling when your elevator drops? Actually, no. There are cables attached to the bottom of each elevator (not just at the top as you might expect), and it's these cables that create that "free-falling" feeling. Here's how it works: When the elevators reach the top, the cables pull the elevators down at a faster speed than you'd experience during an actual free-fall. Even though it feels like you are falling 13 stories, the reality is that the cables are creating that feeling by pulling you down at a speed faster than gravity! Two motors located at the top of the tower bring it all together. The motors are 12 feet tall, 35 feet long, and weigh more than 130,000 pounds each. Speeds inside the Tower can reach 39 mph, and it takes the motors just 1.5 seconds to climb to that maximum speed!

3. One Foot Short

The Tower of Terror soars 199 feet above Sunset Boulevard. Wait, why not go that extra, er, mile and make it an even 200? Well, local ordinances require that any structure 200 feet or higher be affixed with a red light at the top as a warning for low-flying aircraft. The Imagineers felt that would detract from the eerie exterior of the hotel, so 199 feet it was.

4. Second Place

That's still pretty tall, though it actually would have only take an additional seven inches to make it the tallest attraction in Walt Disney World (Expedition Everest beats it out by half a foot).

5. How Many Stories?

Even though there are twelve stories listed on the elevator dial, you'll actually "fall" thirteen.

6. Lightning Strikes...Twice?

According to legend, the ill-fated building was struck by lightning on October 31, 1939. In an eerie coincidence, the Tower was actually struck by lightning in 1997 during its construction.

7. Long Overdue for Inspection

The inspection plaque inside the elevator includes the number 10259, which is a nod to October 2, 1959, the date "The Twilight Zone" TV series first aired. The plaque also states the elevator was checked by Mr. Cadwallader, the deal-maker from the Twilight Zone episode "Escape Clause."

8. The Victims

According to the backstory, five people were originally lost in the fifth dimension. This ill-fated group included Sally Shine (a child star before Shirley Temple graced the movie scene), Emmeline Partridge (Sally's nanny), Caroline Crosson (a glamorous aspiring actress), Gilbert London (one of her many male admirers), and Dewey Todd, Jr. (the hotel bellhop).

9. Researching the Twilight Zone

The Imagineers who worked on the attraction watched each and every episode of "The Twilight Zone" (all 156 of them) at least twice as part of their research.

10. Hollywood Tower Hotel

Be sure to look for the large tapestry that hangs above the fireplace in the queue. It bears the "HTH" logo, which stands for Hollywood Tower Hotel. This is a prime example of how much attention is paid to every little detail when it comes to the theming and backstory for an attraction. Disney Imagineers actually created a logo for the fictional Hollywood Tower Hotel! You'll find the HTH logo scattered throughout the attraction.

Ten Things You May Not Know About
Flight of Passage

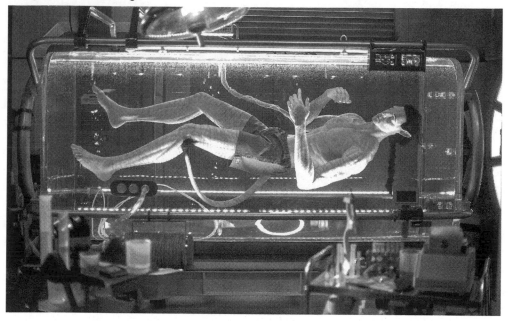

1. An Unassuming Entrance

The entrance to the Flight of Passage is completely different from what most Disney Guests are accustomed. Instead of grand marquees or towering architecture that can visually draw Guests from the entire land, the entrance to Flight of Passage is very understated. This minimal theming helps to blend the attraction into the surrounding environment rather than create an unwelcome visual intrusion.

2. ACE

Look for the pair of "ACE" signs at the attraction's entrance. "ACE" stands for Alpha Centauri Expeditions, and as you would expect, the Imagineers at Disney have crafted an elaborate backstory for ACE: *"Until recently, deep space travel was only an adventure traveller's dream. Now, Alpha Centauri Expeditions, together with Disney's Animal Kingdom Theme Park, has made it possible to travel light years across space to Pandora – a world of beyond-belief expeditions and new possibilities for those seeking interplanetary travel. Our dream is that all those who crave exciting adventures in nature can find that with ACE. We look forward to helping you discover the wondrous beauty that the World of Pandora has to offer."*

3. Cave Art

Throughout the queue, be sure to closely examine the walls of the cave, where you will find numerous primitive drawings of the "Ikran," the Na'vi word for banshees. These caves eventually transform into the long-abandoned barracks of RDA (Resource Development

Administration); the company formerly responsible for the mining operations that took a devastating toll on the Pandora environment.

4. Is He Alive...?

However, the most dramatic portion of the Flight of Passage queue is the ultra-realistic Na'vi Avatar that is floating in a massive water tank. The Avatar is incredibly detailed, and appears to actually be breathing, complete with periodic twitching of his arms and legs.

5. Meeting Your Avatar

You'll eventually enter an area where you will be genetically matched to your respective Avatar (a character that looks like the Na'vi but is controlled by you). But why is this necessary? Simple! Humans cannot ride banshees, only the Na'vi can by virtue of a special mental and spiritual connection. (But you knew that all along of course!)

6. How to Ride a Banshee

The ride "vehicles" for Flight of Passage are unlike any other in Walt Disney World. The best way to describe them is to say that they look like futuristic motorcycles, with each Guest having their very own "bike." You board the ride vehicles by swinging one leg over the center of the vehicle in much the same way as you would ride a motorcycle or bicycle. You'll then rest your chest against a central support.

7. Take Off!

A video screen is located directly in front of you, which displays a multitude of information about the linking process and other information about the attraction experience. When all Guests in the group are ready, the wall in front of the ride vehicles disappears, and the incredible sensation of flight aboard a massive banshee immediately begins! The visuals are displayed on a massive screen that curves around your line of sight, with almost no break in the visual continuity.

8. A Sensory Experience Like No Other

Like Soarin', Flight of Passage also utilizes wind effects, water, and scent to further immerse you into the attraction experience. However, Flight of Passage utilizes these effects in a much more effective manner. For example, the wind effect matches the particular environment, with stronger gusts coming during faster paced moments.

9. Take a Deep Breath...

One of the best features is that the ride vehicles feature an air-bag type mechanism in the seat that expands and contracts periodically throughout the experience, which replicates the breathing of the banshee!

10. Music to Calm the Savage Beast

Although the visuals of the attraction alone are enough to make this is a true headliner attraction, don't forget to listen amongst the eye candy. The London Symphony Orchestra recorded a captivating score for Flight of Passage, and it is a perfect fit for the setting, mood, and feel of the attraction.

Ten Things You May Not Know About
Na'vi River Journey

1. The Journey Begins

The entrance to the Na'vi River Journey mimics that of Flight of Passage in that it is very understated, as compared to other Disney headliner attractions. This technique is very effective in helping to blend the attraction into the surrounding Valley of Mo'ara.

2. Alpha Centauri Expeditions

For the Na'vi River Journey, Guests will see two non-descript entrance points for standby entry and FastPass+ entry, respectively. The attraction entrance to River Journey also includes a sign for "ACE," Alpha Centauri Expeditions.

3. Alien Waterways

Your journey takes place on the Kasvapan River, where you'll enter a world filled with bio-luminescent wonders.

4. Viper Wolves

Keep an eye out for the "viper wolves" as seen in *Avatar,* you can spot them throughout the attraction. Although these exotic beasts are depicted by way of video screens, the effect is so well done that they appear real to the naked eye.

5. Are Those Lizards?

Another astonishing visual effect can be spotted near the ceiling of the attraction as a series of special effects, including lighting, shadows, and fabricated movement, make it appear as though lizards are jumping to and from the leaves that hang above your head.

6. More Wildlife to Discover

As the boats travel further into the cavern, the ambient noises of animals and water in the background begin to increase as video screens display other native Pandoran animal species. It is at this point that Guests begin to hear Na'vi music playing in the background, a precursor to the most stunning portion of the entire attraction: the Shaman of Songs.

7. The Shaman of Songs

Standing at nearly ten feet tall, the Shaman of Songs is the most advanced and most complex Audio-Animatronic figure ever created by Disney. Guests pass by the Shaman of Songs as she is in the middle of a ceremony, playing Na'vi musical instruments and singing native songs. Disney describes this ceremony as follows: *"The adventure comes to a conclusion as the Shaman demonstrates her deep connection to the life force of Pandora – and sends positive energy out into the forest through the power of her music!"*

8. A Beautiful Song for a Beautiful Land

The lyrics for the song were written by Paul R. Frommer, an American communications professor at the University of Southern California, who was also tasked by James Cameron to create a language for the Na'vi to be used in the film *Avatar*. Frommer based some Na'vi grammar on Polynesian languages and used ejectives (voiceless consonants) and word-initial velar nasals that do not occur in Western languages, while omitting common Western sounds like "b," "d," and "g."

9. Sing Along!

The actual translated lyrics are:

> *O beautiful forest, There are tears in the forest.*
> *Woodsprite(s). We cry out, calling,*
> *"O Eywa!"*

> *Connected as one, O Great Mother.*
> *Woodsprite(s). We cry out, calling,*
> *"O Eywa!"*

> *By the People's will, The forest is singing.*
> *Woodsprite(s). We cry out, calling,*
> *"O Eywa!"*

10. Animatronic Magic

The Shaman of Songs moves with a level of fluidity not seen in any other Disney Animatronic, including impressive figures such as the Wicked Witch of the West in the former Great Movie Ride, and Hopper from It's Tough to Be a Bug. This movement, combined with the intricate detailing of the facial features and musculature of the Shaman of Songs, will make Guests feel as if they are literally watching a real Na'vi creature.

Ten Things You May Not Know About
Kilimanjaro Safaris

1. The Heart of the Animal Kingdom

With Disney's Animal Kingdom now on the drawing boards, a safari ride would clearly be the focal point of the new park. The man in charge of bringing this safari themed attraction to life (as well as the majority of the Animal Kingdom park) was Joe Rohde. One of the first orders of business was a field trip to get a feel for the natural environments they would be recreating. A trip to the local zoo? Hardly. Rohde and his team actually traveled to the East African countries of Kenya and Tanzania for what would be the first of six trips to the region. On these trips, the crew gathered valuable knowledge and information, and they also collected a plethora of authentic artifacts to bring back. In addition, they carefully observed all the native customs of the local people, as well as their relationships with the various animals in the region.

2. Animals on Display

One of the challenges of the safari was to provide Guests with an authentic world where they could see the animals in their natural habitats. In doing so, the team realized that artificial fences and walls would ruin the immersive experience they hoped to provide. While there was no avoiding the barriers required to keep the animals separated from Guests and vice versa (as well as keeping the animals apart from each other), the Imagineers strived to keep things feeling as lifelike as possible, carefully designing the barriers so that they blended seamlessly into the surrounding landscape and would be virtually invisible to the naked eye.

3. Animals Everywhere

As with any safari, the main attraction is the animals. You'll find no shortage here on the savanna. In fact, Kilimanjaro Safaris is home to more than forty different species. The list reads like a "who's who" of the savanna, with animals such as cheetahs, elephants, giraffes, zebras, mandrills, hippos, crocs, flamingos, warthogs, wildebeest, black rhinos, white rhinos, Thomson's gazelles, and lions all taking up residence within the confines of the attraction. You'll even find four different species of ducks (much to Donald's delight!). The driver of the safari truck also serves as your tour guide, pointing out all the animals and answering any questions you may have.

4. Simba 1

Every ride vehicle at the attraction is named Simba 1. So if you've ever wondered why you always manage to hitch a ride in Simba 1 and never Simba 2 or Simba 3, this is why!

5. Powering Your Vehicle

The ride vehicles are modified GMC trucks that run not on gasoline but on liquid propane.

6. Refreshing!

Many ecologically-friendly techniques are used to entice the animals to stay in view of the Guests. One of these is a simple misting of the rocks around the lions. The cool mist is a proven favorite amongst the big cats.

7. That's BIG!

With 100 acres of savanna, 800 square-feet of natural terrain, and a total site area of nearly 5 MILLION square-feet, Kilimanjaro Safaris is the largest attraction in Disney history. As we've said before, it's so big that you could actually fit the entire Magic Kingdom inside!

8. Hey, Are Those Eggs Real?

The ostrich eggs visible on the safari do not actually have soon-to-be-born babies in them. Prior to the attraction's opening, the eggs were filled with concrete and placed there for decorative purposes.

9. Foiling the Poachers, Once Upon a Time

In the early days of the attraction, there was an additional Cast Member on each ride vehicle. The Cast Member (equipped with a prop gun!) would save the day, as they played a pivotal role in stopping the poachers who were hunting for elephants. The role was eliminated from the storyline after a few years, and the drivers now serve as the lone Cast Member inside the safari trucks.

10. Lions, Elephants, Giraffes, But No...?

Many people often wonder why there aren't any tigers to be found on Kilimanjaro Safaris. This is because tigers are native to Asia, not Africa. Their presence would compromise the attraction's storyline, thus the reason for their omission. (But if you really want to see some tigers, don't fret. Just wander over to the Maharajah Jungle Trek to catch a glimpse of these regal beasts.)

Ten Things You May Not Know About
Kali River Rapids

1. Not So Fast...

Construction on Kali River Rapids began in the summer of 1997. But when the Animal Kingdom opened on April 22, 1998, the attraction was nowhere near completion. In fact, it would be nearly an entire year before park-goers would get to "ride the rapids." The attraction finally opened on March 18, 1999, nearly two years after construction had initially begun. But it proved to be well worth the wait!

2. Rapid(s) Research

Disney Imagineers undertook a great amount of research while developing the attraction. They traveled to exotic locations like Nepal, Bali, Singapore, Thailand, and Java for information. As a result, traces of these cultures can be found throughout the attraction, most notably in the architecture of the buildings. The Imagineers brought back a treasure trove of artifacts made by the people of these regions and placed them throughout the queue and attraction. This combination of in-depth research and true regional artifacts really make it feel as if you've been transported right into the heart of the Asian rainforest.

3. An Amazing Backstory

Disney Imagineers also managed to create an elaborate and wonderfully themed backstory to go along with the attraction. Long ago, beautiful statues and shrines could be found throughout this little section of jungle. But today, piles of rubble and ruins are all that remain (As you make your way through the queue, keep your eyes peeled for these scattered remnants). However, there are still some signs of human life out here in this isolated stretch of Asian rainforest. A company by the name of "Kali Rapids Expeditions" operates here, and the main goal at Kali Rapids Expeditions is not to make money but to show Guests the rainforest's "natural beauty." The waterfalls, trees, rocky landscape, and wildlife all contribute to this natural beauty, and education on the importance of conservation is a vital key for the forest's survival. But we soon discover that not everyone in the area has the same agenda as Kali Rapids Expeditions. Lurking in the shadows is the ever-present threat of illegal loggers – and we're about to face this threat head on!

4. Mickeys Abound

In the queue area, keep an eye out on your left to find three plates on the wall forming a Hidden Mickey (they're in the room with the bicycle). Also, look above the entrance and exit doors to find a pair of golden Hidden Mickeys.

5. It Wasn't Always Going to Be Kali...

The original name for Kali River Rapids was going to be "Tiger Rapids Run."

6. But Where Are the Tigers?

The name was changed due to the fact that Disney thought the name might confuse or mislead Guests, as it wasn't certain that you would actually see any tigers from either the attraction or the queue.

7. Naming the Rafts

Each of the attraction's rafts has their very own name, and many of the names are quite creative. They include Sherpa Surfer, Java Jumper, Delhi Donut, Himalayan Hummer, Baloo Meaway, Khatmandoozie, and Bali Bumper-Car, to name a few.

8. But What Does "Kali" Mean Anyway?

The word "Kali" means "the black one." In addition, Kali is also the name of a well-known Hindu goddess.

9. Chakranadi

The river is appropriately named the Chakranadi, which in Sanskrit translates to "river that flows in a circle."

10. That's Quite a Drop!

The height of the incline at the beginning of the attraction is 19 feet, while the final drop at the end is a whopping 90 feet! That might sound like a long way down, but it's only 20 feet more than the drop in Pirates of the Caribbean, though admittedly that one is in the dark.

Ten Things You May Not Know About
Expedition Everest

1. A New Disney Mountain

When Disney's Animal Kingdom opened on April 22, 1998, the park promised to immerse Guests into a lush and authentic wilderness that represented the wonder and beauty of nature found throughout the world. The only attraction that could be classified as a thrill ride on that day was Countdown to Extinction (later renamed DINOSAUR), and while Kali River Rapids would open a few years later, Guests were still clamoring for a true headliner attraction to open at Disney's newest park. Fortunately, they wouldn't have to wait long, for plans had always been underway to bring a roller coaster thrill ride to the Animal Kingdom. In true Disney fashion though, this would be a roller coaster the likes of which had never been seen. In fact, one of the early concepts for the new attraction was a dragon-themed roller coaster that would have served as the anchor attraction for the park's proposed Beastly Kingdom section.

2. But Which Mountain?

In the end, the team of Imagineers, led by Joe Rohde, came back to a concept that had proved immensely popular with Guests over the years: the mountain. Over in Disneyland, the Matterhorn was enjoying a renewal in popularity due to the inclusion of the Abominable Snowman in 1978, and it made sense for his Far Eastern cousin, the Yeti, to find a home here at the Animal Kingdom. Since the Yeti was said to prowl the Himalayas, Mount Everest seemed like the logical home for the park's newest attraction. But even so, there was still much debate over that final choice. For one thing, Rohde didn't think that Mount Everest was distinctive enough in appearance, especially when compared to the Matterhorn of Disneyland or Japan's Mt. Fuji, one of several inspirations for the design of Space Mountain. The problem was solved in a uniquely Imagineer-esque way: Mount Everest would indeed appear in the attraction, but only as part of the mountain range that would include the attraction's true mountain...but we'll get to that a little later.

3. Making a Mountain Out of a Molehill

As the team of Imagineers started to design the look of the mountain itself, they started by making several small paper models based on a series of sketches by Chris Turner and his team of designers. These paper models were transformed into a 1/8th-inch scale clay model, and eventually a foam model. The design was revamped several times, and all in all went through 24 iterations before the final look was achieved. At this point, the model was six feet tall, and from there it was digitized into a computer. This process allowed the team to virtually program the ride itself before a single shovel was lifted, and it also allowed for the precise fabrication of the tons of rebar that would form the framework for the actual mountain. Utilizing the latest technology allowed the design process to take only 18 months, compared to the typical three to four years that would have been required using traditional methods.

4. It's All in the Details

This painstaking attention to detail wasn't just reserved for the mountain itself; the same care went into the creation of the surrounding village. The architecture of the buildings was largely based on the Kali Gandaki region of the Annapurna Conservancy area of the Himalayas. Two methods of construction native to the region were used to create the show buildings. One method was "Dry-laid Stone," used in the Tea House, and the other was the "Rammed Earth" method, in which moistened dirt is placed in a four-inch-high framed box and pounded with mallets until the material is as hard as concrete. Over 2,000 handcrafted items were brought in for use as architectural ornamentation, props, and cabinetry. Many of these items were actually made by native Newari wood-carvers from Nepal. Tibetan monks were consulted in regards to the earth-based pigments used to color the attraction's sets.

5. Twisting Tracks

Construction of the new attraction began in March 2003 and would be comprised of three separate structures: the mountain itself, the actual roller coaster, and the Audio-Animatronic Yeti. The mountain and the track presented two opposing challenges. The tracks of the roller coaster needed to be flexible enough to allow for the high speeds and turns of the train, while the mountain needed to be absolutely inflexible since it was covered with layers and layers of the carved plaster that formed the rocky exterior. Great care was taken to ensure that the two structures never got closer than six inches to each other...no small task! 5,000 tons of structural steel went into the ride and structural systems.

6. How to Build a Mountain

The exterior of the mountain was actually an outer shell of sculpted plaster that was put together like a giant puzzle. To accomplish this Herculean task, Imagineers came up with a solution that they called the "chip method." Using the digitized model as a starting point, the Imagineers were able to break this down into 3,307 individual modules, or "chips," each one measuring approximately six square feet. Each chip was assigned a specific place on the mountain's exterior, and the whole thing was assembled like a giant jigsaw puzzle. 27,000 pieces of computer-bent pieces of rebar went into the fabrication of the chips, and, all told, the chips added up to 218,00 square-feet of rockwork. Imagineers then used nearly 32,000 bags of cement to sculpt the individual rocks and peaks, using aluminum foil to mold the wet concrete into the exact shapes they wanted. They then finished off the exterior with more than 2,000 gallons of paint.

7. How Tall Is It?

When it was complete, Expedition Everest topped out at 199½ feet, making it the tallest Walt Disney World attraction. Despite what some people will tell you, it is not Florida's tallest mountain (that honor goes to Walton County's Britton Hill at 345 feet), though it is the Sunshine State's tallest artificial mountain.

8. Mixed Up Mountains

But let's get back to the issue of Mount Everest's innocuous appearance, as described by Joe Rohde. It turns out that the mountain you race through is not Mount Everest, it's the Forbidden Mountain. And unfortunately, the Yeti interrupted your journey before you could arrive at your final destination. Everest is actually the barren peak off in the distance, and that's how we make a memorable mountain!

9. An Historic Moment Immortalized

If you look closely at Mount Everest in the distance, you'll see that the famous final ascent of Sir Edmund Hillary in 1953 is represented in the coloring of the mountain peak. At the 29,000-feet elevation mark, hurricane-force winds often blow the snow off its peak, revealing a raw sheet of rock on the very place were Hillary first set foot at the top of the world.

10. Now We Know Why the Journey Is So Treacherous

"Serka Zong" means "Fortress of the Chasm."

Ten Things You May Not Know About
DINOSAUR

1. Countdown to Extinction

When Disney's Animal Kingdom opened on April 22, 1998, the attraction was called Countdown to Extinction. During the year 2000, Disney released the film *Dinosaur*, which chronicled the adventures of Aladar and Neera, two Iguanodons who travel with a herd of dinosaurs seeking out their breeding ground. The film was very popular, and the Animal Kingdom attraction was quickly renamed DINOSAUR to better tie in with the film. An Iguanodon statue was added to the front of the show building, replacing the original Styracosaurus. The movement of the vehicles was modified to be somewhat less intense – though it's still a wild ride! The attraction was also given a less frightening soundtrack. For instance, in the original soundtrack, you could hear the thunderous roars of the Carnotaurus following you after your first encounter, implying that you were being chased. Now you'll hear those same roars off in the distance, leading you to believe you've escaped – though you shouldn't count on that!

2. Pass the...Ketchup?

Look for the pipes over your head as you approach the Time Rover vehicles in DINOSAUR. The red pipe has the chemical name and formula for ketchup. (Lycopersicon lycopericum is also known as the tomato.) The yellow pipe has the chemical name and formula for mustard, and the white pipe features the chemical formula for mayonnaise! This is a tribute to McDonald's, one of the original sponsors of the attraction.

3. Those Are Some BIG Dinosaurs!

When the attraction opened, the dinosaurs were the largest Audio-Animatronic figures created – a distinction formerly held by the dinosaurs in Epcot's Universe of Energy Pavilion.

4. And Heavy Too!

To support the incredibly large and sophisticated dinosaur Audio-Animatronics, their dino-sized bases were built clear through the building structure down to their own large foundations buried in the ground.

5. Bill Nye

Speaking of the Universe of Energy, Bill Nye the Science Guy provides the narration in the queue/exhibit area. He also starred in Ellen's Energy Adventure, which of course featured its own cast of prehistoric creatures. He must really like dinosaurs!

6. Indiana Jones

DINOSAUR uses the same ride technology as Disneyland's Indiana Jones Adventure: Temple of the Forbidden Eye.

7. What's in a Name?

The vehicle that takes you back in time is called the CTX Time Rover. Why CTX? That's a reference to the attraction's original name, Countdown to Extinction.

8. Who's That Dino?

Even though the original Styracosaurus outside of the attraction building was replaced by an Iguanodon to better tie in to the *Dinosaur* film, a Styracosaurus does figure into the movie. Eema is one of the trio of elder dinosaurs befriended by Aladar.

9. Dinos Dinos Everywhere

You'll find a total of 19 different dinosaurs throughout your adventure; including the Styracosaurus, Alioramus, Parasaurolophus, Velociraptor, Cearadactylus, Saltasaurus, Iguanodon, and Compsognathus.

10. ROAR!

The fearsome dinosaur who bellows out an ear-splitting roar at the end is not a Tyrannosaurus as you might expect, it's actually a Carnotaurus. The Carnotaurus is not only loud, she's fast! Research shows that the Carnotaurus was well adapted for running and was possibly one of the fastest large dinosaurs. Good thing you're in a fast-moving jeep!

Disney Resorts

Ten Things You May Not Know About
Disney's Animal Kingdom Lodge

1. A Wild New Resort

The Animal Kingdom Lodge opened in the spring of 2001, three years after the opening of the Animal Kingdom theme park. The Animal Kingdom Lodge is more than just a resort though. It's a complete cultural experience, meshing African traditions with the building styles, cuisines, decor, animals, birds, and plant life that can be found throughout the continent.

2. Jambo House

The main building of the Animal Kingdom Lodge is the Jambo House, featuring a six-story lobby reminiscent of the Wilderness Lodge, but with a decidedly African theme. (And yes, just like the Wilderness Lodge, the Animal Kingdom Lodge boasts one of the tallest and most beautiful Christmas trees to be found at Disney during the holiday season). Several open-glass areas are scattered throughout the six levels of Jambo House, and each one provides a unique view of the scenery that surrounds this exotic resort.

3. The Savannas

There are three main savannas at the Animal Kingdom Lodge: Uzima, Sunset, and Arusha. Each savanna is about 10 acres in size, and all three are filled with amazing wildlife. You can find more than 30 different species of animals and birds on the savannas, including zebras, giraffes, impalas, wildebeest, and flamingos. At check-in, you'll receive a Wildlife Field Guide with a complete list of the species that can be found at the resort.

4. That Animal Looks Familiar...

Each of these three main savannas features different wildlife. The animals outside the rooms in one savanna are completely different from the animals in the other savannas. Well, all but one anyway. Which one? The Giraffe!

5. Kilimanjaro?

You may think that the animals you're seeing are the same ones found on Kilimanjaro Safaris at Disney's Animal Kingdom, but in fact these two areas are a significant distance apart and don't overlap at all.

6. Watching the Animals

If you don't have a room overlooking one of the savannas or if you're just visiting, don't worry. There are several viewing areas located around the Animal Kingdom Lodge. You'll find the start of the pathway at the far end of the lobby.

7. Under the Moonlight

After the sun goes down, artificial moonlight lights up the savannas, offering a unique view of the animals at nighttime.

8. Starlight Safari

One of the most spectacular experiences to be found at the Animal Kingdom Lodge is the Starlight Safari. The Starlight Safari takes you on a tour of the savannas, with a unique chance to see the animals in way you've never seen them before. You'll be given night vision goggles, and as you peer into the evening landscape you might see zebras, giraffes, gazelles, wildebeests, flamingos, ostriches, and more. The experience is open to all Walt Disney World Guests.

9. The View from the Water

You can even see the wildlife while you enjoy a swim, because the pool overlooks part of the Uzima Savanna.

10. Animal Kingdom Lodge Hidden Mickeys

The Animal Kingdom Lodge features plenty of Hidden Mickeys. In the main lobby, carefully study the log work. Also, look closely at the hallway carpeting all around the resort. For Hidden Mickey fun inside the Guest rooms, be sure to check out the bedspreads.

Ten Things You May Not Know About
Disney's Beach Club Resort

1. A Seaside Resort

The architecture of the Beach Club is reminiscent of the "stick-style" architecture found in seaside cottages from the 1860s and 70s. You'll find wicker furniture, limestone floors, and a seashell motif throughout this elegant resort.

2. Beautiful Gardens

The landscaping at the Beach Club is also reminiscent of a New England seaside resort, featuring magnolias, Japanese elms, Bradford pear trees, crape myrtle, gardenias and roses lining the courtyards and walkways.

3. Stormalong Bay

The Beach Club Resort's crown jewel (which it shares with the Yacht Club) is the Stormalong Bay pool. Stormalong Bay features a natural sand bottom and holds an impressive 750,000 gallons of water. The complex is separated into three lagoon sections. The first lagoon is mild and relaxing. The second lagoon is for thrill seekers, as it's filled with whirlpools and other exciting aquatic obstacles. The third lagoon allows you to snorkel the area around the Shipwreck. For the bravest Guests, the Shipwreck also features a gigantic waterslide known as the Flying Jib.

4. That's a LOOOOONG Slide

Just how gigantic is it? The Flying Jib stretches 150 feet into the air. That's only 30 feet shorter than Spaceship Earth, which stands at a height of 180 feet.

5. Getting to Epcot

In addition to taking a boat launch, you can walk to Epcot from this resort and enter the park through your very own entrance, the International Gateway. At one time, Guests could take a tram from the resort to the International Gateway. The tram no longer runs, but you could still see the Epcot tram station near the dock for the water launches. In recent years, that area was occasionally used for special events, such as a special DVC reception held around the holidays.

6. Getting to the Studios

You can also walk to Disney's Hollywood Studios from this resort! The path, which follows a scenic canal, is located behind the nearby BoardWalk Inn. The relaxing stroll takes about 10-15 minutes and affords you a breathtaking view of the Twilight Zone Tower of Terror.

7. Opening day

Despite what you might think, the Yacht Club and Beach Club Resorts didn't open on the same day. The Yacht Club opened on November 5, 1990. The Beach Club opened on November 19, 1990, a whole two weeks later.

8. Small and Cozy

Of all the Walt Disney World Deluxe Resorts, Beach Club's room total ranks as the second smallest. The Deluxe Resort with the lowest room total is the BoardWalk Inn, with 378 rooms.

9. Beach Club Hidden Mickeys

Countless Hidden Mickeys are scattered throughout Disney's Beach Club Resort. On your way to your room, be sure to check out the carpeting in the hallways. And in your room, look closely at all the paintings!

10. The Best Room of All

The Beach Club holds the distinction of being home to the Disney resort room closest to the entrance of a Disney park (discounting the suite in Cinderella Castle). Found on the extreme end of the first floor, room 1501 puts you a short walk away from the International Gateway entrance of Epcot.

Ten Things You May Not Know About
Disney's BoardWalk Inn

1. Atlantic City Nostalgia

Inspired by the New Jersey resorts of the 1920s, 30s, and 40s, the BoardWalk Inn transports you back to an era of carnivals, seaside entertainment, and Victorian nostalgia. From the outside, the Inn boasts a striking comparison to Atlantic City circa 1940. In fact, if you look at a picture of the Inn and compare it to an old shot of Atlantic City, you'll find that the two are hauntingly similar, from the striped awnings, white picket balconies, and string lighting down to roofs topped with flashy signs and flagged turrets.

2. The Tuxedo Sofas

Once you enter the majestic lobby you'll find hard wood flooring as well as chandeliers and other period-style lighting fixtures. The color scheme is bright and warm, with various shades of white interspersed with a very light shade of sea foam green. You'll find an assortment of interesting period furniture throughout the Inn, including a circular sofa, chairs with vibrant floral patterns, and tuxedo sofas (a style of sofa invented in the 1920s in Tuxedo Park, New York).

3. The Hippocampus Electrolier

Make sure to look for the whimsical chandelier in the lobby. That's the "Hippocampus Electrolier" (Hippocampus is a mythological creature; electrolier is a chandelier for electric lamps), and it weighs 3,000 pounds! The unique piece of art is finished entirely in 22-karat gold leaf, hand-cut Austrian crystal and custom-blown glass. The crystal globe at the bottom of the chandelier is a time capsule scheduled for opening during the 50th Anniversary celebration of the Walt Disney World.

4. Luna Park

The Luna Park Pool was named after an amusement park on New York's Coney Island. The original New York Luna Park operated from 1903 until 1944, when a series of fires sealed the amusement park's fate.

5. Bird Houses

If you make your way to the courtyard found outside toward the rear of the resort, you'll find a number of Garden Suites. The Garden Suites have a little birdhouse at the entrance to each private courtyard. The birdhouses each have their respective room number on it, so that way Guests will know which courtyard is theirs.

6. Coney Island Carousel

The carousel on display in the lobby is not a re-creation made for the Inn...it's actually an authentic carousel from the 1920s! The carousel was created for New York's Coney Island by carousel designer M.C. Illions.

7. The Convention Center

There are five Convention Centers at Walt Disney World, and one of them just happens to be located at the BoardWalk Inn. This Conference Center features 20,000 square feet of indoor space, as well as two outdoor pavilions. As impressive as that sounds (and it is), it actually makes the BoardWalk's Conference Center the smallest of the five.

8. BoardWalk Inn Hidden Mickeys

When it comes to Hidden Mickeys around the BoardWalk, the hunt is on at almost every turn. Look closely at the painting hanging over the middle Registration Counter and you'll discover that the foliage of one of the trees is a classic Mickey head! Now venture over to the white carousel horse with brown spots to find two classic Mickeys. One can be found on the horse's neck, while the second is located on his hind-end.

9. Antique Arcade Fun

A favorite destination of early visitors to the Magic Kingdom was the Penny Arcade, a replica of the arcades that popped up around the country in the early years of the 20th century. Guests could step inside and play modern and vintage games, as well as watch moving pictures in Mutoscopes and Cail-o-scopes. The Arcade closed in 1995, and the majority of the machines were placed in storage. However, a few of the machines can now be found at Disney's BoardWalk Inn (as well as the Main Street Train Station at the Magic Kingdom).

10. Gingerbread, Seaside Style

During the Christmas season, the BoardWalk Inn is home to a giant gingerbread house, which is made from 350 lbs. of gingerbread, 240 mini marshmallows, 240 large marshmallows, 80 lbs. of rolled fondant, 15 lbs. of modeling chocolate, 5 lbs. of dark chocolate, and... since we're at a seaside resort...90 lbs. of salt water taffy!

Ten Things You May Not Know About
Disney's Contemporary Resort

1. A True Original

The Contemporary and Polynesian resorts were only two of the original five resorts planned for the Magic Kingdom. The other resorts were going to be the Asian Resort, the Persian Resort, and the Venetian Resort.

2. A Unique Design

Disney's Contemporary Resort was created as a modern backdrop to Tomorrowland. The first structure to be constructed at the Contemporary Resort was the elevator shaft. Once that was completed, 13 steel-trussed A-frames were placed in position around it, forming a 150-foot-high skeleton. The rooms themselves were assembled a few miles away in the form of modules that were later transported to the construction site.

3. Learning the Business

When the Contemporary opened, Disney was new to the hotel business. To learn their way around, Disney leased the recently opened Hilton Inn South in Orlando, and used the 140-room hotel as a learning center, developing everything from training manuals to restaurant menus and everything in between.

4. The Grand Concourse Mural

The giant mural in the Grand Canyon Concourse was designed by Mary Blair, who also created the distinctive shapes and colors found on "it's a small world." The mural consists of 18,000 hand-painted tiles and is 90 feet tall. See if you can spot the five-legged goat in the mural. It is best viewed from the seventh and eighth floors on the monorail side of the tower.

5. Walking to the Magic Kingdom

If you want to walk from the Contemporary Resort to the Magic Kingdom, you'll find a path outside the main entrance leading to the park. The walk takes about 10 minutes, and you'll be able to see the monorail gliding overhead!

6. That's A Lot of Tomatoes!

The California Grill at Disney's Contemporary Resort serves 70 pounds of tomatoes every night during tomato season, which is July through November.

7. Chef Mickey's

In July 1990, the Village Restaurant, located in the Disney Village Marketplace (now known as Disney Springs), was renamed Chef Mickey's Village Restaurant. The restaurant closed on September 30, 1995 and was replaced by the Rainforest Cafe. In 1996, Chef Mickey's buffet, featuring character meals with Mickey and his pals, opened on the Grand Canyon Concourse in Disney's Contemporary Resort.

8. "I Am Not a Crook."

On November 17, 1973, President Richard Nixon delivered his "I am not a crook" speech from one of the ballrooms at the Contemporary Resort.

9. Bay Lake Tower

Opening in 2009, Bay Lake Tower is the luxurious DVC companion to the Contemporary Resort. The tower is connected to the main building via the Skyway Bridge. The bridge contains 167 miles of post-tensioning cable running through the concrete slabs. These cables could stretch from Bay Lake Tower to Disney's Vero Beach Resort and back. There are 1,398 tons of reinforcing steel, known as rebar, within the structure. This is equal to the weight of 254 full-grown elephants. Bay Lake Tower rests on a foundation of more than 800 concrete piles that are 16 inches in diameter and extend 70 feet into the ground. Stacked on top of one another, these would reach more than 10 miles into the sky.

10. Bathing in Style

Talk about class! Some of the rooms in Bay Lake Tower have movable partitions in the bathrooms so that you can watch the Magic Kingdom's evening fireworks from the luxury of your bathtub!

Ten Things You May Not Know About
Disney's Grand Floridian Resort & Spa

1. Victorian Elegance

Disney's Grand Floridian Resort & Spa is perhaps the most elegant of all of the Walt Disney World resorts, styled after the fabled beach resorts of the 19th century. The buildings are reminiscent of the Victorian era, embellished with intricate lattice work and balustrades and 120 miles of scrolls, turn posts, and curved moldings. Snow white towers and red-shingled roofs complete the distinctive facade, while an open-cage elevator, aviary, palms, and ferns set the mood in the Grand Lobby.

2. A Breathtaking Lobby

The lobby is a wonder unto itself, soaring five stories high to a breathtaking ceiling adorned with three illuminated stained-glass domes, ornate chandeliers, and metal scrolls. This distinctive style extends to the monorail platform, which is designed to resemble a Victorian train station.

3. The View from the Magic Kingdom

You can actually see the Grand Floridian from the Magic Kingdom monorail station, and in keeping with the attention to detail found throughout Walt Disney World, the Victorian-influenced architecture found in both provides Guests with a harmonious view.

4. The White Cadillac

The resort opened on June 28, 1988, and it was originally known as the Grand Floridian Beach Resort. (It was renamed a few years later.) The Grand Floridian was modeled after the Hotel del Coronado in California, and as you might expect it boasts a number of interesting features. For example, look for an elegant 1929 white Cadillac and horseless carriage outside the main entrance.

5. A Special Suite

The resort is home to the Walter E. Disney Suite, which is dedicated to the life and times of Walt Disney. The suite contains vintage photographs of Walt and his family, as well as a replica of his Carolwood Pacific Railroad locomotive in an enclosed presentation case.

6. Familiar Faces

As you wander about the second floor of the Grand Floridian lobby, take a look at the marble floor and see if you can find Peter Pan, Mrs. Potts, Pluto, and other beloved Disney characters in the elegant designs.

7. Alice in Wonderland

The Grand Floridian offers several pool areas for splashing good fun. One is a miniature "water park" geared toward children, inspired by the famous Disney animated classic, *Alice in Wonderland.*

8. Out and About

The Grand Floridian resort comprises several buildings, all individually named. In addition to the Main Building, you'll find Sago Cay, Sugar Loaf, Conch Key, Boca Chica, and Big Pine Key.

9. The Orchestra

In addition to the piano player that occasionally delights Guests relaxing in the main lobby, you may also hear a 6-piece band, Disney's Grand Floridian Society Orchestra, playing classic favorites on the second floor. The band's music features a wide range of styles, though they are all appropriate to the Victorian setting of the lobby. You might hear old-fashioned Dixieland music, with a mix of Chicago-style and a slower New-Orleans-style tempo. Or you might hear the sounds of swing, or even jazz standards flavored with bossa nova accents. The tunes may be familiar, but these are Disney classics performed in a way you've probably never heard before. The unique arrangements of these Disney songs are the work of the pianist, John Katalenic, who finds creative ways to make these songs fit the grandeur of the hotel.

10. A Surprise From a Princess

The Grand Floridian is a favorite spot for couples to be married (specifically at the nearby Wedding Pavilion), so don't be surprised if you see a beautiful bride and her entourage descending down the grand staircase. But that's not the only elegant surprise you might experience; occasionally you'll see a Disney Princess or two, accompanied by their princely husbands, wander into the lobby for an impromptu ball...and yes, you're invited to join in!

Ten Things You May Not Know About
Disney's Polynesian Village Resort

1. An Ever-Changing Name

When Disney's Polynesian Resort originally opened in 1971, it was known as the Polynesian Village Resort. The "Village" moniker was dropped from the title in 1985, though in 2014 the name was reverted back to the Polynesian Village Resort as it underwent its DVC expansion.

2. The Ceremonial House

The main building of the resort is called the Great Ceremonial House, and it was built in the style of a Tahitian royal assembly lodge.

3. The Customs Office

Be sure to check out the Customs Office outside the shop on the second floor. You'll notice a sign that says "Out to Lunch: Back in February." But if you come back in February it will say "August." Actually, it seems the proprietor is never coming back, so you're probably out of luck!

4. The Longhouses

Ten of the eleven longhouses have also undergone name changes since the resort opened. In 1999, many new longhouse names were introduced, such as Rarotonga, Tuvalu, and Rapa Nui. Most of the remaining longhouses flip-flopped their names, such as Samoa and Hawaii. Through the years, only one longhouse has managed to keep the same name it had on opening day: the Fiji longhouse.

5. Mahalo

You'll frequently hear the word "mahalo" at the Polynesian Resort, that means "thank you" in Polynesian. In fact, many Polynesian words are used at the resort to fully immerse you in the island experience.

6. Polynesian Hidden Mickeys

Disney's Polynesian Resort is filled with Hidden Mickeys to discover. In the Great Ceremonial House, look at the floor upon entering, as well as the carpeting at the Kona Café. You'll also find a Hidden Mickey on the back of the statue in the Boutiki store on the first floor. For Hidden Mickey fun inside the Guest rooms, checkout the paintings on the walls and the shower curtains in the bathrooms.

7. Paddling on Seven Seas Lagoon

At one point, Guests could rent a 40-foot long canoe to paddle on Seven Seas Lagoon. The canoe is long gone, but you can still enjoy a tranquil boat ride (especially in the evening) aboard the launch boat that takes you to the Magic Kingdom.

8. Bora Bora Bungalows

The Polynesian is home to the Polynesian Village Bora Bora Bungalows, part of Disney's Vacation Club. Located right on Seven Seas Lagoon, each bungalow has its own private deck, complete with a plunge pool. A what? Yup, you read that right! From your own private miniature pool you can watch the Magic Kingdom fireworks, and you can even hear the music thanks to the piped-in sound. Now that's luxury!

9. The Eastern Winds

In the early years of the Polynesian, Guests could take a cruise on an authentic 65-foot Chinese Junk, The Eastern Winds, which was docked at the resort and offered chartered excursions that included a cocktail lounge and fine dining. The ship left Disney in 1978.

10. The Strangler Fig

On the grounds of the Polynesian Village Resort, you'll find a giant tree marked with a plaque. The plaque makes reference to a particular plant that is taking over the host tree (a sable palm), giving the tree a unique appearance. The invading plant is known as the Ficus Aurea, but is better known by its common name, The Strangler Fig.

Ten Things You May Not Know About
Disney's Wilderness Lodge

1. That Incredible Lobby

The Wilderness Lodge has the highest "wow" factor of any of the Disney resorts, with a jaw-dropping 7-story, timber-framed lobby featuring towering totem poles, massive western-themed chandeliers, and a spectacular 82-foot tall stone fireplace. Breathtaking! And those timbers aren't just for decoration. That's all a part of the authentic construction. Those six-story bundled log columns support the roof dormers, and as you walk among the many balconies you can catch a glimpse of how all those timber frames tie in together.

2. Old Faithful Lodge

The main building is modeled on the historic Old Faithful Lodge in Yellowstone National Park, built in 1904, as well as other lodges from that era, created under the direction of Stephen Mather. Nature was the inspiration for this spectacular resort, and the rustic design took its cue from the Arts and Crafts movement of the early 1900s that sought to unify many of the elements of the untamed wilderness; harmony with nature, wildlife, and Native American culture.

3. The Grand Canyon Fireplace

Nowhere is that more evident than with the towering fireplace in the main lobby. The layered stone of the fireplace symbolizes the strata of the Grand Canyon, giving you a glimpse into two billion years of natural history. (See if you can spot the authentic fossils of some prehistoric plants and animals!)

4. The Original Totem Poles

The two original totem poles on either side of the lobby were carved in Washington State and were known as the Eagle and the Raven. And while you're soaking it all in, make note of the four massive chandeliers, topped with glowing tepees!

5. Wilderness Lodge Hidden Mickeys

The Wilderness Lodge is filled with lots of Hidden Mickeys. You can ask for an official list at the front desk to assist you in your search. Here are a few of the more famous ones: Look on the right side of the fireplace about a third of the way up to find a Hidden Mickey in the rocks. In the geyser pool, look closely in the rocks and see if you can spot a familiar shape. If you visit the Territory Lounge, look up at the ceiling and look for something special in the mural. You'll also find another Hidden Mickey in the mural on the wall as you enter the lounge.

6. Winnie the Pooh and Friends

Artist Point at The Wilderness Lodge used to host a character breakfast that featured Winnie the Pooh, Tigger, and other members of the Hundred Acre Wood gang. You could even get an "I Bounced with Tigger" sticker!

7. Wilderness Lodge Suites

The Wilderness Lodge contains several beautifully appointed suites, including the Yosemite Suite, the Yellowstone Suite, and of course, the Honeymoon Suite,

8. Watch Out for the Geyser!

The Fire Rock Geyser has a wind gauge that can moderate the height of the water eruption. Why is this necessary? Soon after the Wilderness Lodge opened, it was noted that water would sometimes blow onto Guest's balconies during particularly windy days, so a wind gauge was installed to monitor weather conditions and to adjust the geyser height accordingly.

9. Christmas Magic

The Wilderness Lodge is home to one of the most beautiful Christmas trees to be found at Walt Disney World, not to mention one of the tallest. How tall? 60 feet tall! Yes, you'll need a REALLY big ladder to place the ornaments at the top of that tree!

10. A Tranquil Journey on the Water

If you love boats, you can cruise the waters of Bay Lake by hopping on the boat that takes Guests from the Lodge to the Contemporary Resort and Fort Wilderness. There are two boats that continuously circle the lake in opposite directions.

Ten Things You May Not Know About
Disney's Yacht Club

1. The New England Seaside

The Yacht Club Resort, nestled on the shores of Crescent Lake behind Epcot, was designed to evoke the shingle-style New England seaside summer cottages of the 1880s. The architecture and decor are filled with all sorts of nautical touches. Sophisticated details can be found everywhere, from dark hardwood floors, rich millwork, and brass accents to leather couches, antique chandeliers and beautifully detailed ship models. The gray and white clapboard exterior evokes the classic style of Martha's Vineyard, and, like its sister resort the Beach Club, the grounds are surrounded by walkways lined with Japanese elms, crepe myrtle and magnolias.

2. The Lighthouse

A distinctive lighthouse, perched majestically at the end of the launch boat dock, beckons Guests from all around Crescent Lake.

3. Fun at the Shore

The Yacht Club shares one of the most spectacular pools at Walt Disney World, Stormalong Bay, with its sister resort, the Beach Club. Epcot and Disney's Hollywood Studios are both within walking distance (or take a launch boat if you prefer), and the nearby Boardwalk is a great place to visit for some nostalgic beachside fun.

4. Evenings by the Campfire

The sprawling resort features an additional quiet pool, the Ship Shape Health Spa, the Lafferty Place Arcade, the Bayside Marina, and a quiet beach right on Crescent Lake, where you can enjoy Movie Nights and Campfire Sing-Alongs.

5. Look Closely at the Furniture...

Look for a distinctive chest of drawers in the lobby. You'll find the names of many favorite Disney characters on the plaques on each drawer.

6. The Faux Elevator

There is a bank of four elevators in the lobby, or at least there appears to be. One of them is actually a faux elevator, can you tell which one? (HINT: you might want to call someone for a clue.)

7. The Breathless II

The Breathless II at the marina is an authentic replica of a 1930 "Chris Craft Runabout," one of only fifteen that were ever built. It is 27' long and is constructed of solid wood.

8. Look Carefully at the Flags

The nautical flags found in the Fittings & Fairings store (as well as those on the guest room bedspreads) aren't random. They actually spell out "Disney's Yacht Club Resort."

9. Where Did That Sand Come From?

The sand on the beaches of Stormalong Bay was imported, not from New England as you might expect, but from New Mexico!

10. The Lobby Globe

The globe in the lobby was designed for the Yacht Club by Disney Imagineers to resemble globes from the 19th century, but it also includes some fictitious names and places (look closely!). You'll also find a Hidden Mickey somewhere in the southern seas.

People & Characters

Ten Things You May Not Know About
Walt Disney

1. Walt's Tie Clip

The Partners statue in the Magic Kingdom features an odd monogram on Walt Disney's tie. You might expect it to be Walt's initials or Mickey Mouse, but it's not. It actually stands for the Smoke Tree Ranch in Palm Springs, California, where Walt owned a vacation home.

2. Partners Statue Quote

You might also think that the plaque on the statue would immortalize one of Walt's most famous quotes: "My only hope is that we never lose sight of one thing, that it was all started by a mouse," considering he's standing hand in hand with Mickey. But it doesn't. It says "We believe in our ideas: a family park where parents and children can have fun - together."

3. Walt's Earliest Animations

Technically though, it didn't even start with a mouse. Walt's earliest animations included the Alice Comedies, where he mixed live action with animation. Mickey wasn't even Disney's first named animated character; earlier creations included a cat named Julius (from the Alice series) and Oswald the Lucky Rabbit, created in 1927. Mickey wouldn't come on the scene until 1928.

4. Mortimer?

He may have been a mouse, but he wasn't always Mickey. The original name Walt had chosen for his new character was Mortimer. Walt's wife Lillian suggested a shorter, better name. Good thing too, or else the song would go: "Who's the leader of the club that's made for you and me? M-O-R-T-I-M...", well, you get the idea.

5. To the Library

When Walt first delved into the world of animation, he borrowed a book from the Kansas City Library called "Animated Cartoons: How They Are Made, Their Origin and Development" by Edwin G. Lutz. The book detailed the methods of animation technique used in New York, then the center of animation.

6. The Animation Table

Walt did make a significant improvement, however. In the New York method of animation, the pegs that held the paper in place (to keep them aligned) were placed at the top of the board to keep them away from the animator's hands. Walt moved them to the bottom so the animators could easily flip the pages to see the action they were animating. It would be the first of a long list of innovations that Walt would introduce.

7. Walt's First Foray into the Art World

Walt's first art job was as an apprentice at the Pesmen/Rubin commercial art shop, where he drew roughs for advertisements and catalogs. One of his first assignments was to create an ad for a donut shop. The job didn't last long; Walt was terminated after the holiday season.

8. Laugh-O-Grams

He didn't fare much better in subsequent ventures. Walt opened his own studio to produce Laugh-O-Gram cartoon shorts. Though initially successful, the company soon went bankrupt. Walt's fortunes would change soon.

9. Walt's Triumph

Less than eight years later, *Snow White and the Seven Dwarfs* was released, earning more than $8 million. The film also earned Disney one of his 26 Academy Awards (this one was accompanied by seven smaller statuettes). It was not his first; he had already won eight Short Subject-Cartoon awards.

10. Twinkle Twinkle Little Planet

The next time you wish upon a star, you might think about a planet instead. In 1980, a minor planet was discovered by L.G. Karachkina. It was named Disneya in honor of Walt Disney.

Ten Things You May Not Know About
Mickey Mouse

1. Happy Birthday!

Mickey's birthday is November 18, 1928, the day that the short *Steamboat Willie* was released. But that wasn't Mickey's first appearance. He made his debut in *Plane Crazy* and had a follow-up short called *The Gallopin' Gaucho*. However, *Steamboat Willie* was the first Mickey Mouse cartoon to find a distributor, and that's when his career really started.

2. A True Star

Fifty years later, Mickey celebrated his birthday by getting a star on the Hollywood Walk of Fame, making him the first cartoon character to be so honored.

3. You Knew We Had to Mention Those Ears

Mickey's ears have the unusual characteristic of always appearing perfectly round, no matter which way he is facing.

4. But Those Fingers...

He also has three fingers on each hand instead of four. Why three? It's not a bizarre quirk of mouse anatomy; it just makes his hands easier to draw.

5. 3D Mickey

Mickey made his CGI debut in the Magic Kingdom attraction, Mickey's PhilharMagic. The 3D film actually follows the adventures of Donald Duck as he searches for Mickey's sorcerer's hat as seen in the film *Fantasia* during the Sorcerer's Apprentice sequence.

6. The Sorcerer's Apprentice

The Sorcerer's Apprentice scene was also the inspiration for the giant Mickey hand that adorned Spaceship Earth for many years. The Mickey hand held a giant magic wand, despite the fact that Mickey never held a wand in the film itself.

7. Steamboat Willie

Steamboat Willie was the first cartoon to feature a synchronized sound track. However, Mickey himself wouldn't speak for six more shorts. And what were his immortal first words? "Hot dogs, hot dogs!"

8. The Mickey Watch

The first Mickey Mouse watch was manufactured in 1933 and sold for $3.25. Looking for something a little more extravagant? Today, you can purchase a diamond studded, hand-painted Mickey watch with a Mother of Pearl dial for a mere $4500.

9. Mickey's Voice

Mickey Mouse's voice was originally provided by none other than Walt Disney himself, who took great pride in perfecting Mickey's falsetto vocal style. For many years, Mickey's voice was provided by Wayne Allwine. Bret Iwan (Mickey's current voice actor and a former Hallmark greeting card artist), was cast as Allwine's understudy. Sadly, Allwine passed away in 2009 before the two had a chance to meet. Coincidentally, Allwine was married to Russi Taylor, the current voice of Minnie Mouse.

10. Mickey Ears (The Cap, Not His Actual Ears...)

The name Roy Williams may not be familiar to Disney fans, but he's responsible for one of the most familiar Disney symbols of all. A long time Disney employee, Roy was handpicked by Walt Disney to be a new (but much older) Mouseketeer on the "Mickey Mouse Club." Why? According to Roy, Walt "looked up at me and said, 'Say, you're fat and funny looking. I'm going to put you on [the show] and call you the Big Mooseketeer.'" But his greatest contribution would come not through his acting but from his idea (inspired by a gag in the 1929 short *The Karnival Kid* where Mickey tips his ears to Minnie) of creating a little cap for Guests that would let them tip their own set of ears. And thus was born one of the most endearing Disney souvenirs of all time, the famous Mickey Mouse Ears.

Ten Things You May Not Know About
Minnie Mouse

1. Minnie's Debut

Like her beau, Mickey Mouse, Minnie's first appearance was in the 1928 short *Plane Crazy*.

2. Always Second Fiddle

While Minnie would go on to appear in 73 cartoons with Mickey and Pluto, she is the only member of the famed Fab Five (Mickey, Minnie, Donald, Pluto, and Goofy) to never have headlined her own film.

3. Minnie's Real Name

In the comic strip story "The Gleam," published in 1942, it was revealed that Minnie's full name is Minerva Mouse. Walt Disney later admitted that Minnie was named after Minnie Cowles, the wife of Dr. John Cowles, who was an investor in one of Walt's earliest animation ventures, Laugh-O-Gram studios.

4. A Name All Her Own

Speaking of names, Minnie was a very popular name in the United States in the late 1800s. When the Social Security Administration began keeping track of baby names in 1880, Minnie was the fifth most popular name in the country. It remained a top 10 name until 1892, when it began to decline in popularity. Today the name doesn't even appear in the top 1,000 names in the country, which definitely puts Minnie Mouse in a class by herself!

5. Minnie's Voice

The first voice of Minnie Mouse was Marcellite Garner, originally from the Ink and Paint Department at the Disney Studio. She is currently voiced by Russi Taylor, who was married to Wayne Allwine, the third voice of Mickey Mouse, until he died on May 18, 2009. Interestingly,

Taylor provided the voice for another Disney mouse, though admittedly one who wasn't quite as famous. She played Nurse Mouse, the assistant to Doctor Mouse and a competent second-in-command in 1990's *The Rescuers Down Under.*

6. Minnie's "Other" Voice

Like Mickey, Minnie's voice was sometimes provided by Walt Disney himself in the early days!

7. She's a Busy Mouse!

In addition to Minnie's duties as editor of Minnie's "Cartoon Country Living" magazine, she also quilts, paints, and gardens.

8. Minnie's Year

The year 1986 was declared "Minnie's Year" throughout the Disney parks, giving Mickey's sweetheart the recognition that she deserved.

9. Mrs. Mouse?

Mickey and Minnie are sweethearts, but the big question is, are they married? While they've never been married on-screen, Walt Disney, in a 1933 interview with "Film Pictorial" magazine, said, "In private life, Mickey is married to Minnie...What it really amounts to is that Minnie is, for screen purposes, his leading lady." So that settles the question, right? Not quite. Two years later in 1935, Walt told Louise Morgan in the News Chronicle "There's no marriage in the land of make-believe. Mickey and Minnie must live happily ever after."

10. Relatively Speaking...

Minnie's marital status might be a mystery, but we do know that she has two nieces, Melody and Millicent. She has also had several pets, including Figaro, Fifi, and Frankie. Interestingly, one of her first pets was a familiar looking dog named Rover. That playful canine was soon renamed Pluto, and he went on to have quite a career of his own.

Ten Things You May Not Know About
Donald Duck

1. Happy Birthday Donald

Donald Duck's birthday is June 9, 1934, making him nearly six years younger than Mickey Mouse. Unlike Mickey, who had a name change after he was created, Donald's moniker has always been the same. But Donald has something that Mickey doesn't have: a middle name.

Quick quiz. What is it?

2. The Wise Guy

Donald Duck was created partly because Mickey Mouse had become too "nice." Audiences expected Mickey to behave and to be the good guy, so Donald was brought in to be his mischievous counterpart. But why a duck? You might expect that a great deal of market research and testing went into the decision, but the simple fact is that Walt Disney overheard voice actor Clarence Nash reciting "Mary Had a Little Lamb" in a peculiar duck voice, and Walt liked it. Thus, Donald was born.

3. Donald's First Film

That must have been some reading! Donald Duck went on to recite "Mary Had a Little Lamb" in the 1934 cartoon *Orphan's Benefit*, which was his first appearance alongside Mickey Mouse. It wasn't Donald's first role however; that distinction goes to the 1934 short *The Wise Little Hen*. Donald wouldn't star in his own feature until 1936's *Donald and Pluto*.

4. Donald's Rise to Fame

Once Donald got that first leading role, he quickly rose to stardom. In 1937, he started headlining his own cartoons, and by the mid-1940s, he had become more popular than

Mickey himself, starring in more than 100 cartoons over the next two decades.

5. No Wonder He Acts Confused

Not only does Donald have flat feet (which you might expect; he is a duck after all), he's also color blind.

6. The Love of His Life

Daisy Duck may be Donald's true love, but she wasn't his first. That honor goes to Donna Duck, who appeared in the 1937 cartoon short *Don Donald*. Daisy would make her debut three years later in *Mr. Duck Steps Out*.

7. But Oh, Those Nephews...

Donald of course has a trio of famous nephews, Huey, Dewey, and Louie, and an equally famous uncle, Uncle Scrooge. But he also has a cousin, Gus Goose, and a grandmother, Elvira Coot. Not to be outdone, Daisy has a set of triplet nieces: April, May, and June.

8. Hollywood Stardom

Like Mickey Mouse, Donald Duck has a star on the Hollywood Walk of Fame. He received his in 2005.

9. Sports Stardom

Donald may have followed in Mickey's footsteps when he got his star, but Donald has one honor that Mickey doesn't have: that of being a mascot for a college athletic program. Donald serves as the fighting duck mascot for the University of Oregon, whose team is officially known as the Ducks.

10. Donald Comes to Epcot

Donald also holds the distinction of being the first classic Disney character to have a starring role in an Epcot attraction, when Gran Fiesta Tour Starring the Three Caballeros opened in 2007. (By classic, we're referring to the older animated characters. Nemo doesn't quite fit the bill, even though the Seas with Nemo & Friends opened six months earlier.)

By the way, of the Three Caballeros, Panchito Pistoles (the rooster) is the only true Mexican character of the trio. José Carioca (the parrot) is from Brazil, and of course Donald is from the good old U. S. of A.

Oh, did you think we forgot? Donald Duck's middle name is Fauntleroy.

Ten Things You May Not Know About
Goofy

1. What IS Goofy?

Okay, once and for all, Goofy is most definitely a dog. How do we know? Because his original name was Dippy Dawg, of course! But why does Goofy talk while Pluto does not? Because Pluto is Mickey's pet, and as everyone knows, pets don't talk.

2. Happy Birthday Goofy

Goofy's birthday is May 25, 1932. That's when he first appeared (as Dippy Dawg) in the cartoon short *Mickey's Revue*. His first appearance as Goofy was two years later in *Orphan's Benefit*, which also saw the debut of Donald Duck.

3. Mr. Goofy?

So, is Goofy his first name or his last name? It's hard to say. His full name has variously been given as George Geef, Goofus D. Dawg, and G.G. Goof. His son's name is Max Goof, and his father's is Benjamin Goof, leading one to believe that Goofy is simply a nickname. But in recent years, his proper name has evolved to Goofy Goof, so first name it is!

4. Hee-Yuk

Goofy's distinctive "hee-yuk" was originally voiced by Pinto Colvig, who was also the voice of both Sleepy and Grumpy in *Snow White and the Seven Dwarfs*, as well as the pig who built the house of bricks in the classic Disney short *Three Little Pigs*.

5. Goofy's TV Show

Even though Goofy was the last member of the Fab Five to come on the scene, he was the first to star in his own television series, "Goof Troop," which debuted in September 1992.

6. The Common Man

For a time in the 1950s, Goofy was known as Mr. George Geef, a common man contending with the perils of modern living. Gone were his big teeth and floppy ears, and even his voice was changed to a more normal tone.

7. A True(?) Athlete

Goofy took an interest in personal fitness in the 1980s, taking on the persona of Sport Goof. How did he do? He must have fared pretty well because he was eventually named the official mascot of the French Olympic team!

8. Super Goof

Goofy also has a secret identity, Super Goof, able to leap tall buildings in a single bound, most of the time anyway. Often he would lose his powers at the last minute, leading to hilarious results. And how did he get his super powers? Super goobers, of course! (Those are peanuts to you and me.)

9. Goofy's Place in Animation History

Goofy has a film-making connection with his smaller canine cousins, the puppies in *One Hundred and One Dalmatians*. The 1961 film was the first to use the xerography technique, which replaced the painstaking process of hand-inking each animation cel. (It sure beat having to draw all those spots by hand!) Coincidentally, Goofy's last "classic" solo animated short, *Aquamania*, was made the same year, and it was the only time a solo Goofy cartoon used xerography in its production.

10. The Joke's on Him

You might spot Guests wearing familiar floppy-eared Goofy hats around the Magic Kingdom, but one of Goofy's first merchandising appearances was in a deck of playing cards. Which card? The Joker, of course!

Ten Things You May Not Know About
Pluto

1. Pluto the Planet, er, Dwarf Planet, er...

Pluto was discovered in 1930 while scientists were searching for a new planet beyond the orbit of Neptune. Once known as the ninth planet, Pluto has since lost its planetary status and is now considered to be a dwarf planet. Pluto has five moons and, hold on a minute; this is supposed to be a piece on the Disney dog, not the astronomical body...!

2. Which Came First?

But that does beg the question, was the one-time planet named for the dog or was the dog named for the planet? Pluto made his film debut in 1930 (the same year as the planet's discovery) in the cartoon short *The Chain Gang*, though, at the time, he was unnamed. It would be another year before he was formally called Pluto the Pup (in the cartoon *The Moose Hunt*). So the first part of the mystery is that the planet came first (and was in fact named for the Roman God of the Underworld). But how was the dog named? No one is quite sure. It's possible, and likely, that the recent discovery of the (then) ninth planet was the inspiration, but no one remembers for certain.

3. Mickey's Pet

As we mentioned in our Goofy Top Ten List, Pluto was not given human characteristics when he was animated; he appeared more or less like a regular dog. Why? In the classic Disney hierarchy, Pluto is a notch below Mickey, Minnie, Donald and Goofy, seeing as he is clearly Mickey's pet. As a result, he shows many dog traits such as walking on all fours (though more on that later) and not being able to speak...apart from the occasional growl or bark.

4. Speak!

Well, that's not quite true. Pluto did speak on one occasion in the 1931 short *The Moose Hunt* (which you may recall was the first short in which he was referred to by his proper name). He has been silent ever since. And what were those infamous words? "Kiss me."

5. Pluto in the Parks

Astute observers will also note that, unlike real dogs, the Pluto we see in the theme parks walks on two legs rather than four. Good thing too, or that would make for some awfully dirty autograph books.

6. Who's Rover?

Even more astute observers will also recall that Mickey wasn't always Pluto's owner. His first owner was actually Minnie Mouse, and at the time he was called Rover (he might not have had his final name yet, but at least he wasn't nameless!). We learn this from Pluto's second appearance in the short *The Picnic*.

7. Tomorrowland Pluto?

Wait, Rover? Hmm, where have we seen that name before...why, at the Carousel of Progress in Tomorrowland of course (look on the dog bowls throughout the presentation if you don't believe us)! Let's see, Rover the dog can be found inside a futuristic building at the end of the Avenue of the Planets...dog, Disney, planet...a coincidence?

8. We Thought He Sounded Grumpy

In his early days, Pluto was voiced (OK, "barked") by Pinto Colvig. If those barks sound familiar, well, you have better hearing than the rest of us. But to give you the benefit of the doubt, you might have heard traces of the "house of bricks" pig, the dwarfs Sleepy and Grumpy, and even a Munchkin from *The Wizard of Oz* in Pluto's growls. They were all voiced by Colvig, who was also the original voice of fellow Disney dog Goofy.

9. Pluto's...Son?

Did you know that Pluto has a son? Yep! While the astronomical Pluto has five moons with the mysterious and exotic names of Charon, Nix, Styx, Kerberos, and Hydra, our canine pal's son goes by the simpler name, Pluto Jr. (Which, for our money, still would have been a better name for the dwarf planet's biggest moon.)

10. Cuddly Co-stars

Pluto also paved the way for a couple of other cuddly Disney characters. His 1943 short *Private Pluto* introduced Chip 'n' Dale to the world. Like Pluto, however, they were unnamed in their first cinematic appearance.

Ten Things You May Not Know About
Tinker Bell

1. What's with that Name?

Tinker Bell's name came from the fact that she was originally a fairy who fixed pots and kettles, just like a tinsmith or tinker. In the original play, she communicated with a tinkling bell sound.

2. Her First Appearance

Tinker Bell first appeared in the 1904 play, "Peter Pan: or, The Boy Who Wouldn't Grow Up" by Sir James M. Barrie. In the play, as well as in later depictions, she is seen as kind and helpful one minute while vindictive and jealous the next. Why such disparate emotions? It's simple, her diminutive size prevents her from holding more than one feeling at a time!

3. Pixie Dust

Tinker Bell is known for sprinkling pixie dust around, and indeed, pixie dust has become synonymous with magical happenings throughout Walt Disney World. However, pixie dust is purely a Disney creation. In the original play it was merely fairy dust.

4. Tinker Bell's Wand

One of the first pieces of Tinker Bell merchandise ever offered at Disney parks was a glow in the dark wand, even though she never actually used one in the 1953 Disney film *Peter Pan*.

5. Taking Flight

Millions have dazzled at the sight of Tinker Bell flying down from the top of the castle before the evening fireworks. This tradition started in 1961 in Disneyland, when the part of Tinker Bell was performed by Hungarian-born circus performer Tiny Kline, who was 71 years old at the time!

6. Marilyn Bell?

Legend has it that Marilyn Monroe was the inspiration for the look of Tinker Bell, but that's not true. Her real-life reference model was Margaret Kerry, who was also the voice of Spinner and Paddlefoot in the "Clutch Cargo" animated TV show.

7. Tink's Voice

She is currently voiced by Mae Whitman, whose voice work also includes the part of Katara in the animated television series "Avatar: The Last Airbender."

8. Tinker Bell in the Jungle

You could once get Tinker Bell's autograph in Adventureland at Tinker Bell's Magical Nook (along with some of her fairy friends). Her Meet and Greet Nook has since been moved to Main Street U.S.A., next to that of a rather famous mouse.

9. Tinker Bell's Talent

Each fairy has her own special talent, but what is Tinker Bell's talent? In keeping with her origins, she is a problem-solver and inventor. And what has she invented? Why, an acorn crusher and the flower sprayer of course!

10. A Baby's Laugh

So where exactly did Tinker Bell come from? Sir James Barrie once said that "'When the first baby laughed for the first time, the laugh broke into a thousand pieces and they all went skipping about...and that was the beginning of faeries." This idea was echoed in the *Tinker Bell* film, where she was born from the first laugh of a baby and brought by the winds to Pixie Hollow. And she's been spreading pixie dust ever since!

Ten Things You May Not Know About
Winnie the Pooh

1. Winnie's Birthday

Winnie the Pooh was born on October 14, 1926, when A.A. Milne's original book, "Winnie-the-Pooh," was published. That makes Pooh older than Donald Duck, Goofy, and even Mickey Mouse himself!

2. Hyphens or Not?

Winnie the Pooh wasn't always Winnie the Pooh. When A.A. Milne first wrote the tale of this lovable bear, he was called Winnie-the-Pooh, hyphens and all. When Disney adapted the beloved stories into the classic series of featurettes, the dashes were dropped – a boon to typists everywhere.

3. So Where Did the Name Originate?

Milne's son Christopher (yes, that is how Christopher Robin got his name) had a toy bear that he named after a real bear he often visited at the London Zoo. The bear's name? Winnipeg – or Winnie for short.

4. What about "Pooh"?

Pooh was the name of a swan who was also a resident at the zoo, but Milne crafted a more prosaic explanation in the first chapter of his book. *"But his arms were so stiff...they stayed up straight in the air for more than a week, and whenever a fly came and settled on his nose he had to blow it off. And I think – but I am not sure – that that is why he is always called Pooh."*

5. The Toy Bear Today

The original Winnie at the London Zoo has long since left us, but you can still visit Christopher Milne's toy bear at the main branch of the New York Public Library.

6. Pooh Sticks

Winnie the Pooh fans are familiar with the game Pooh Sticks, where players stand over a bridge and drop their sticks at the same time, and the first stick to emerge from underneath the bridge is the winner. But did you know that you can play Pooh Sticks in a real competition? Enthusiasts gather every year at Day's Lock near Dorchester-on-Thames, Oxfordshire, England, for the Pooh Sticks Championships held on the river Thames.

7. Winnie in the Movies

The Many Adventures of Winnie the Pooh, released on March 11, 1977, was a collection of three previously released featurettes: *Winnie the Pooh and the Honey Tree* (1966), *Winnie the Pooh and the Blustery Day* (1968), and *Winnie the Pooh and Tigger Too* (1974). Strictly speaking, it was the last film in which Walt Disney had personal involvement, since *Winnie the Pooh and the Honey Tree* was released before Walt passed away (the scene where Rabbit decorates Pooh's rump to look like a moose was a favorite of Walt's), and he was involved in the production of *Winnie the Pooh and the Blustery Day.*

8. And the Oscar Goes To...

Winnie the Pooh and the Blustery Day won the 1968 Academy Award* for Best Animated Short Film, and to date it is the only Winnie the Pooh film to win the award.

9. An International Bear

If you think Winnie the Pooh is popular in the United States, then venture over to Warsaw, Poland, where you'll find a street named after him, Ulica Kubusia Puchatka. (You'll also find a street named after him in Budapest, Micimackó Utca.)

10. Popular Pooh

Just how popular is Pooh? He generates nearly $1 billion in features and merchandising sales annually, which is estimated to be more than Mickey Mouse, Donald Duck, and Goofy combined. Not bad for a silly old bear.

Ten Things You May Not Know About
The Disney Princesses

1. The Official Lineup

There are 11 official Disney Princesses: Snow White, Cinderella, Aurora (Sleeping Beauty), Ariel, Belle, Jasmine, Pocahontas, Mulan, Tiana, Merida, and Rapunzel. (Or is it 12? Elena of Avalor is a newly announced sixteen-year-old Latin American princess. She is an official Disney princess but is not part of the merchandising lineup.)

2. Wait, What about...

Why not Anna and Elsa? It turns out that the *Frozen* franchise is so successful that it was felt unnecessary to add them to the Disney Princess lineup. The popularity and recognition that both Anna and Elsa constantly receive would have overshadowed the rest of the members of the franchise.

3. But How About...

Some may wonder why other female Disney characters haven't joined the ranks of the Disney Princesses. Sometimes it's because their films didn't perform well at the box office (and consequently aren't very well known, as is the case with Kida from the film *Atlantis*). Others are deemed to be too young (e.g. *Sofia from Sofia the First*), or because they're not human (e.g. Nala from *The Lion King*). We're still holding out hope for Vanellope von Schweetz though!

4. Enchanted

But what about Giselle from *Enchanted*? She seems to fit all of the criteria of being a Disney Princess, and in fact her character was inspired by Disney's own princess franchise. Though her film was a success and she was initially intended to join the line-up, plans were dropped when Disney realized that they would have to pay royalties to Amy Adams for using her likeness. And to be technical, it is her friend, Nancy, who ends up marrying the Prince.

5. That'll Buy A Lot of Tiaras

In 2006, the total sales of Disney Princess merchandise topped $3 billion. Yes, that's billion with a "B!"

6. True Royalty

Despite the moniker of "princess," there is one Disney Princess that isn't royal by virtue of blood or marriage. That would be Mulan, though she did receive a grace of honor from the Emperor of China, the only female to earn that distinction. Some may protest that Pocahontas belongs in the same category, but since she is the daughter of the chief of her tribe, she is considered to be royalty by English standards.

7. How Old Are They?

Snow White is the youngest of the Disney Princesses at 14, while Tiana, 19, is the oldest.

8. Left Out

There was one character that was dropped from the official Disney Princess lineup. That dubious honor belongs to Tinker Bell, but don't feel badly for her. The reason she was dropped was that because she was so popular, it was decided that she would head up her own group, the Disney Fairies.

9. Where's Their Crown?

Five princesses didn't wear a tiara or crown in their respective feature films. They would be Snow White, Belle, Jasmine, Pocahontas, and Mulan (though all of them do wear crowns in their roles as Disney Princesses).

10. A New Princess on the Way

Princess Moana (from the movie of the same name) is expected to join the line-up soon, which would bring the official Disney Princess count to 12.

Disney Films

Ten Things You May Not Know About
Snow White and the Seven Dwarfs

1. A Boy and a Dream

The origins of *Snow White and the Seven Dwarfs* go back to 1917, when a young Walt Disney saw a film version of a play starring Marguerite Clark in the Kansas City Convention Hall. As Walt would later write, "My impression of the picture has stayed with me through the years, and I know it played a big part in selecting Snow White for my first feature production."

2. A Legend in the Making

And what a production it was. *Snow White and the Seven Dwarfs* was the first feature length cel-animated film, the first in full color, and the highest grossing film of 1938. The film received its official premier on December 21, 1937, at the Carthay Circle Theatre, attended by such Hollywood legends as Charlie Chaplin, Clark Gable, Shirley Temple, and Judy Garland. The film has been re-released on numerous occasions throughout the years, and it continues to inspire our imaginations. To this day, *Snow White* is still among the top ten money-making films of all time when inflation is taken into account.

3. Bringing the Dwarfs to Life

One of the biggest challenges that the animators faced was giving each dwarf his own personality. They initially tried to give each dwarf his own quirk so that they would have signature behaviors. It was soon realized that this approach was too superficial, so the animators sought to dig deeper and to understand their individual personalities. To do so, they turned to real life inspiration, using Will Rogers as the personality of Bashful, and Roy Atwell for Doc, who would eventually provide his voice. (Walt said of Atwell, "He is, like Doc, a windbag type. He loves to talk of 'the good old days when...'")

4. Dopey, Always the Odd One Out

Dopey presented the biggest challenge of all the dwarfs because, as Walt explained, "We are depending on him to carry most of the belly laughs." Many different approaches were tried, including modeling him after Harpo Marx and Charlie Chaplin, but nothing seemed to work. Oddly enough, inspiration finally came not from an actor, but from an old friend. Walt had the idea of making Dopey a "human with dog mannerisms and intellect," and for that, the animators needed to look no further than to Mickey Mouse's friend Pluto. By giving Dopey some canine traits, they were finally able to transform into the lovable dwarf we know today.

5. Animation Innovation

The production of *Snow White and the Seven Dwarfs* led to the development of another technological innovation, the multiplane camera. The new camera allowed four levels of animation to be filmed simultaneously, and for the first time ever viewers could move through a scene with a sense of real perspective and three dimensionality. The multiplane camera was first put to use on the 1937 animated short, *The Old Mill*, and the result was a resounding success. The multiplane camera was subsequently used to great effect in *Snow White*, helping to bring to life Walt's vision in a way that the world had never seen before.

6. Well. That's One Way to Do It!

Lucille La Verne, who provided the voice of the Queen, assumed the voice of the peddler woman by removing her false teeth.

7. Blabby?

Other names considered for the dwarfs included Wheezy, Sniffy, Puffy, Blabby, Dirty, Tubby, Cranky, Dizzy, and Scrappy.

8. A Touch of Makeup

Despite the animators' best efforts, Walt still felt that the look of Snow White seemed too harsh. One of the ink and paint artists suggested that they add some rouge to her cheeks, and demonstrated what she meant on an animation cel. Walt was impressed, but he asked how they would possibly be able to do that on thousands of frames of animation and get it right every time. She responded, "What do you think we've been doing all our lives?"

9. Mirror, Mirror

Animator Wolfgang Reitherman had the task of bringing the Magic Mirror to life, but had a lot of trouble achieving the right look. Finally, he folded his drawing paper in half, drew one half of the face, then turned the paper over and traced the other half. In the end though, much of his effort was obscured by the fire and smoke effects seen in the final film.

10. The Voice of Snow White

During the auditions for the actress who would voice Snow White, Walt would listen to the auditions of prospective candidates through a speaker in a different room so that her appearance wouldn't affect his judgment. Upon hearing Adriana Caselotti, he remarked, "She sounds like a fourteen-year-old girl." She was in fact 19, but she got the part anyway.

Ten Things You May Not Know About
Pinocchio

1. A Classic Tale

The well-known story of a wooden puppet who dreams of becoming a real boy goes all the way back to 1881, when he first appeared in a serial written by Italian author Carlo Collodi. The stories were soon published as a children's book called "The Adventures of Pinocchio."

2. Next in Line

Pinocchio was originally intended to be the third animated feature produced by the studios, but work on it was moved up when the studio realized that *Bambi* (the original follow-up choice to *Snow White*), would require more work than originally planned.

3. How to Animate a Marionette

Despite Walt's enthusiasm for the story, Pinocchio presented a set of challenges that had to be overcome. The biggest problem was Pinocchio himself: How do you bring a puppet to life? There was much debate over whether to portray him as an actual marionette or more like a real boy. The first animations treated him like a puppet, but the results were, pardon the pun, wooden and unsatisfactory. After much deliberation, it was decided to start over again, this time making Pinocchio behave and move more like a real boy. The newly revised character was much more lifelike, with the only real indication of his puppetry being the appearance of his arms and legs.

4. Making Pinocchio Likable

The other problem was that Pinocchio was a rather unlikable character, unable to discern the difference between right and wrong. Walt himself said that "people know the story, but they don't like the character." In fact, the Pinocchio of the original story could be quite cruel, such as when he killed a small cricket (who was then nameless) when it offered him advice. Yet it was that very cricket who ended up solving Pinocchio's personality problem.

5. Jiminy to the Rescue

One of the early (and later discarded) scenes from the film showed Pinocchio terrorizing Figaro the cat. Animator Ham Luske remarked that audiences would be unsympathetic to Pinocchio as long as he had no moral center. That was the spark of inspiration that led to the development of Jiminy Cricket, whose minor role was greatly expanded to be that of Pinocchio's conscience.

6. Jiminy Becomes a Star

Jiminy Cricket was also the inspiration behind another key decision, which would lead to one of the greatest pieces of animation ever created. As Jiminy's character expanded, Walt hit upon the idea of him being Pinocchio's moral center, and also the narrator of the film itself. This led to the creation of the opening sequence of the film, where Jiminy sings "When You Wish Upon a Star" and starts to tell the story.

7. An Animation Milestone

During the song, a dramatic shot was introduced, with the camera pulling back from a bright star in the night sky and slowly panning over a quaint village. The camera then slowly zooms in on a lone cottage, the home of Geppetto. This sequence was a technical marvel (making great use of the multi-plane camera to add three-dimensional depth), and it also served to draw the viewer into the story in a way never before achieved in an animated motion picture.

8. Turquoise?

The Blue Fairy was known as the Fairy with the Turquoise Hair in the original tale. Additionally, J. Worthington Foulfellow and Gideon, the fox and cat who try to lead Pinocchio astray, were originally nameless.

9. New Techniques

Disney developed new innovations for the coloring of the film, including a new technique called "blending," which incorporated a combination of dry brushing and air brushing. Jiminy Cricket alone was composed of 27 different colors.

10. Pinocchio in Disneyland

While Pinocchio has a minor presence in the Magic Kingdom (you can dine at the Pinocchio Village Haus in Fantasyland and watch the boats as they enter "it's a small world"), visitors to Disneyland can enjoy the dark ride Pinocchio's Daring Journey. Opening in 1983, it was the first Disney attraction to use holographic technology.

Ten Things You May Not Know About
Fantasia

1. A Simple Idea...

Fantasia had not started out as a sweeping statement on the possibilities of animation. It had not even started as a feature film, but rather as a short called *The Sorcerer's Apprentice*. This short was to be very important for the Disney studio, combining the storytelling of the Mickey Mouse series with the artistic music of the Silly Symphonies. The very best of each respective field would now be joined for the first time.

2. Leopold Stokowski

Disney's earliest work on the short had actually begun with a recording by Arturo Toscanini, but a chance encounter between Walt and the renowned Leopold Stokowski changed everything. Walt quickly recognized a kindred spirit in Stokowski for the conductor sought to spread awareness and respect for classical music, much as Disney endeavored to do for animation. The pair quickly agreed to collaborate. Toscanini was out, Stokowski in.

3. A Classic is Born

Just two months later, the time had arrived to record the titular composition. Working through the night, Stokowski put his newly-assembled one-hundred-piece orchestra through its paces. By morning, Stokowski's recording was finished...though in reality his work had just begun. Unbeknownst to the conductor, Walt and Roy Disney were coming to an important realization: *The Sorcerer's Apprentice* had grown far too expensive to remain just a short. They both decided, although Roy needed a little convincing, that the only path to profitability lay in expanding the project into a full-blown feature. Considering the studio had already spent nearly four times the cost of a normal Silly Symphony short on *The Sorcerer's Apprentice*, that was probably a good call.

4. Enlisting Assistance

Fantasia, internally dubbed *The Concert Feature*, had instantly grown exponentially larger – and Disney needed reinforcements. Walt and Stokowski successfully recruited Deems Taylor, the famed radio personality and music critic, to complete the creative triumvirate of *Fantasia*. With the guidance of Taylor and Stokowski, Walt and his staff then spent several weeks immersing themselves in classical music. They listened to countless selections, allowing artistic inspiration to choose what would ultimately be included in the feature film.

5. The Final Lineup

When the dust finally settled, seven classical pieces had been chosen for *The Concert Feature*. (1) *Toccata and Fugue*, a celebration of abstract animation; (2) *The Nutcracker Suite*, eschewing the tradition of children's toys for a reflection on the changing seasons; (3) *The Sorcerer's Apprentice*, wherein Mickey Mouse grapples with the awesome responsibility of unlimited power; (4) *Rite of Spring*, tracing the creation of life on Earth up through the extinction of the dinosaurs; (5) *The Pastoral Symphony*, a comic romp through Greek mythology; (6) *Dance of the Hours*, parodying ballet's grace and litheness; and (7) *Night on Bald Mountain/Ave Maria*, a powerful juxtaposition between the depths of evil and the ultimate redemption of faith.

6. Audio Innovations

One listen to Stokowski's recording of *The Sorcerer's Apprentice* proved that Disney's current sound set-up would be wholly inadequate for *Fantasia*. Although the conductor had done his best under the circumstances, Walt knew a better system would be necessary for future recordings. To accomplish this, Walt turned to Bill Garity of the studio's sound department. Garity, who was also instrumental in designing the aforementioned multiplane camera, and his engineers developed a two-tiered system known as Fantasound. Fantasound used multiple recording devices to capture all of the different parts of the orchestra. The system then stored the recordings separately on discrete tracks. The recorded music could later be played back in the theater on more than sixty speakers arranged from the front of the hall to the back. Several speakers would even be stealthily positioned behind the movie screen itself. Fantasound would bombard listeners with rich music from all angles...but this breakthrough did not come cheap. The studio went through numerous Fantasound prototypes and, by the end, the sound budget accounted for nearly one-fifth of *Fantasia's* $2.28 million cost.

7. Nearing the End

Deep into its third year of production, the thousand-strong workforce of the Disney studio had to believe they were heading into the home stretch. Fantasound had been tweaked to perfection and most of the animation was completed and filmed. With just the *Ave Maria* section left to complete, Walt and his animators could be forgiven for thinking the worst was over.

8. A Case of the Jitters

Before long, however, it became apparent that *Ave Maria* might just bring the entire project – and its looming world premiere – crashing down. The problems began innocuously enough. During the finale's procession of pilgrims, the filmed animation seemed to jitter when played back. Because the painted cels were being filmed so closely, any minute change in camera speed would cause the frames to jump around. Costly retakes were inevitable, but even Walt remained unsure if they would solve anything. The real problem lay with the camera – it needed to move both slowly and smoothly in one long continuous motion to avoid the jittering dilemma. Disney's biggest problem? Such a camera did not yet exist.

9. Quick Thinking

Rolling up its collective sleeves, the Disney studio quickly constructed a horizontal rendition of its multiplane camera. Instead of providing depth, this camera would be placed on a carriage and rolled along a set track, filming all the while. This process would theoretically allow the camera to gracefully glide on its own procession through the forest of Ave Maria. With this newest creation complete and operational, all that was left was to film the scene.

The first attempt lasted six days and nights. The result? The jitter was gone, but the wrong lens had been used – rendering the footage worthless. The incorrect camera lens had indeed beautifully captured the animation – but it also captured the camera's track and even some of the cameramen.

Take two did not go much better. This time it was not human error, but rather an act of nature that intervened. On the third day of filming, an earthquake rumbled through the Disney Studio. No camera equipment had been broken, but the stands holding the completed cels had definitely moved. There was no way to discern if the filmed animation had been ruined or not. If they forged ahead with this second attempt, the entire ending of *Fantasia* could be distorted.

10. Whew!

With the premiere just days away and only one more chance to get it right, the stars finally aligned and the third try worked. The completed footage was flown directly to New York City, the site of *Fantasia's* grand opening, and arrived with only four hours to spare.

Ten Things You May Not Know About
Cinderella

1. Cinderella's First Appearance

The full-length feature was not Walt Disney's first treatment of *Cinderella*. While running his Laugh-O-Gram Studio in Kansas City, Missouri, Walt produced a seven-minute short film of Cinderella. The film was accompanied only by piano, and the characters communicated through dialogue balloons.

2. Prince Who?

Prince Charming's name is never mentioned in the film.

3. Fur Slippers

Cinderella is well known for her glass slippers, but were they always glass? A popular tale is that her slippers were originally made of fur, and the notion that her slippers were glass came from a mistranslation of an early French manuscript.

Not so fast...

The supposed mistranslation stems from a version written by Charles Perrault in 1697. The story as written includes the phrase "pantoufle de verre," which means glass slipper. However, many assume he meant "pantoufle de vair," meaning fur slipper. But did he? This supposed fact has been examined at length, with some concluding that it was indeed a mistranslation, and others deciding that he really meant "glass slipper" after all.

Too confusing? You can always opt for the Grimm Brothers version of the tale, which had Cinderella wearing gold slippers!

4. Cinderella's Origins

The actual tale goes back much farther than 17th century France. About 400 versions of the story have been documented, with the earliest going all the way back to the first century B.C.

Examples have been discovered in the early literature of China and Vietnam, and a variation was included in the "One Thousand and One Nights" collection of stories (also known as Arabian Nights). A version of the famous tale was also a sub-plot in Shakespeare's "King Lear."

5. A Return to Form

The Disney film was released in 1950 and represented a return to feature length animation for the studios. Disney's last major release had been *Bambi* in 1942, with World War II and other factors forcing Disney to release six package films made up of various shorts in the intervening years.

6. A Princely Sum

The film cost $3 million to produce, more than double the final budget for *Snow White and the Seven Dwarfs*.

7. Only One Dance for Our Disney Princess

The Disney film was based primarily on Charles Perrault's version of the story, but there is one major difference between the original story and the film. In Perrault's version, Cinderella attends two balls, leaving the first before midnight strikes. She loses her slipper the next night when she returns to attend a second ball. In the film, of course, there is only one ball.

8. That Unforgettable Voice

Cinderella's voice was provided by Ilene Woods, who actually won the part after Walt Disney heard the demo recordings of her singing "Bibbidi-Bobbidi-Boo," "A Dream Is a Wish Your Heart Makes," and "So This is Love." He was so enthralled with her voice that he asked her to take on the title role, beating out more than 300 actresses who were vying for the part.

9. Live-Action Reference

The vast majority of the film was produced using live sets and actors as visual references. The part of Cinderella was performed by Helene Stanley, who would go on to supply live action references for *Sleeping Beauty* and as Anita Radcliff in *One Hundred and One Dalmatians*. So if you ever thought those three Disney damsels looked similar, now you know why!

10. Cinderella Saves the Day

If it weren't for *Cinderella*, Disneyland and Walt Disney World might never have come into existence. At the time of the film's release, the studio was in financial straits. The production of *Cinderella* was a big gamble, and if it had bombed the studios would likely have closed. As with all fairy tales though, this story had a happy ending, and the enduring success of *Cinderella* propelled Disney to new heights and new innovations.

Ten Things You May Not Know About
Sleeping Beauty

1. A Long Time Coming

The Disney team began working on *Sleeping Beauty* in 1951, and though the story had generally been decided upon by 1952, which was unusually early in the process, the movie spent eight years in development. Six of those years were devoted almost entirely to animating the film. This unprecedented length of time in producing the film was, in many ways, affected by the diverse paths the Studios had begun to take. A great deal of Walt Disney's attention and time were understandably caught up with the creation of the television series "Walt Disney's Wonderful World of Color," which premiered in 1954, as well as the significant demands of the opening of Disneyland a year later.

2. The End of an Era

Sleeping Beauty was the final Disney film to utilize the ink and paint technique of creating animation cels. *One Hundred and One Dalmatians*, released in 1961, would be the first in which animators used xerography, an electromagnetic process that transferred pictures onto celluloid, rather than all the pictures being hand-drawn. Additionally, *Sleeping Beauty* would be the last fairytale to be adapted for a Disney film until *The Little Mermaid* in 1989.

3. The Power of Color

The use of color also played a big part in the conceptual design of the film. The designers wished to provide strong visual contrast between good and evil, so for the palace, forest, and cottage, as well as the good people and fairies of the kingdom, bright colors were used, such as vivid reds, blues, pinks, emerald greens and yellows. Maleficent, her castle, and her cronies were painted in darker hues – browns, deeper greens, and shades of gray and black.

4. Live-Action References

Like *Cinderella*, *Sleeping Beauty* was first staged with actors performing the roles in a studio, complete with costumes and props. With *Cinderella*, it had been a cost-saving measure for the financially struggling studio: the scenes were enacted, filmed, and then traced onto animation paper in order to avoid having to correct and re-draw any errors. In *Sleeping Beauty*, this was done so that animators would not have to imagine the characters' actions but would be able to see the events first-hand. Structures were built to represent the palaces of King Stefan and Maleficent, as well as the fairies' cottage; stairs were even constructed to form the mountain from which Prince Philip battled Maleficent!

5. Well, That Makes Sense

"Maleficent" means "harmful or evil in intent."

6. You Can't Rush Perfection

It is ironic that the production process for *Sleeping Beauty* was the longest to date (around eight years), as Peter Tchaikovsky composed the entire ballet score for his take on the classic tale in forty days, the shortest length of time for any of his pieces. (Those forty days were over a five-month period.)

7. Alice Davis

Disney Legend Alice Davis, perhaps best-known as the costume designer for the attractions "it's a small world" and Pirates of the Caribbean, had her first Disney assignment with *Sleeping Beauty*. Costumes were constructed for the live actors playing out the scenes of the film. Using designs by her husband (and fellow Legend) Marc Davis, she created the gray dress worn by Briar Rose in "Once Upon a Dream" and the subsequent birthday scene.

8. The Three Fairies

Walt Disney wanted the three fairies to be similar in personality. It was the animation staff who talked him into allowing each fairy to have her own distinct characteristics: the matriarchal Flora, fluttery Fauna, and sweetly naïve Merryweather.

9. Briar Rose

The physical appearance of Princess Aurora/Briar Rose was based on the actress who modeled her dances, Helene Stanley, as well as her voice actress, Mary Costa.

10. A Castle for Disneyland

Sleeping Beauty Castle, which opened on July 17, 1955, is the centerpiece of Disneyland. It is the smallest of the Disney Parks castles and is the only castle with a working drawbridge. In 1957, the Castle opened a walk-through attraction featuring animated dioramas that were based on the movie. This attraction closed in 2001 but re-opened in 2008, replacing the dioramas with rooms with special effects and animated scenes.

Ten Things You May Not Know About
The Little Mermaid

1. The Dark Days of Disney Animation

As the 1980s unfolded, Disney was sorely in need of a hit animated film. A number of changes had occurred in the highest levels of the company: a hostile takeover was only narrowly averted, Disney stock had plummeted, and perhaps the most discouraging point of all, Disney desperately needed a life jacket for an animation studio that was frantically treading water. The team of animators was in a state of unrest as the younger artists, eager to generate new ideas, were at odds with the veteran staff, clinging to long-held traditions. A line of films was released whose critical and financial successes did not measure up with the animated features of the previous decades, the low point being *The Black Cauldron* (1985), which cost $44 million to make and grossed less than half of that amount. Discouraged with the direction in which Disney Animation seemed to be going, many of the older animators retired and some of the younger staff left for other jobs. There was deep concern that their successors would not be able to live up to the standards long held by the company.

2. A Renaissance is Born

Instead of eliminating the animation division, however, the new leadership team of Chief Executive Officer and Chairman of the Board Michael Eisner, President and Chief Operating Officer Frank Wells, and Vice President Roy E. Disney worked with Jeffrey Katzenberg, Chairman of Walt Disney Studios, to bring Disney animation back to its former glory. The animation team hoped to create a film that could stand with classics such as *Snow White and the Seven Dwarfs*, *Pinocchio* and *Cinderella*, so they returned to the medium that had served

Disney so well in the past: the musical fairytale. While looking for inspiration for a new animated feature, writer Ron Clements stumbled upon "The Little Mermaid" in a book of fairytales by Hans Christian Andersen. He was immediately drawn to the cinematic potential of the story. Like many older stories, though, including *Cinderella* and *Sleeping Beauty*, the ending of Andersen's tale was very dark, with the mermaid dying on the morning of her wedding.

3. Mermaids Aplenty

Clements re-worked the story with a happy conclusion and pitched the idea at the next staff meeting, where incredibly it was turned down! The success of *Splash* (1984), starring Tom Hanks and Daryl Hannah, had prompted the studio to begin work on a sequel, and it was feared that *The Little Mermaid* was too similar to the live-action mermaid film. Katzenberg, however, was impressed with Clements' treatment of the story, and the next day called him into his office to discuss moving forward with the project. Though Katzenberg originally thought of looking outside of Disney for a screenwriter, Clements convinced him that he and his frequent writing partner, John Musker, were up to the task, and the two became co-writers and co-directors of the film.

4. Memorable Music

When recording the songs, a new technique was utilized in which the actors sang accompanied only by a synthesizer, which was later edited out and replaced with an orchestra. (The same procedure was famously used for the 2012 film *Les Misérables*.) While this system seemed more efficient at first, it actually proved to be rather challenging, as it was difficult for the orchestra to accurately time individual musical moments within the songs that accompanied actions occurring in the animation.

5. Old Technologies...

The animation itself was quite traditional, using the Xerox process that had been utilized for every Disney animated film since *One Hundred and One Dalmatians*: instead of hand-drawing each animation cel, pictures were photocopied onto cels and then painted by hand. The animators insisted, however, that in order to achieve the look of the older classic films, the bubbles – which numbered around a million – should be hand-drawn, which was completed by an animation company in China. (Due to political tensions in China at that time, there was concern that the cells would not be completed and returned for the scheduled opening of the film, but Disney did indeed receive the work in time.)

6. ...And New

A new technique was utilized for the wedding scene: Computer Animation Production System, or CAPS. With this process, cels were colored digitally instead of being painted by hand. This process would be used exclusively in Disney's next animated feature, *The Rescuers Down Under* (1990).

7. A Close Call...

During an early screening for a group of children, it was noticed that some of the children did not stay particularly attentive through "Part of Your World," and Katzenberg ordered the song cut from the film. He remained firm despite the pleadings and arguments of a number of members of the creative team, but Glen Keane, supervising animator for Ariel, convinced him to allow them to finish animating the scene and reserve judgment until then. Subsequent screenings tested very well, and Katzenberg himself later admitted that he could not imagine the film without the song!

8. But Why Red Hair?

It was decided that Ariel would have red hair primarily because it was markedly different from Daryl Hannah's character in *Splash*, and because red is a complementary color to the green of Ariel's tail, making for a sharp and aesthetically appealing contrast.

9. Ursula

When animating Ursula, animators studied footage of the octopus from *Mysteries of the Deep* (1959), an episode of Disney's *True-Life Adventures* series. However, while the filmmakers and many fans think of Ursula as being based on an octopus, her voice actress, Pat Carroll, insists that she is a squid, as she has six tentacles instead of eight.

10. A Statue Comes to Life

Near the end of the movie, Ariel is positioned on a rock, gazing at Eric. Her pose mimics that of The Little Mermaid statue in Copenhagen, Denmark, Den Lille Havfrue, sculpted by Edvard Eriksen in 1913.

Ten Things You May Not Know About
Beauty and the Beast

1. Unprecedented Accolades

Beauty and the Beast was the first of two animated films ever to be nominated for the Academy Award Best Picture. The other film to be nominated was Pixar's *Up*, which wouldn't be released until 2009, 18 years later!

2. The Story's Origins

Beauty and the Beast is based on the traditional fairy tale of "La Belle et la Bête" by Jeanne-Marie LePrince de Beaumont, which is the most popular written version of the story. The idea for creating a film based on this fairy tale was present for long time. In fact, Walt Disney himself had tried to develop the story in the 1930s and 1950s. After *Who Framed Roger Rabbit* was finished in 1988, the concept was brought to the table once again. Richard Purdum was asked to direct a non-musical version, and a script was written. This was a first for the company since storyboards were always created first, but Michael Eisner insisted on the traditional live-action process of scriptwriting. After a year, then-chairman Jeffrey Katzenberg saw some early storyboarding and decided the film needed to be trashed and started over. Kirk Wise and Gary Trousdale were asked to fill in as directors. Eventually, the story started taking shape with Howard Ashman and Alan Menken coming in to write songs for the newly-established musical rendition of the story.

3. That's A Lot of Drawing!

The film contains 1,295 painted backgrounds and 120,000 drawings. Lumière's flames alone necessitated about 19,000 drawings. A total of 370 people were involved in the creation of the film, including 43 animators.

4. And A Lot of Music!

The songs themselves make up about 25 minutes of the movie. Adding in the score, only five minutes of the film are without music.

5. Blue Belle

Belle wears her blue-colored outfit to make her stand out from the rest of the villagers, who have brown, red, yellow, or green in their palette. Her blue clothes mark her as different. Then she meets the Beast, somebody just as different from everyone as she is, who also wears blue.

6. An Unexpected Star

Chip started out with only one line, but he was given a bigger role when the producers heard and highly enjoyed Bradley Pierce's voice.

7. Animation innovation

This was the second film to fully use the new Computerized Animation Production System (CAPS), which was put to significant use during the waltz sequence, in which Belle and Beast dance through a computer-generated ballroom as the camera moves around them.

8. Mrs. Potts

Angela Lansbury, the voice of Mrs. Potts, didn't think her character should be the one to sing during the dancing ballroom scene. The director asked her to make a recording just in case as a backup, and they ended up using that recording in the final piece.

9. How Do You Make Realistic Smoke?

The smoke used during the Beast-to-Prince transformation is actual real smoke, not animated.

10. Belle's Inspiration

Screenplay writer Linda Woolverton said that she drew her inspiration for Belle from the 1933 film *Little Women* (specifically Katharine Hepburn's portrayal of Jo March), not from the 1946 Jean Cocteau film version of the famous tale.

Ten Things You May Not Know About
Aladdin

1. Aladdin's Origins

Creating an animated version of *Aladdin* was originally suggested by Howard Ashman, lyricist and co-producer of *The Little Mermaid* (1989), while that film was still in production. He and *Mermaid* composer Alan Menken began working on songs to accompany the story, while simultaneously, the co-writers of *The Little Mermaid*, Ron Clements and John Musker, put together their own ideas for an *Aladdin* treatment. Plans for the film were temporarily put on hold while Menken and Ashman worked on *Beauty and the Beast* (1991), but after that film was completed, it was time to revisit the idea of *Aladdin*. Sadly, Ashman would not live to see his ideas come to fruition, as he passed away shortly after completing the music for *Beauty and the Beast*. Hired to step in was renowned lyricist Sir Tim Rice, who had famously worked with Oscar- and Tony- Award-winning composer Sir Andrew Lloyd Webber, creating some of the most renowned musicals in theatre history, including *Joseph and the Amazing Technicolor Dreamcoat*, *Jesus Christ Superstar*, and *Evita*.

2. Aladdin's Black Friday

After the story had been developed, the songs written, and the animation story-boarded, the creative team took their ideas to then-Disney chief Jeffrey Katzenberg, who did not like their original concept at all. On what was dubbed "Black Friday," Katzenberg told the staff that they would need to completely start over with their vision for the film, from the characters to the music to the look of the film. Amazingly, in only eight days the production team was not only able to rework the entire movie, but they did it so well that they got Katzenberg's approval.

3. Redesigning Aladdin

One of the changes Katzenberg wanted was in the appearance of the title character. Aladdin was originally drawn as quite small in stature, looking like a boy rather than a young man that would be a believable love interest for Jasmine. Katzenberg suggested to the artists that he wanted "less Michael J. Fox" and "more Tom Cruise." The challenge in the new approach was to keep him as an underdog, in spite of his more heroic appearance. The artists found their answer in creating Aladdin's character to be outwardly confident, while hiding his insecurities underneath his layers of bravado.

4. Graceful Architecture

A beautifully-exotic setting was necessary to support the colorful characters of Agrabah. The animators based their curved building structures on the architecture of the Middle East, using lines such as those used in Arabic calligraphy, beginning with a slender stroke, thickening in the middle, then tapering back to a thin line.

5. Computer Animation

The use of computerized animation began to take more of a prominent role during this era. In creating the Cave of Wonders, the animators drew on their experiences with the ballroom scene from *Beauty and the Beast*, using the same camera and computer techniques that had been utilized for that landmark moment.

6. The First Computer Animated Character

New techniques were pushed even further with *Aladdin*. While, in the past, computerized animation was used for background images, this was the first time it was used for animating a character, the magic carpet. Yes, with its own movements and personality, the carpet was indeed considered a character! In fact, it was one of the most complex of the film's characters to construct. The elements of its ornate design – lamps, tiger heads, and flames – represented Aladdin's journey through the story. With all the carpet's movement, it would have been exceedingly difficult, if not downright impossible, to draw all these images by hand, so the design was computer-animated and layered over a hand-drawn picture of the carpet. A technique called "texture mapping" was utilized: the pattern was "painted" over the computer-drawn picture, so that when the object moved, the textures did as well, creating a more life-like effect. The tassels, which were used to express the carpet's emotions (See? It really is a character!), were drawn and layered over the computer drawing as well.

7. Under the Sea

When Aladdin asks the Genie to make him a prince, the Genie checks his book of "Royal Recipes" and conjures up "chicken a la king," "Caesar salad," and a "king crab." Listen carefully when the Genie holds the crab, and you'll hear a snippet of "Under the Sea," which of course is sung by the crooning crustacean Sebastian from *The Little Mermaid*! (Aladdin composers Menken and Ashman made their Disney debut writing the music of *The Little Mermaid*.)

8. Starting Off with a Joke

The opening scene of the merchant's monologue was included so that when Robin Williams returned later as the Genie, his fast-paced improvisatory style would not be such a startling transition for the audience. In order to create that scene, Williams was presented with a table full of objects, covered by a sheet. The sheet was lifted, and he improvised a comic bit on each of the items on the table.

9. For the Birds

For the recording sessions, Disney had a parrot in the studio for Jonathan Freeman, who voiced Jafar, to look at during his scenes. Rather than making the process easier for Freeman, however, it actually caused him more stress, as he is afraid of birds.

10. Princess Legends

The two actresses providing the speaking and singing voices of Jasmine, Linda Larkin and Lea Salonga, were inducted as Disney Legends together at the D23 Expo in 2011, alongside fellow princess voices Jodi Benson (Ariel), Paige O'Hara (Belle), and Anika Noni Rose (Tiana).

Ten Things You May Not Know About
The Lion King

1. An Original Tale

The Lion King was the first Disney feature to be based on an original story, which had its origins four years earlier as a project originally titled *King of the Jungle*. Unlike previous Disney films which dealt with traditional love stories, the writers sought to tell a story of the relationship between father and son. Like many other Disney films (particularly those from that era), this emphasis on story and character development was vital to the success of the film. The writers even looked to Shakespeare's "Hamlet" for inspiration for this story of loss and redemption.

2. Animation Challenges

One of the challenges of *The Lion King* was in bringing the exotic wilderness of Africa to life. More than 600 artists, animators, and technicians contributed to *The Lion King* over its lengthy production. In the end, they produced more than one million drawings, including 1,197 hand-painted backgrounds and 119,058 individually colored frames of film. In 1991, codirector Roger Allers, story head Brenda Chapman, and production designer Chris Sanders traveled to Kenya to experience Africa firsthand, knowing that a key to the film's success would be in convincingly recreating that exotic landscape.

3. Bringing the Animals to Life

In a nod to the production techniques first used in 1942's *Bambi*, Disney's animators studied real animals in great detail. Jim Fowler, a renowned wildlife expert, visited the studio with real lions and other jungle wildlife. He helped the animators understand animal behavior, particularly how lions greet each other in the wild and how they express fear, aggressiveness, and affection. CGI technology also played an important role in the creation of the film. Animators used it to great effect in the memorable wildebeest stampede sequence. The new technology allowed the animators to create the breathtaking scene by multiplying one drawing into hundreds, and then programming the individual animals to move distinctly and independently – and just as importantly, not to run into each other!

4. Conveying Emotions

Another challenge the animators faced was conveying the complex emotions experienced by the characters. This was made especially difficult because they have no hands! The artists instead relied on facial expressions, mannerisms, and even the way the characters walked. Take note of how Scar slinks along in a menacing, low-to-the-ground manner, in direct contrast to Mufasa and the other lions, who walk about with their heads held high.

5. A Mickey Cameo

One of the bugs that Timon pulls out of a knothole during the "Hakuna Matata" sequence is wearing Mickey Mouse ears.

6. Jeremy Irons

Jeremy Iron's physical traits had a great influence on Andreas Deja's design for Scar. "There was darkness around his eyes that fascinated me and gave him an eerie look in his films," Deja said. "I wanted to keep that quality, so I gave Scar dark circles around his eyes and combed his mane as if it were slicked back."

7. Snubbed for a Princess

At one point, it was felt that *The Lion King* was a lesser project than *Pocahontas*. Both movies were in production at the same time, and many felt that *Pocahontas* would be the more successful of the two. *Pocahontas* did perform quite well, earning more than $340 million, but *The Lion King* more than doubled that, becoming the highest grossing traditionally-animated film in history, when dollars are adjusted for inflation.

8. What did Rafiki say?

The song lyrics that Rafiki chants, "Asante Sana! Squash banana! We we nuga! Mi mi apana!" came from a schoolyard chant made up as a child by the guide who accompanied members of the production staff on their African research trip.

9. What Do Those Names Mean?

"Simba" means lion in Swahili. The name "Mufasa" means king in the Manazoto language, and it was also the name of the last king of the Bagada people of precolonial Kenya.

10. They Did What?

Jonathan Taylor Thomas, who performed the voice of the young Simba, achieved the sound of sliding down the elephant's backbone in the graveyard scene by having several studio aids pound on his back as he did his voice-over.

Ten Things You May Not Know About
Toy Story

1. The Dawn of Pixar

Toy Story was the first Pixar feature-length animated film, released back in 1995, and the technology used to create *Toy Story* is quite staggering. New software programs and hardware had to be designed and built to create this whimsical fantasy world in which toys come to life when the humans are gone. With ties to George Lucas's Industrial Light & Magic visual effects company, Pixar was at the forefront of innovative animation technologies, even working with Disney on the development of the CAPS project, which was created to replace the laborious task of hand-inking and painting individual animation cels. After creating several innovative shorts (including *Luxo Jr.*, which features a brightly colored ball that makes a cameo appearance in *Toy Story*), the stage was set for Pixar's first full-length feature. Despite some early rocky moments (Disney executives initially tinkered with the storyline so much that the project was shelved, until Executive Producer John Lasseter gathered his team together and remade the film the way they envisioned), the results were a smashing success.

2. It's All About Story

But despite all the technological glitz, *Toy Story's* true genius is in its storytelling. Like every Pixar movie created since, story and character development are never secondary to the technology. It might have been tempting to load the film with a never-ending stream of visual acrobatics, but while the film is most certainly a delight to watch, the visuals are there to support the story, not the other way around. *Toy Story*, like the other films in the Pixar library, endures not because of the technology used to produce it, but because of the emotions it conveys. Just think of the scene where Buzz realizes that he's only a toy after all, plummeting down the stairwell when he fails to fly. Every Pixar film has similar, poignant moments, and these are achieved not through dazzling animation and special effects (of which there are plenty), but through characters and situations that we care about.

3. Tinny the Toy

The star of the Pixar short film *Tin Toy*, Tinny, a wind-up musician, was originally going to be Andy's new toy. He was, of course, replaced by good-old Buzz. Good thing, too, because "Tinny the Tin Toy's Space Ranger Spin" doesn't have quite the same ring to it.

4. Buzz...?

But Andy's new toy almost wasn't named Buzz either. Other names that were considered included Lunar Larry and Tempus from Morph.

5. You Mean He Wasn't Always a Sheriff?

Woody also went through some changes. He was originally going to be a ventriloquist's dummy.

6. An Historic First

Toy Story was the first full-length animated feature film to be created entirely on the computer. This process introduced a whole new set of challenges. While fewer animators were required (about an eighth of the number used on a typical Disney animated feature), the process to bring the characters to life was much more involved. Hundreds of computer models were generated, each with a complex system of 3-D motion controls. For example, animating Woody's mouth alone required 58 separate controls.

7. Computer Overload

The film required 114,240 frames of animation, with a staggering 2 to 15 hours of computer time required to render each and every frame. Three hundred computers worked simultaneously to handle the tremendous load.

8. A Big Mistake

Billy Crystal was originally approached to be the voice of Buzz Lightyear, but he turned it down. He later said that it was one of the biggest mistakes of his career. Pixar gave him a second chance by offering him the opportunity to voice Mike Wazowski in *Monsters, Inc.*, which Crystal eagerly accepted.

9. Honors

Toy Story was the first animated film to be nominated for the 'Best Writing, Screenplay Written Directly for the Screen' Academy Award'.

10. The Pizza Planet Truck

The Pizza Planet truck, first seen in *Toy Story*, can be found in nearly every subsequent Pixar film. For example, in *Monsters, Inc.*, you can find it in the Louisiana swamp to which Randall gets banished parked next to the motor home.

Ten Things You May Not Know About
Finding Nemo

1. Just a Couple of Fish

Finding Nemo came onto the scene in 2003 with two top-notch filmmakers directing it, Andrew Stanton and Lee Unkrich. Stanton was the second animator to join Pixar. (The first was John Lasseter.) Stanton said that he came up with the idea for the film when he saw two clownfish playing around an anemone. "It was so arresting," he said. "I had no idea what kind of fish they were, but I couldn't take my eyes off them. And as an entertainer, the fact that they were called clownfish – it was perfect. There's almost nothing more appealing than these little fish that want to play peek-a-boo with you."

2. Animating the Ocean

Pixar had to figure out how to create an underwater world that would look believable to the audience. New technologies allowed for small particles to be seen in the water, as well as to recreate the reflection and refraction effects necessary to provide realistic views of the water surface. Amazingly, the team actually created the water surface too realistically. They were concerned that the audience might think that they had simply filmed the ocean, so they made the water more cartoon-like.

3. Under the Sea

Finding Nemo was definitely a technological milestone for Pixar – and for animation in general. To make sure the team could understand the ocean and its many creatures, Lasseter made the key members become trained scuba divers. By diving in Monterey and Hawaii, going to innumerable aquariums, and listening to an ichthyologist (a fish biologist), Pixar created a living and breathing underwater environment for all to enjoy.

4. Bubbles, Bubbles, Bubbles...

Crush and Squirt are named after two popular citrus soda beverages in the United States.

5. Woof!

The animators studied the movements of the eyes of dogs to figure out how to animate the eyes of the fish.

6. Just That Easy

Andrew Stanton gave an exhausting, hour-long pitch for this movie. When he looked to John Lasseter, the head of Pixar, for approval, Lasseter said, "You had me at 'fish.'"

7. Dude!

There are about 200 turtles in the Eastern Australian Current (EAC) sequence.

8. Jellies!

For the jellyfish, Pixar created a new system called, "transblurrency," which allows one to see through an object, but not completely...similar to a fogged-up window.

9. Will She Ever Get That Name Right?

Throughout the film, Dory refers to Nemo as Fabio, Elmo, Bingo, Chico, and Harpo.

10. Pixar Cameos

In the waiting room of the dentist's office (modeled after a dentist's office in Emeryville, CA, where Pixar is located), you can see a Buzz Lightyear doll on the floor. A boy in the waiting room is reading a Mr. Incredible comic book. During the credits, Mike Wazowski can be seen swimming by with a snorkel.

Ten Things You May Not Know About
The Incredibles

1. Beyond Toys and Animals

The Incredibles was the first Pixar film to feature an all-human cast. This was no small feat, as it required the creation of new technology to realistically depict everything from skin, hair, and clothing, as well as to accurately replicate human anatomy. Realistically rendering the appearance of the characters' skin was made possible through the use of "subsurface scattering," where light penetrates the surface of a translucent object, is scattered by inter-acting with the material, and exits the surface at a different point.

2. Out of Breath

Director Brad Bird made actor Spencer Fox run laps around the studio in order to give his character, Dash, a realistic out-of-breath voice.

3. Violet's Hairdo

Of all the challenges faced by animators, hair has always proven to be among the most difficult. From Rapunzel to Merida and even to Sulley, new technological advances were always required to animate the character's hair. Violet's long black locks were no exception, and, in fact, throughout most of the film's production it was feared that animating her hair was simply not possible, especially since it had to move convincingly underwater and in the wind. These difficulties were overcome, of course, and the techniques that were used paved the way for characters to come.

4. Talk About Flexible

Elastigirl can stretch any part of her body up to 100 feet (that's taller than Splash Mountain!). She can also squeeze into a space as small as one millimeter.

5. Edna Mode

While the voice cast for most of the film's characters was settled on early, the production team had a difficult time finding the right voice for Edna Mode. At one point, actress Lily Tomlin was brought in to audition for the part, and to assist her Brad Bird read a few lines to demonstrate how he thought she should sound. Tomlin told Bird that he did the voice so well that he should take on the role himself, which he did.

6. Frozen with a Vengeance

Fans of Samuel L. Jackson, who played Frozone, may find the scene where he is confronted by the police in the jewelry store familiar. The scene is an homage to a similar scene in the film *Die Hard with a Vengeance*. In *Die Hard*, Jackson's character is similarly threatened by a nervous police officer (in this case, as he attempts to answer a telephone). The sequence is nearly identical to the one in *The Incredibles*, right down to the officer's facial expressions.

7. Milt Kahl

Brad Bird was mentored by Milt Kahl, one of Disney's legendary Nine Old Men. Kahl, considered to be one of the finest draughtsman in Disney history, was responsible for the final look of many classic Disney characters, including Peter Pan, Pinocchio, Lady and the Tramp, Tigger, and Alice.

8. Nine Old Men

A tribute to the Nine Old Men can be seen near the end of the film. Frank Thomas and Ollie Johnston, the last of the legendary group of Disney animators, make an animated cameo appearance after the Omnidroid is destroyed. After the Incredibles defeat the Omnidroid, Frank tells Ollie, "That's the way to do it. That's old school," an homage to the rich tradition of animation the pair helped to create.

9. A113

The classic Pixar Easter Egg, A113, makes two appearances in *The Incredibles*. First, Mr. Incredible is told to go to conference room A113 where he is attacked by an Omnidroid. Later, if you look carefully you'll see that as Elastigirl is trying to find her husband, she finds that he is being held in cell 13 on floor A1. But what does A113 mean? It's a reference to the classroom used by Graphic Design and Character Animation students at the California Institute of the Arts, whose alumni include John Lasseter and Brad Bird.

10. Where's the Pizza Planet Truck?

Curiously, this is the only Pixar film that doesn't feature another Pixar trademark, the Pizza Planet truck (first seen in *Toy Story*). While some think the truck can be spotted in one of the street scenes, animators have confirmed that the truck does not appear in the final film.

Ten Things You May Not Know About
Ratatouille

1. Researching, um, Rats

Disney films are typically noted for the extraordinary research conducted by their animation crew, and *Ratatouille* is no exception. Naturally, rats were brought in to be observed, both singularly and in groups, in order to see how they would interact. The movements of their bodies were studied so that their subtle nuances, such as the squeezing and contorting that occurs when the animals move through tight spaces, could be replicated in the animation.

2. Researching Food (Yes, That Sounds Much Better!)

A far brighter and undoubtedly more fragrant venture was to dine in some of Paris's most acclaimed restaurants in order to make Gusteau's as realistic as possible. The final restaurant seen in the film incorporated elements from Guy Savoy on the rue Troyon; La Tour d'Argent, the famed inn that first introduced forks to France during the reign of Henry III; the ornate Le Train Bleu, built for the 1900 World's Fair; and Taillevent, located in what was once the private mansion of the Duc de Mornay, built in 1852.

3. Let's Cook!

Disney's animators not only enjoyed fine French cuisine, but they learned to create it as well! Members of the animation team took cooking classes to learn the finer techniques of the culinary arts, including the types of utensils, pots, and pans used by trained chefs, as well as the interpersonal dynamics of a restaurant kitchen. *Ratatouille* producer Brad Lewis even worked as an intern for a few days at The French Laundry in Yountville, California, widely regarded as one of the best restaurants in the country.

4. Animation Innovations

Liquids are difficult to animate in order to make them appear to move naturally, so sauces and wines were a particular challenge. Fortunately, Pixar had recently completed another feature that included a great deal of water: *Finding Nemo. Ratatouille's* animators found that by adjusting the parameters of the software used in creating the watery world of the Great Barrier Reef and the East Australia Current, they were able to swirl wine and stir sauces with a high degree of realism. Software had been developed to create realistic fabric, fur, and hair for *Monsters, Inc.* and *The Incredibles.* The team expanded upon the same software to accommodate the amount of fur being animated for *Ratatouille,* as well as the extent of how the rats' interactions with objects and each other would affect the look of the fur.

5. Not as Fuzzy as We Thought

Real-life rats can have up to 500,000 individual hairs; *Ratatouille's* rodents were given "only" around 30,000.

6. Classical Painting Techniques

The colors created for the rats' fur utilized a French painting technique called pointillism. Pointillism is credited to painters Georges Seurat and Paul Signac, and consists of using small dots of paint rather than full brush strokes. From a distance, the effect is a rich hue; close inspection will reveal tiny points colors. For example, Remy's "blue" fur actually consisted of purple, yellow, and green hairs that blended together to create his distinctive blue coloring.

7. Up on Your Paws!

Remy is the only rat who walks on two legs instead of four. This was done for two reasons: so that he would not be cooking and handling food with paws that had been on the ground, and to show that he was developing increasingly human qualities as he spent time with Linguini and the other cooks.

8. Say That Again?

Because Disney was concerned that the public would not know to pronounce Ratatouille, it was spelled phonetically ("rat-a-too-ee") under the title on trailers and posters.

9. What IS Ratatouille Anyway?

The title entrée is a stew made of tomatoes, zucchini, yellow squash, peppers, onion, and garlic. As Colette mentions in the film, it was once considered "a peasant dish," but refined renditions have been appearing in high-end French restaurants for many years. Thomas Keller, the multiple James Beard Award-winning owner of The French Laundry, designed the version of Ratatouille used in the film, which is called confit biyalid. Chef Keller also served as a consultant on the movie and provided the voice for one of the diners at Gusteau's.

10. Umm, Perhaps Not the Best Idea...

Though *Ratatouille* had successful product promotions with books, video games, and toys, plans to have Remy grace wine and food merchandise were scrapped after it was realized that consumers were turned off by the idea of rats advertising edibles.

Ten Things You May Not Know About
WALL-E

1. What's in a Name

WALL-E's name was going to be W.A.L.-E., but Steve Jobs (co-founder of Apple and CEO of Pixar at the time) didn't like that particular spelling, so it was changed to the familiar WALL- E. But what does WALL-E mean? A reference to Walt Disney perhaps? Actually, the name is an acronym for Waste Allocation Load Lifter – Earth-Class). Apparently, "loadlifter" was one word in the original spelling!

2. Ben Burtt

WALL-E's "voice" was created by legendary sound designer Ben Burtt, most famously known for creating the sounds of R2-D2 and the other audio effects from *Star Wars*. In the course of creating WALL-E's different sounds, Burtt recorded 2,500 pieces of audio, more than twice the number he recorded for Star Wars.

3. From the Oddest Places...

And what were some of those sounds? They included a hand-cranked electrical generator (to create the noises WALL-E made while moving about), an automobile self-starter (for when WALL-E went fast), and, curiously, the sound of cars being wrecked at a demolition derby. Why? That's how Burtt recreated the sounds of WALL-E compacting trash!

4. Apple's Influence

However, the most recognizable sound to most viewers was the familiar Macintosh start-up chime that sounded when WALL-E has fully charged up. Coincidentally (or not), the design of his companion Eve is highly reminiscent of Apple's distinctive product design.

5. Let's Go Shopping!

Finally, when WALL-E runs from the shopping carts aboard the Axiom, Burtt went straight to the source to create the clattering sound effect. He and his daughter actually went to a supermarket, placed a recorder in a shopping cart, and sent it careening down a hill!

6. Why Yellow?

WALL-E's main coloring was yellow, the better to mimic the typical coloring of a construction or maintenance vehicle. (Remember that WALL-E was a utilitarian "machine" whose only purpose was to collect and compact trash.) Since WALL-E himself was largely yellow, Production Designer Ralph Eggleston avoided using that color (as well as green) when designing the color palette for the background settings in the film, particularly those on Earth. As a result, the garbage-strewn Earth is largely devoid of color.

7. WALL-E's Cameo

As with most Pixar characters, WALL-E makes a cameo in another Pixar release, the short film *Your Friend the Rat* that was included with the DVD release of *Ratatouille*.

8. Play Ball!

The concept of WALL-E's distinctive eyes came from, of all places, a baseball game! Inspiration came from a pair of binoculars director Andrew Stanton was given at an Oakland Athletics/Boston Red Sox game. He was so mesmerized by them that he missed an entire inning of the game.

9. Inspiration From...a Printer?

At one point, WALL-E was going to have elbows, but it was quickly realized that a robot whose sole function was to pull garbage into itself would have no need for them. Not to mention that test animations of him waving (with elbows) made him look flimsy. Instead, Animation Director Angus MacLane had the idea to attach his arms to a track on the sides of his body, similar to the inkjet printers his father designed.

10. Hello, Dolly!

WALL-E had quite a collection of gadgets and gizmos in his "home," but his most prized possession was an old VHS tape of *Hello, Dolly!*, which instilled in him the concept of love, which he would ultimately convey to Eve when he reached out to hold her hand, reminiscent of his favorite scene from the old film.

Ten Things You May Not Know About
Frozen

1. Frozen's Origins

Frozen was a return to fairy tales for Disney, the story being loosely based on "Sneedronningen," or "The Snow Queen," written by Danish author Hans Christian Andersen. Various treatments of "The Snow Queen" were developed over the years, including a stage production with Disney Legend composer Alan Menken attached to the project, but none of the concepts ever came to fruition. While the title character could certainly be considered a villain, there was no climactic show-down between good and evil. The encounters that Gerda (the character from the original fairy tale) made with other characters on her journey made for a charming story, but they would not necessarily translate well on the screen. John Lasseter encouraged Disney's writers to further develop the characters that had been considered for a potential animated film. As discussions continued, it was suggested that Gerda's new persona, Anna, and the Snow Queen's counterpart, Elsa, could be sisters. This opened up a number of plot possibilities, and so the story began to take shape, ultimately developing into Disney's 53rd animated feature.

2. An Ice Castle

To get a better grasp on how to bring an ice castle to life on-screen, the art and lighting teams was sent north to the Hôtel de Glace, or Ice Hotel, in Québec City. The hotel, which opened in 2001, welcomes guests from January through March each year, and is constructed entirely of ice and snow. The Disney crew visited the hotel for inspiration in designing Elsa's castle in order to get a first-hand look at the ways light traveled through the structure and reflected about.

3. The Science of Snow

To accurately portray the properties of ice and snow, Disney consulted with Dr. Ken Libbrecht, chairman of the Physics Department at the California Institute of Technology (CalTech). Nicknamed "Dr. Snow," he explained to the Disney team how ice crystals form in the air. When the air temperature and humidity conditions are just right, the crystals will plate and then branch into snowflakes. The animators utilized this knowledge in animating the film, particularly during the scene in which Elsa creates her palace of ice, so that the audience could see the intricate process of snowflakes taking shape.

4. Snowmaking

Snow-creating programs were developed to further immerse the audience into the frosty Nordic kingdom of Arendelle. One of the challenges of working with snowy scenes in an animated movie is to have the characters look as though they are part of the scene and interacting with the snow. To solve the problem, an animation program called Snow Batcher was developed, which would preview where snow would fall, thus allowing animators to add further details to the scene. Snow-generating software called Matterhorn was created for *Frozen* and allowed different textures of snow to be seen throughout the film.

5. Creating Royal Hairstyles

The hairstyles of Anna and Elsa, typical of Scandinavia in the mid-1800s, were created by software designed for *Frozen* called "Tonic." Not only did the program help animators design the ladies' braids, but also made hair styling easier and faster to render in animation.

6. That's A Lot of Brushing

Elsa has more than 400,000 strands of hair. In contrast, Rapunzel had "only" 27,000 strands of hair in *Tangled* (2010).

7. Bringing the Characters to Life

The rigging required for *Frozen* was the most extensive of any Disney feature to date. In animation, rigging refers to what is basically the characters' skeletons. Before they are rigged, the characters are essentially digitally-created, three-dimensional statues. Rigging provides the characters with digital "joints" and "muscles" so that they can move and have facial expressions. Due to the amount of characters in Frozen, 312 character rigs, 245 cloth rigs, and 63 hair rigs were designed for the film.

8. Oh That Sven...

In order to animate Sven, a reindeer was brought to the animation studio so that artists could see how the animal naturally moves.

9. Let It Snow

There are 2,000 different kinds of snowflakes seen in the film.

10. Biting Her Lip

Have you noticed that Anna frequently bites her lip? While recording the script, animators noticed that this is a habit of Kristen Bell, and therefore, added it to Anna's character.

Miscellany

Three Attraction Details You May Never Have Noticed

Walt Disney World is filled with amazing sights, attractions, and iconic structures. It's easy to marvel at the towering spires of Cinderella Castle, the grand geodesic sphere of Spaceship Earth, or the magnificent glamour of Hollywood Boulevard. But as we've talked about many times before, Disney's true magic lies in the details. Oftentimes these details can be found in the references to the history and the people who brought Walt Disney World to life, and even those who helped build the Disney empire from its earliest days. Other times they can be found in the hidden jokes and puns written on crates, barrels, signs, and other decorative items. But sometimes these details are nothing more than the seemingly ordinary items that you would normally overlook. But although they may not be readily noticeable, they add much to the theming of the surrounding area and are just as important in creating a totally immersive setting as the attractions themselves.

1. Futuristic Finds

At the Tomorrowland Transit Authority PeopleMover, be sure to take a close look at the dioramas that you pass. In one of them, you'll note references to the Red and Green lines that, along with the Blue line that you are currently riding, serve as the intergalactic transportation system for Tomorrowland. It may not be evident as you look at the scene, but this is a reference to the land's fictional backstory in which the Green line takes you to the outer Hover-Burbs, while the Red line takes you to other-worldly destinations. The Blue line, or the TTA, serves as the inner-city transportation system. This is not only a reference to the backstory of Tomorrowland, but also a nod to Walt Disney's original vision of EPCOT, the city of the future. He envisioned a city where transportation would be provided by monorails taking citizens from the outer living areas into the heart of the city, and once in the city, people could travel around via transportation systems much like the TTA.

You'll also find some odd-looking writing throughout Tomorrowland, most notably at the newspaper stand near the entrance to the TTA. You can also see this alphabet – or, at least you used to – at Stitch's Great Escape!, as this was the alphabet used by the alien beings of Stitch's universe. You may not know what the letters mean on the newspaper as you glance at them, (though they do tell a story which is fun to decipher), but just seeing this alien writing lends an authentic detail, albeit a small one, which helps to reinforce the idea that you are in the middle of an intergalactic community.

2. Ghouls and Scallywags

Over in the Haunted Mansion, be sure to pay attention to the objects in the loading area as you head toward your Doom Buggy. It may seem like an ordinary queue, but on closer inspection you'll notice that the post tops are actually bats, in keeping with the haunting theme of this foreboding mansion. While you're in your Doom Buggy, be sure to take a close look at the wallpaper, chairs, and other fixtures found throughout the mansion. You'll find that everything is not as it seems, and some of the seemingly innocent decorations are actually sinister faces staring back at you, adding to the ghoulish atmosphere found inside this classic attraction.

Likewise, over at Pirates of the Caribbean, you'll see many small details in the queue that you might overlook as you make your way toward the loading area. But if time permits, take a closer look inside the dungeons and through the prison bars to view the incredible details that can be found within. You can famously see the pair of skeleton pirates playing an eternal game of chess of course, but you'll also see cannon balls, barrels, and even Jack Sparrow's long-lost rum.

3. Lighting the Way

While touring World Showcase, take note of the streetlamps found throughout the pavilions. While the main streetlamps on the major walkways share a common look, you'll notice that the lamps take on unique designs as you enter each pavilion. For instance, observe the intricate ornamentation of the lanterns in the China pavilion, as well as the elegant and romantic craftsmanship of the lamps found in the France pavilion.

Indeed, light fixtures throughout all of Walt Disney World often take on the theming of the attraction or land in which they are located. Whether it's the flickering lamps on Main Street U.S.A., the old-fashioned lights in Frontierland, or the futuristic fixtures found in Tomorrowland (including the palm trees!), the lights found throughout Walt Disney World not only serve a functional purpose, but also go a long way towards adding to the theming and detailing of each area, helping to transport you to lands far far away.

The Ten Best Animatronic Figures

1. The Dancing Man

Though not a true Animatronic figure, the Dancing Man deserves to kick off our list because of its importance in the development of Animatronic figures. In the late 1940s, Walt Disney became enamored with a small mechanical bird he had recently acquired. He set a team of Imagineers from WED Enterprises (now Walt Disney Imagineering) to figure out how to improve on this model. The figure they came up with was called the Dancing Man, modeled after a vaudeville dance routine by Buddy Ebsen, who's perhaps best known as Jed Clampett from "The Beverly Hillbillies." While this figure wasn't a true Audio-Animatronic, it was a good first attempt at robotics. It was operated by a system of cams and levers. This system worked for the small dancing figure (Dancing Man was only nine inches tall), but it wouldn't work for larger figures because the cams would have to be much larger. Also, cams took a lot of time to cut. But it was a vital early step that paved the way for the Animatronic figures you see today.

2. Stitch

Our next two entries are no longer around, but they still deserve special mention. Stitch's Great Escape! was home to two new A-100 Animatronic figures, Sergeant C4703BK2704-90210 (or S.I.R. as he was known in the ExtraTERRORestrial Alien Encounter), and of course Stitch himself. Stitch was the most advanced A-100 AA figure created at that time, which is even more impressive considering he was only 39 inches tall. He "walked" around on the elevated platform, his arms moved in incredible life-like fashion, and his ears and spine spikes even twitched. Stitch could blink, laugh, growl, and turn a full 360 degrees. Stitch also has the dubious distinction of being the first Audio-Animatronic figure to spit. (And yes, he could let out a good chili dog burp too!)

3. Wicked Witch

The figure of the Wicked Witch in the *Wizard of Oz* scene in the Great Movie Ride was the first in a new series of Animatronics known as the A-100 series. The A-100 series boasted a number of technological advances. For example, while the previous incarnation of Animatronic figures (the A-1 series) had a single actuator in their hand that controlled the fingers, the A-100 had an actuator for each finger that allowed them to move independently. The A-100 series also featured compliance technology. Previously, Imagineers had to be very careful with how fast an Animatronic figure moved in order to avoid unwanted shaking. The A-100 series utilized compliance technology that fixed the problem, allowing Imagineers to produce faster and smoother movements in their characters. But how did she appear and disappear on the platform? Actually, it's the same trick that was used in the original film! Hidden behind a dense cloud of smoke, the Wicked Witch would ascend and descend on an elevator; her movements out of sight of Guests. Yep, it's a simple trick; she may be magical, but she's not that magical!

4. The Yeti

On Expedition Everest, you'll find yourself face to face with the fearsome Yeti, which at the time of the attraction's opening was the largest and most complex Animatronic ever built, incorporating nineteen separate functions throughout its framework. The framework itself was clad with 6,000 pounds of various furs, forming a 1,000 square foot "skin" held in place with more than 1,000 snaps and 250 zippers. The Yeti proved to be so massive that an entirely new system was devised to mount it, as it wasn't possible for the massive creature to be self-supported. A long boom was attached to the Yeti's back, and it would travel along massive horizontal and vertical slides to allow the creature to move. The Yeti itself was powered by a 3,000-psi hydraulic thruster that can be recharged in twenty seconds. (That amount of thrust is greater than that found in a 747 jet engine!)

Unfortunately, a problem with the frame occurred soon after the attraction opened, resulting in the Yeti's inability to function in its fully operational mode. The problem was caused by damage to the Yeti's concrete base structure, and since the design of the attraction limits access to the affected sections (without shutting down the entire attraction for an extended length of time), repairs seem unfeasible, at least in the immediate future. In the meantime, the Yeti is operating in its alternative "B-mode," which incorporates strobe-lights to achieve the illusion of movement.

5. Ariel

The Journey of the Little Mermaid in Fantasyland features a whole host of impressive Animatronic figures, with Ursula being the most fearsome of all. But the star of the show is, of course, Ariel, and she can be seen several times throughout your journey. Advances in technology provided Ariel with a fluidity of movement never seen before in an Animatronic... you'll even notice that her hair moves!

6. Lumière

Lumière, found in Enchanted Tales with Belle, is one of the most impressive Audio-Animatronic figures ever created, and he's even more impressive considering his tiny size! The secret behind Lumière's fluid movements is the use of external controls, or actuators, that are concealed behind the curtain and connected by rods to Lumière's head, arms, and base. While typical Animatronic figures are completely self-contained, the use of external actuators allowed the Imagineers to recreate Lumière in his proper (small) scale, while giving him complete freedom of movement that would otherwise be impossible. The rods and external mechanics are concealed by the aforementioned curtains as well as clever lighting effects, and they all combine to create one of the most breathtaking Animatronic characters ever.

7. Mr. Potato Head

Found at Toy Story Mania!, the famous toy spud from all three *Toy Story* movies is dressed in his best barker outfit, complete with a straw hat. What makes Mr. Potato Head so advanced is his fluid motion and unique interactive ability. Voiced by legendary actor Don Rickles (who also voiced the character for all three *Toy Story* films), Mr. Potato Head interacts with individual Guests. During his routine, Mr. Potato Head can pull his ear out and put it back, which is an incredible sight to behold, not to mention an incredible engineering feat!

8. Benjamin Franklin/Mark Twain

Serving as your hosts for The American Adventure, the figures of Ben Franklin and Mark Twain are two of the most advanced and life-like characters in the history of Audio-Animatronics. Franklin and Twain do things that no other Audio-Animatronics had ever done before them, such as (seemingly) shaking hands, walking across the stage, and even climbing up a flight of stairs. Another major innovation is that the characters' voices are projected from inside the Audio-Animatronic characters themselves, rather than through the theater's sound system as in other attractions. If all of that still doesn't make the characters seem alive, look closely at Mr. Twain's cigar!

9. Jack Sparrow

In 2006, Pirates of the Caribbean received a new addition to its plundering gang of scoundrels, Jack Sparrow himself. The incredibly lifelike Animatronic figure appears several times throughout your journey: you'll find him hiding in the crowd in the well-dunking scene, peering out of a barrel over a pirate's shoulder for a sneak peek at a treasure map, and finally at the end as he sits in a room full of treasure, toasting to his good fortune. On April 26, 2017, Johnny Depp surprised Disneyland Guests by appearing in full costume in place of his Animatronic double. This was done as part of the promotion for *Pirates of the Caribbean: Dead Men Tell No Tales.*

10. Shaman of Songs

One of Disney's newest and most impressive Audio-Animatronic figures can be found in the Na'vi River Journey. Standing at nearly ten feet tall, the Shaman of Songs is the most advanced and most complex Audio-Animatronic figure ever created by Disney. The Shaman of Songs moves with a level of fluidity not seen in any other Disney Animatronic. This movement, combined with the intricate detailing of the facial features and musculature of the Shaman of Songs, will make Guests feel like they are literally watching a real Na'vi creature.

Ten Favorite Attraction Queues

1. Dumbo the Flying Elephant

The first interactive queue to be rolled out as part of the New Fantasyland expansion was Storybook Circus' Dumbo the Flying Elephant. In its previous location, Dumbo's queue was infamous, its main characteristics being long, slow, and very, very hot. The new queue resides inside a big top tent between the attraction's dual spinners. Inside, you'll find a playground perfect for climbing, swinging, and other circus shenanigans. Kids can slide, spin, and swing around as "Amazing Acrobats" above the heads of their parents waiting below. There is something for everyone – older Guests are treated to benches and air conditioning while the kids play. Guests are given a "ticket" upon entering the circus playground (an electronic pager). The little ones get to play and the not-so-little ones get to enjoy some cool air while their feet enjoy a welcome break from plodding around the park. When it's time for your party to board, the pager will buzz, letting you know that it's time to take a ride on everyone's favorite flying elephant.

2. Under the Sea – Journey of The Little Mermaid

As you approach the entrance to Prince Eric's castle, you'll be welcomed by a beached ship and a smiling Ariel waving from the prow. The queue is filled with all sorts of details, including light posts constructed to look like ship masts hung with lanterns, railings embellished with fishing nets, and walls that are weathered and barnacled. A note from Ariel explains that a storm has left her collection of human artifacts in shambles and asks Guests to help put everything back as it was before. Little blue crabs skitter across screens disguised as portholes and windows throughout the waiting area, bringing out objects for Guests to put in their proper places. It's up to you to make sure that everything goes back where it should!

3. Seven Dwarfs Mine Train

This is one of the best interactive queues at the Magic Kingdom, and here you'll find three interactive stations where you can help the dwarfs as they mine for jewels. The first station is a fifteen-foot long trough where you can sort out gems as they float past. The second station features musical water spouts that are activated by passing your hands beneath carved wooden animals. The third is in the "vault," where the dwarfs are storing their jewels. Doc's note instructs you to spin the glittering barrels of gems clustered around a support beam. A glance up at the ceiling will reveal that spinning the barrels creates kaleidoscopic projections above your head. Keep an eye on the ceiling to catch a glimpse of some familiar characters from the film!

4. Peter Pan's Flight

In this new interactive queue, you'll enter through a hall of portraits depicting scenes from the 1953 film before approaching the Darling home. Before going into the house, you'll pass by some windows where a silhouetted Mr. and Mrs. Darling are getting ready for a party. Inside the house are portraits of the entire family (Nana the Saint Bernard included), but the highlight is the Darling children's nursery. Tinker Bell flitters around the room, where her handiwork provides entertainment for everyone inside. You can play with your own shadow as it mingles with projected shadows on the wall. You can actually make your shadow ring silhouetted bells and have shadow butterflies land on your fingers. Be on the lookout for the shadow of a few familiar characters – they've been known to pop in!

5. The Twilight Zone Tower of Terror

As you approach the entrance to the Tower of Terror, you'll wander through the hotel's cultivated garden, patterned after the Griffith and Elysian parks in Los Angeles. The queue path winds upward, offering occasional glimpses of the towering hotel. The music you hear is classic Big Band–era instrumentals, featuring Duke Ellington and Glenn Miller. Soon you'll enter the lobby of the Hollywood Tower Hotel, and you'll see that it's covered with a heavy coating of dust and cobwebs. There's a concierge desk with an elegant gentleman's hat and cane, a rotary dial phone, and an ink blotter. On the wall hangs an AAA 13-diamond award, an unlucky twist on the coveted five-diamond rating. Two champagne glasses sit abandoned on the table, one with a trace of lipstick. Alongside the glasses are a diamond ring and white gloves, quickly left behind by the celebrating couple in the chaotic aftermath of the lightning strike. Also in the lobby is a table featuring a Mahjong game. Disney Imagineers brought in professional Mahjong players to begin a game, and at a random moment the Imagineers instructed the players to stop playing and leave the tile pieces intact – much like it would have been on that unfortunate Halloween night. The front desk also shows signs of a past life. Envelopes are tucked into the room slots of the elegant mahogany hutch behind the counter, offering us a glimpse of life before voicemail. A set of authentic alligator-skin luggage sits by the front desk, left behind by hotel guests who were checking in. You'll next enter the library, where you'll see a "lost" Twilight Zone episode playing on an old television, with Rod Serling describing the fateful night when tragedy struck the hotel. A number of props in the library pay homage to some of the show's more memorable episodes, including Burgess Meredith's broken glasses from "Time Enough at Last," Jack Klugman's trumpet from "A Passage for Trumpet," and the grim cookbook from "To Serve Man." Rod Serling concludes his speech by telling us that the service elevator is still functional, and that it's our passage to the fifth dimension. The final stage of the queue takes us through an authentic recreation of the hotel's dimly lit boiler room, with grimy walls and a still- active furnace. From here, we finally board the service elevator for our meeting with destiny.

6. Muppet*Vision 3D

The exterior of the building shows plenty of signs of "Muppetization." For example, look for the drain spouts and water pipes that have been playfully painted and decorated to appear as Muppets. Look up high to the clock tower, which features Gonzo hanging onto the minute hand just like Harold Lloyd did in the 1923 silent film *Safety Last*. Once inside, see if you can find the sign that says "Back in 5 minutes; key is under mat" sign. Surely Muppets aren't this trusting? Yep. Take a look under the mat...there's the key! Across from the office is the directory of Muppet*Vision 3D World Headquarters, featuring the Institute of Heckling and Browbeating (Statler and Waldorf: Curmudgeons- in-Chief). Kermit, Miss Piggy, Sam the Eagle, and Animal also have their own clever directory entries. Further down the hallway, you'll pass by several doors, including that of the Department of Artificial Reality entrance that boasts "This is not a door." The pre-show area opens up into a large room set up as the backstage to the theatre, complete with overhead catwalks and theater props. Monitors hang from the ceiling for the preshow film, in which Scooter tries valiantly to organize the backstage crew for the big 3D show. Fozzie Bear, Sam the Eagle, Kermit, and other Muppets participate in the film. Mickey Mouse himself makes a cameo appearance in the film, or so it seems. As entertaining as the film is, the props and gags are the real stars of the show. Look up at the spaceship from Pigs in Space and see if you can spot the cargo netting holding a large amount of colorful gelatin blocks, nicely paying homage to the most famous original Mouseketeer, Annette Funicello ("a net full of Jell-O," get it?). Around the room are crates and boxes of props for the show, including luggage for Miss Piggy's "sat in" gowns, Muppet Labs experimental dryer lint, and a box of flat pictures of oranges and lemons, better known as 2D fruities.

7. Toy Story Mania!

When you first enter the attraction building for Toy Story Mania!, the first thing you'll notice is the giant nightlight plugged into an equally large electrical outlet. Wow, everything sure is big in here! Or is it? No, they aren't oversized, you've shrunken down to the same size as Andy's toys! Larger-than-life toys (well, larger than life to your new, tiny self anyway) are scattered throughout this whimsical queue. Part of the ceiling is crafted as a checkerboard, with the red and black checker pieces stacked tall in a corner. Classic children's games are prominently displayed, such as Candy Land, Chutes and Ladders, Tinkertoys, Lincoln Logs, and Battleship. A spin art creation is proudly displayed on a wall, and another wall features a crayon drawing of a bright red race car with orange flames, taking the checkered flag. Andy's favorite toys, Buzz Lightyear and Sheriff Woody, are drawn on another wall in a youthful style. Elsewhere in the queue, you'll discover several View-Master discs, telling us that Andy has a preference for Peter Pan and Walt Disney World's Tomorrowland. (But where is the actual View-Master? Why, over in the queue of Buzz Lightyear's Space Ranger Spin, of course!) Even Andy's crayons are on display. It's hard to tell what his favorite color is, but it's easy to tell which one he likes least. The pink crayon still has its factory-sharp tip. Elsewhere, look for the simple balsa wood flyer propped against a wall, with "blue sky" written on the left wing. This is a sly nod to the Imagineering concept that all ideas have full merit and should first be fully fleshed out without limitations. If you look carefully, you'll also find a "Hidden Nemo" on the wall. After you pick up your 3D glasses, you'll proceed up a hallway that takes you over and into the loading area. This oversized space is Andy's bedroom. The large painted murals depict his bed and dresser and feature the blue-sky-with-clouds wallpaper and white wainscoting panels seen in the films. His latest game is the Toy Story Midway Games Play Set, and all his other toys have taken it out of the box. The toys don't want Andy to catch them in the act, so they propped the bedroom door shut with the Little Golden Book "Tin Toy," which is another nod to Pixar's vast animation history. The toys left the Toy Story Midway Games Play Set box out, and it serves as the entrance into the attraction itself.

8. Expedition Everest

So here you are, fearless adventurers seeking the services of a local company named Himalayan Escapes Tours and Expeditions ("There and back with the flying yak"), which will take you and your mountaineering gear to the base camp of Mount Everest. As it turns out, Himalayan Escapes has converted the former Anandapur Tea Company steam trains into transport vehicles. Trouble is, they've modified the train track so that it passes over the Forbidden Mountain, which, legend has it, is protected by the mighty Yeti. What could possibly go wrong? The standby line formally begins when you enter the building that housed the offices of the former Anandapur Tea Company. Because you haven't yet booked passage with Himalayan Escapes, your journey starts in the booking office, a ramshackle room with western (computer and printer) and local (wood carvings) influences on the desk. A simple note taped to the chair reads "Be right back." Unfortunately, no one is available to assist you, so it's on through an open courtyard and the Mandir, an authentic recreation of a Nepalese temple. Bells of all shapes and sizes adorn the ceiling, to be rung upon entry to announce your presence to the deities. Images of the Yeti are found throughout the Mandir in carvings and in shrines, complete with offerings of fruit, which are common in Asian cultures. Next up is the Yeti Museum, which is located in a converted tea warehouse. The museum provides a stark contrast between the legend of the Yeti and the entrepreneurs of Himalayan Escapes. The curator of the museum, Professor Pema Dorje, insists that the Yeti is real. As proof, he presents books by noted cryptozoologist Loren Coleman, a plaster cast of an oversized Yeti footprint, and graphic evidence of the "lost expedition" of 1982. The remains of the lost expedition include shredded tents, mangled camping gear, and photos that were developed from a recovered camera, showing you terrifying, albeit blurry, images of a Yeti with bared fangs. Norbu and Bob, the proprietors of Himalayan Escapes, don't want to lose business to the Yeti, real or imagined, and they counter that "The curators of the 'Yeti Museum' in no way reflect the views of the owners and operators of Himalayan Escapes Tours and Expeditions." Hmm, you should still probably be nervous...

9. The Jungle Cruise

The fictitious Jungle Navigation Company, Ltd. is the proprietor of this remote Amazon River outpost circa 1930, and throughout the boarding area you'll find an impressive collection of artifacts. Steamer trunks, leather suitcases, and wooden crates are abundant, and various other supplies can be found, such as canteens, lanterns, fuel canisters, and pith helmets. Signs in the queue indicate that the staff of the Jungle Navigation Company might not be the most reliable boat captains. Apparently, skippers have been known to use their boats for "daredevil trips over Schweitzer Falls," although the company frowns upon that. Another sign suggest that the citizens of this outpost are apparently very generous. They're offering free kittens to a good home! However, these kittens are a bit oversized, and they can evidently shred a shirt. You can also hear the antics of Albert Awol, who operates as "the voice of the jungle" on the DBC. Albert Awol's office is the centerpiece of the queue, although he's not there at the moment. But you can still see his desk, complete with a vintage manual typewriter, books, binoculars, pipe, and his radio gear. There are several hidden gems in the queue, all paying homage to Imagineers and real-life explorers. For example, keep an eye out for the barrel addressed to Dr. Winston Hibler, of the Special Arachnid Unit. Winston Hibler, along with Ted Sears, created the *True Life Adventure* series that served as the inspiration for the Jungle Cruise.

10. Kali River Rapids

Kali River Rapids draws its architectural influence from Thailand, Nepal, and India, and cultural inspiration from Bhutan, Nepal, India, Bali, and Java. The story puts Guests on a rafting expedition organized by Kali Rapids Expeditions, which is a local company specializing in eco-tourism packages that highlight the local ecology. Unfortunately, illegal logging is occurring in the region, which threatens the stability of the ecosystem and the river within it. The queue takes you along a wandering path through the jungle. Although paved, the original underlying bricks occasionally peek through. Keep a close eye out for ornate decorations in the pavement. Prayer shrines and large statues can be seen along the walkway as well. As you reach a clearing, you'll see the temple ahead, with its red-tiled roof and white peak. As is the religious custom in Asia, footwear is not worn inside the temple, and we see sandals lined up outside the entrance. Inside is a rich cornucopia of artifacts. An ornate feline statue is the centerpiece of one room, surrounded by prayer flags, with ornamental bells above and a fruit offering at its feet. Large, intricately detailed brass plates and woodcarvings hang on the wall. A decorative cobra serves as a fountain, spitting water out of its mouth. This temple serves many purposes, including as the office for the Kali Rapids Expeditions Company. The tour operator's desk is unoccupied, with a simple "Gone to temple, return soon" sign.

Some easily overlooked details include a framed 100 Rupee bill, which is a sign of pride for their first sale. The manual typewriter on the desk and the film available for sale tell you that the office hasn't quite caught up with our digital and electronic world. A chart on the wall lists all the rafts and whether they're in use. In another section of the queue, you'll find a multitude of birdcages, which serves as the local bird market. Another segment of the queue is dedicated to a local businessman, Mr. Panika, who has many local wares for sale. He even offers his services to ship what we buy. His scale is set up with a box that is being prepared for shipping. Bollywood-style movie posters are plastered along the wall, giving us a glimpse into the local film scene. Eki's Hotel is nearby, conveniently offering "fans in most rooms" and "mattress and toilet paper, just a little extra," according to a colorful sign. You'll next proceed through a smaller temple that highlights the Jataka Tales, which are a series of folklore-like morality tales from India, dating back to 3,000 B.C. that honor Buddha in animal and human forms. Eventually you'll enter the oar room, and all along the walls are wooden cutouts of boat paddles, all autographed by former customers who have conquered the rapids. Nearby are richly-illustrated images of the rafts owned by Kali Rapids Expeditions, with clever names such as Raja Runaround, Monsoon Momma, and Himalaya Hummer. Your final stop before boarding your raft is the boat room, where you'll see a video from a member of Kali Rapids Expeditions telling you that you'll be seeing beautiful scenery and nature, but that we need to be aware of illegal logging and its negative impact on the local ecology. (Unfortunately, they neglect to tell you that you might get a little wet along your journey!)

Ten Favorite Attraction Scenes

The attractions at Walt Disney World are filled with memorable moments and details; from dazzling special effects and stirring music to incredible Animatronic figures and immersive storytelling. But there are some attraction scenes that really stand out; the ones that instantly come to mind when you think of Disney. This list is admittedly very subjective, and we're sure you have favorites not listed here. But nevertheless, here are our picks for the attraction scenes we want to see again and again.

1. Haunted Mansion Ballroom

The Haunted Mansion is filled with memorable scenes, and it's really difficult to think of one that stands out from the rest. From the stretching rooms to the ghoulishly delightful graveyard, this attraction is brimming with sinister scenes and all those happy haunts who are just dying to welcome you to their swinging wake. And that's our pick for our favorite scene in the Haunted Mansion; the Ballroom Scene. Dancing ghosts sweep their way across the dilapidated dance floor, while other spirits partake of the lavish birthday feast as well as some personal hijinx. (Who can ever forget the two ghosts engaged in their eternal pistol duel?) The special effects here, though relatively simple in concept (but groundbreaking at the time), still dazzle and amaze us. But perhaps the greatest aspect of this scene is the sheer wealth of detail found throughout this cavernous dining hall. You could ride through the scene hundreds of times and see something new with each visit. One thing to keep an eye out for; since the dancing ghosts are really reflections off a giant piece of glass between you and the actual Animatronics (which are in fact located directly beneath the balcony), the images you see are reversed...meaning the ladies are leading the men in this ghoulish waltz!

2. Pirates of the Caribbean

This is another classic attraction filled with memorable scenes (for some reason the dirty pirate leg always comes to mind...), but our favorite comes after your plunge down the blackened tunnel as an ominous voices intones that "Dead Men Tell No Tales." As you emerge from the pitch-black tunnel, you find yourself in a whole other world; a nighttime scene where the town is being besieged by Captain Barbossa and his band of scallywags on the hunt for Jack Sparrow. The sheer scale of this room is jaw-dropping; everything seems larger than life, and the Animatronic of Captain Barbossa is absolutely stunning. You'll also notice that the haunting, ethereal music that echoed through the caves has been replaced by the more upbeat "Yo Ho (A Pirate's Life for Me)" And what about those exploding cannons? If you didn't get splashed on your drop through the darkness, you may still catch a stray spray of water as the cannonballs fall into the water, barely missing your boat.

3. "It's a small world"

This is another attraction graced with countless scenes filled with rich details and dazzling colors; how could one possibly pick a favorite? Actually, it's not that difficult, as everyone is fairly unanimous in picking the final white room as their favorite scene in the entire attraction. And for good reason! The "white room" is a bit of a misnomer, as the room's props and the outfits worn by the dolls are comprised of various shades of blue and white. But after seeing all the whimsical, colorful designs created by Disney Legend Mary Blair and the costumes created by Alice Davis in the previous rooms, the uniformity and brightness of this room simply takes your breath away. And it also perfectly encapsulates the theme of the attraction; world unity. Here are all the children of the world, coming together to bid you a fond farewell, and while they're still decked out in their homeland attire, they are all now coordinated in a pure and unifying color palette that brings all the countries together in one final display of togetherness. And the Ferris wheel is pretty cool, too!

4. Spaceship Earth

We're going to cheat a little bit with this one and go back a bit in time (but, hey, isn't that the point of the attraction?). We're going to travel backward to the version that featured Jeremy Irons as your narrator. Virtually every scene in Spaceship Earth is a classic, but our all-time favorite (with a close honorable mention that we'll get to shortly) was the grand reveal of the Earth floating in a vast expanse of stars at the top of the giant sphere. What made this version so spectacular was the perfect timing of the narration, your entrance into the grand planetarium, and the stirring musical score. As the distinctive voice of Jeremy Irons intones "But will these seemingly infinite communications become a flood of electronic babble? Or will we use this power to usher in a new age of understanding and cooperation on this, our Spaceship Earth," your vehicle emerged from the data tunnel, turning in perfect synchronization with the narration to reveal the glorious sight of planet Earth hovering in the heavens. Oh, and that honorable mention we talked about? That would be the dazzling fiber optic city of the future that you saw moments later...we can only dream of what it would be like to live there someday!

5. Peter Pan's Flight

This charming Fantasyland attraction is filled with whimsy and all the charm that makes the Disney Dark Ride such a magical experience. But our favorite scene in the attraction is when your ship soars over London on its way to Neverland. The reverse forced perspective of the Big Ben tower really makes it feel as if you're flying through the skies, but the best part is the moment you notice all those little cars driving through the streets below...complete with honking horns. (How did they do that? The answer is surprisingly simple; they're glow-in-dark spots on a continuously moving bicycle chain!).

6. Splash Mountain

You may think we're going to go with the plunge into the briar patch as our favorite scene in this Frontierland attraction, but to be honest, we usually have our eyes squeezed shut as we plummet toward that giant splash. No, our actual favorite scene takes place moments before, as you take a double-dip plunge deep into the heart of Chickapin Hill and into one of the most whimsical settings in all of Disney, the Laughing Place. This fun-filled "secret hideaway" is filled with all sorts of playful critters, from the chortling turtles gleefully riding fountains of water to the gophers that pop their heads from the ceiling. Great fun indeed (but the two vultures looming ahead are about to put an end to your merriment...)

7. Tomorrowland Transit Authority PeopleMover

This is one of our favorite attractions in all of Walt Disney World, and it's certainly filled with memorable scenes (the Epcot model continues to dazzle us to this day). But for this list we're going to get uncharacteristically specific, for this is a "scene" that can only be experienced at a certain time of year. And even more oddly, the "scene" isn't even in Tomorrowland. If you ride the TTA in the evening during the holidays, there's a point in your journey where you're traveling outside, heading around the curve that leads to the Tomorrowland Speedway. You'll need to pay attention, for this sight is fleeting. Look off to your left as you round the bend, and you'll get a glorious view of Cinderella Castle decked out in its Dream Lights. Glistening like a giant ice palace in the distance, this view is simply breathtaking, and for most Guests totally unexpected. Have your cameras at the ready, or better yet, tuck them away and simply behold this Christmas wonder with your own eyes...it's a sight you'll never forget!

8. Jungle Cruise

Ah, the jokes! The puns! The merriment! The Jungle Cruise is certainly one of the most fun-filled attractions in the Magic Kingdom, courtesy of your Cast Member skippers who always add a little bit of extra magic to every cruise. But there's one part of the journey that's not funny at all; the journey into the crumbling temple. Suddenly, all is silent and the jokes give way to dimly lit scenes of snakes, tigers, and golden treasure filling this ancient temple. In stark contrast to the rest of your journey, this section of the tour is delightfully spooky, especially at night. But lest you think things are starting to get too creepy, you'll emerge back into the friendly (?) jungle and your upcoming encounter with Trader Sam.

9. Carousel of Progress

This sometimes-overlooked treasure in Tomorrowland is filled with nostalgic charm and plenty of clever details (see how many times you can spot Rover's food bowl!). But in another nod to the holidays, our favorite scene by far is the final Christmas room. Even in the middle of summer, this scene definitely puts you in the holiday spirit. Some may quibble on whether the scene should be updated (to reflect that latest and greatest technologies), but to us the room has a delightful nostalgic charm to it, even though it's meant to show off some of the technological marvels of today and of those to come. It's an idealistic Christmas scene we always imagine; the family gathered together (including Uncle Orville), the beauty of the Christmas decorations (including a Mickey Mouse nutcracker tucked away on the mantle), and the inevitable kitchen mishap. (All of a sudden I'm in the mood for pizza...)

10. Mickey's PhilharMagic

This 3D film takes you on a whimsical journey through some of the most beloved Disney films of all time. As we follow Donald Duck in his quest to retrieve Mickey's Sorcerer's Hat, we visit the worlds of *Beauty and the Beast, Aladdin, Peter Pan,* and *The Lion King,* just to name a few. But our favorite moment is when we go under the sea to visit with Ariel as she sings of longing to be part of our world. At one point she tosses out a handful of jewels into the audience (courtesy of the magic of 3D technology), and while we're all busy grasping at the phantom rubies and sapphires, Ariel herself comes straight off the screen, arms stretched, singing "I want more...". Beautiful, emotional, and visually spellbinding, this scene always brings a tear to my eye (and admit it, you've wiped away a tear or two yourself).

Seven Best Attraction Exits

Y ou've blasted your way across the cosmos, survived your encounter with 999 happy haunts, and discovered your future with the help of some innovative technology. So now it's off to the next attraction, or for some of us, a much-needed helping of funnel cake. But wait, why are you in such a hurry? Just because the attraction is over doesn't mean the experience is too. More often than not, just when you think you've seen it all, you'll find that there's a lot more to discover. And thus we arrive at one of the great overlooked features of Walt Disney World: the magic of the attraction exits.

1. The Haunted Mansion

Take some time to look around as you exit the foreboding Gothic structure. To the left you'll find a mausoleum, and upon further examination you'll discover a treasure trove of pun-filled inscriptions. Say a few out loud if you can't figure them out! Continuing on, you'll soon come across the Pet Cemetery. The gravestones are a bit further back and positioned a bit higher than their counterparts that stand guard at the Mansion's entrance, but they are just as much fun to study. For the keen-eyed among you, look all the way back to the left and see if you can spot the tombstone of Mr. Toad, a one-time resident of Fantasyland. During Mickey's Not-So-Scary Halloween Party, the Pet Cemetery takes on a whole new aura, with black lights illuminating the cryptic memorials and ominous fog slowly cascading down the hillside. Even as you finally exit, take a peek on the ground and see if you can spot the horseshoe prints in the concrete. Memories of the Headless Horseman? Or the ghostly tracks of the bearer of the morbid hearse that sits nearby?

2. Frozen Ever After

Speaking of hoofprints, once you leave the gift shop, (which features Frozen-themed merchandise as you would expect, but also a host of souvenirs from Norway...be sure to check out the candy selection!) head on over to the nearby Wandering Reindeer shop. As you enter, look on the ground and you'll see more prints in the sidewalk...but these aren't horseshoe prints. No, these are the distinctive prints of Sven himself, who apparently wanted to get some early souvenir shopping down while the cement was still wet!

3. Space Mountain

Here, your exit takes you up a long moving sidewalk (or Speedramp as it's known to the local astronauts) that brings you back to the surface. You'll see several futuristic scenes depicting life in the far-off future. TTA fans will recall these scenes from their journey through Space Mountain, but now's your chance to see them up close. By the way, if you ever wondered why the ramp dips down and then back up again, that's because you're actually traveling underneath the Walt Disney World Railroad tracks.

(Pirates of the Caribbean / Star Tours)

We're going to take a slight detour with our next entry. Several attractions have exits that take you into a gift shop, including the Many Adventures of Winnie the Pooh, Buzz Lightyear's Space Ranger Spin, and Mickey's PhilharMagic, to name a few. There are two shops that merit special attention; the Pirates Bazaar at Pirates of the Caribbean, and Tatooine Traders at Star Tours – The Adventures Continue. Both are brimming with unique collectibles and hard-to-find treasures, and both are nearly as much fun to explore as the attractions themselves. In fact, you'll find lots of people that come to visit the shops in their own right, and whether you're looking for a personal souvenir or a gift for someone special, both shops offer a wealth of merchandise sure to please any pirate or wannabe Jedi. Tatooine Traders, in particular, is a must-visit for any Star Wars fan. In addition to the expected clothing, toys, and action figures, you'll also find lots of collectible items including autographed memorabilia and rare trinkets. Just be warned, both of these stores are a gold mine for young visitors, so be sure to set the ground rules ahead of time before you venture inside! You'll often find yourself spending much more time in the shops than you did in the attraction, and if the little ones are trying to pick out a souvenir it'll be difficult for them to stop at one. (Don't be too smug though. You'll discover plenty of kids your own age rummaging through the racks and shelves!)

4. Spaceship Earth

Upon exiting your time machine, you'll get to see yourself projected up on the giant globe (it may take a moment for your image to appear). Once your face is on display, it will stay for a few seconds and then be whisked away to your hometown (now you know why you entered your place of residence at the beginning of your journey through time!). For repeat visitors, it can be fun to pretend you live in a different place and see your image race over to Australia or Japan.

5. The Seas with Nemo & Friends

Here, the post-show area is actually home to the main attraction; the giant aquarium that's home to hundreds of a fish and sea mammals. This is definitely one pavilion you'll want to explore, and if you look around long enough you'll even discover Nemo's real-life counterpart.

6. Mission: SPACE

Once you safely make it back to Earth, you'll come across a number of interactive games and play areas in the attraction's post-show area. So many, in fact, that the pavilion is a wonderful attraction even if you don't think you have the right stuff for the flight to Mars. The pavilion features one of the lesser known play areas for children (though arguably one of the coolest), and a cooperative game for space explorers of all ages.

7. Test Track

The other thrill attraction in Future World East also features an expansive post-show area, and it's here you'll find some of the latest automotive innovations on display. And yep, you can climb in one of those new cars and see how it feels! (But no, you can't take it for a test drive.) You'll also find several interactive pavilions, such as a virtual racing game table. And, of course, you can check out your souvenir photo. (You remembered to smile, right?)

Ten Best Overlooked Disney Snacks

No trip to Walt Disney World would be complete without the food; and when you talk about Disney snacks, there are plenty of classics to be enjoyed. Who can forget that first bite of your Mickey Ice Cream Bar? Or the tantalizing smell of popcorn on Main Street U.S.A.? No Disney vacation would be complete without the classic churro, and how can we forget that most infamous of Disney snacks, the turkey leg? But there are lots of other delectable snacks to be found at Walt Disney World, and we thought we'd share some of our favorites.

1. Lemon Blueberry Cupcake

This refreshingly delicious dessert can be found at the Gasparilla Island Grill at the Grand Floridian Resort & Spa. The golden yellow cupcake is topped with a generous dollop of lemon icing, but the best part is what's inside; a surprise center of sweet blueberry filling. And let's not forget the proverbial icing on the cake; a juicy blueberry perched on top. By the way, if you're up for a different sort of citrus confection, you can also try the Piña Colada cupcake, complete with coconut shavings!

2. Zebra Domes

Over at the Animal Kingdom Lodge, you'll find a unique treat called a Zebra Dome. A what? Think of it as an exotic Tiramisu, comprised of an Amarula Cream Liquor mousse covered with white chocolate and drizzled with chocolate and chocolate shavings, all sitting atop a base of scrumptious cake. While it may not be for everyone, it's definitely worth a try! You can find this exotic treat at Boma, but you can also pop over to the Mara, the Animal Kingdom Lodge quick service eatery named for a river flowing through Kenya and Tanzania.

3. Peanut Butter and Jelly Shake

We'll give you fair warning; this one will make your knees buckle. This mouth-watering treat can be found at the 50's Prime Time Café at Disney's Hollywood Studios. You'll find lots of tempting treats here, including a warm apple crisp and a chocolate-peanut butter layered cake, but our favorite by far is the peanut butter & jelly milkshake. If you've never tried it, it may sound like an odd choice for a milkshake flavor, but you'll quickly be taken in by the explosion of flavors in this confectionery concoction. Best of all, you can get one to go if you don't have time to stay for lunch or dinner!

4. LeFou's Brew

This one-of-a-kind beverage can only be found at Gaston's Tavern in New Fantasyland, and its unique flavor is one you'll never forget. What is it exactly? Well, it's made with apple juice and a hint of toasted marshmallow, topped off with a passion fruit-mango foam. That's all well and good, but what does it taste like? Surprisingly, it may remind you of bubble gum! For a truly unique snacking experience, visit Gaston's around Christmastime and pair LeFou's Brew up with a peppermint cupcake. Now that's festive!

5. Mango Green Tea Slush

This unusual but refreshing beverage can be found at the Joy of Tea stand on the lagoon side of the China Pavilion in World Showcase. The Joy of Tea actually offers two varieties of smoothies; Strawberry Oolong Tea and Mango Green Tea (along with a variety of other great snacks from China). We're partial to the Mango Green Tea ourselves, but the Strawberry Oolong Tea is just as delicious. Just beware of the brain freeze that will hit you right around the time you reach the Italy pavilion...

6. Cheese Danish

This scrumptious delight is a bit harder to find these days, at least in the classic form that used to be commonplace throughout the Magic Kingdom. Cheese Danish can be found nearly everywhere at Walt Disney World, but the true classic consists of a cinnamon-laced frosted pastry topped with a heaping dollop of the most delicious cream cheese filling you've ever tasted. This is the classic Disney Cheese Danish, and while it may take some hunting to find that true original, it's well worth the search!

7. Mickey Krispies Treat

There are plenty of classic Disney treats to be found in the Main Street Confectionery, everything from cupcakes and candy apples to cotton candy and fudge. But our vote for favorite Confectionery snack has to be the classic Mickey Rice Krispies Treat Bar. Even in its simplest form, this is a true ooey-gooey classic that will take you right back to your childhood. But the confectioners at Disney have created countless variations on this classic treat. You'll find Rice Krispies treats decorated as some of your other favorite Disney characters, and you'll always find some special ones created just for the holidays (whether it be Christmas, Halloween, or any other special time of year).

8. Pocky

One of our favorite shops in all of Walt Disney World can be found in the Japan pavilion at Epcot, the Mitsukoshi Department Store. Tucked away in the back is an entire room devoted to food and other culinary items (and yes, even sake), and it's here you'll find one of our favorite snacks...pocky! The basic version consists of a chocolate-covered biscuit stick, but you'll also find a wide variety of other flavors; everything from strawberry and cookies and cream to almond and even green tea. If you're really hungry, you can get a jumbo box, which should last you, oh, for at least a few days.

9. Beverly

OK, we're kidding a little bit here, but no visit to Epcot would be complete without a stop at Club Cool in Future World. Here you can enjoy (for free!) Coca-Cola beverages from around the world; everything from Sparletta (a raspberry cream soda from Zimbabwe) to Fanta Pineapple from Greece. There are eight flavors to choose from, every one of them (well, nearly every one of them) a delicious taste treat that takes you on a flavorful tour around the world. But seriously, do try the Beverly at least once...it's not that bad!

10. Dole Whip

Speaking of pineapple, we couldn't help but include one classic in our list, the tropical treat that is the Dole Whip. The proper Dole Whip is the simple, classic cup of pineapple-flavored soft serve ice cream, but for a truly refreshing experience, we highly recommend the Pineapple Float. The float is made up of a generous helping of Dole Whip served up in a tangy cup of pineapple juice. There's nothing quite like that "bottom of the cup" mixture of melted pineapple ice cream and sweet pineapple juice; the perfect treat to enjoy in the tropical setting of Adventureland!

Eight Favorite Special Effects

1. Enchanted Mirror

One of the most astounding special effects to arrive at Walt Disney World in recent years was the mirror portal in Enchanted Tales with Belle So how does the mirror portal work? Well, magic of course! Disney magic, that is. We'll leave the details for you to figure out (or not, if you don't want to spoil the fun!), but we can tell you that it's a very sophisticated combination of 3D projected imagery, moving (and hollow) walls, sliding mirrors, and highly precise optical technology. The mirror portal utilizes similar techniques used in the Haunted Mansion's stretching room and the expanding stage in Mickey's PhilharMagic to "open" the doorway, with additional visual effects used to conceal the seam in the mirror itself. Many of the visual effects are enhanced by the darkness of the room; since you've just come from a brightly lit room your eyes aren't dark-adjusted so you don't notice some of the subtler motions of the mirror's components as they slide in and out of place. The one thing we will tell you is that the "doors" of the mirror slide open like an elevator, rather than swinging open as they seem to do. More Disney magic? Sure, and some very creative 3D animation and ultra-precise projection to boot.

2. Haunted Mansion Hitchhiking Ghosts

The recent refurbishment of the Haunted Mansion introduced several new innovations, such as the new figure of Constance Hatchaway (the bride in the attic), and a new Escher-like staircase room, filled with the footprints of otherwise invisible ghosts lighting and extinguishing the many candelabras found throughout the room. But the most humorous addition was the update of the final scene, where a hitchhiking ghost would follow you home. Previously, your ghost guest was simply a projection on the mirror in front of you that moved in synchronization with your Doom Buggy. But the new characters made use of advanced CGI technology and are now able to interact with Guests in delightfully mischievous ways. For example, you might find them switching your head with that of your fellow Guest! You'll never know what sort of hijinks the hitchhiking ghosts have in store for you, so each Haunted Mansion experience will be different.

3. Leota's Crystal Ball

Madame Leota's crystal ball is one of Disney's classic special effects, and it's actually undergone quite a few changes over the years. Originally, the image of Imagineer Leota Toombs was projected by a 16mm film loop onto a bust inside a crystal ball, creating the illusion of a living, speaking disembodied head. Imagineers revisited the effect in the 1990s, utilizing new technology that allowed the now-digitized footage to be sent through fiber optics to the back of Madame Leota's "head." The image then shone out from a wide-angle lens with a small focal length. The new method of projection allowed the table holding the crystal ball to move about in the séance room without disturbing the image of Leota's face.

Less than a decade later, Madame Leota received yet another upgrade at the Disneyland version of the Haunted Mansion. The advent of high-definition video projection technology allowed the crystal ball to float around the room while still holding the projected image. Imagineers programed the ball's course into a computer, and the projector used the path as a virtual screen, following the ball as it moved around the room. Walt Disney World's Magic Kingdom never utilized this upgrade. Instead, Imagineers implemented a new internal, LCD projection program in 2007 that eliminated issues with the earlier rear projection attempt, such as poor light and image quality.

4. Misty Pirates

Water screen projections have been used to great effect in shows like Fantasmic! and the new Rivers of Light show at Disney's Animal Kingdom. But the effect was also put to use in the refurbished Pirates of the Caribbean. As you start off on your journey, you'll pass through a waterfall. Don't worry, the "water" is actually fog. But another surprise awaits you at this point; the appearance of Blackbeard projected on the fog, warning you of the dangers ahead. When the effect first appeared, the haunting apparition was that of Davy Jones, Blackbeard was added to the attraction to coincide with the release of *Pirates of the Caribbean: On Stranger Tides*.

5. Nemo and His Aquatic Friends

The Seas with Nemo & Friends makes great use of Animatronic figures and film projections to create a fun-filled world for you to get lost in. (Well, don't get too lost; we're still looking for that little orange fish...) While the EAC scene with Crush is exhilarating (or "righteous" as Crush would say), a more subtle but no less stunning effect can be found near the end of the attraction. Here you'll see several scenes of various characters from the film singing "In the Big Blue World," happily swimming in the aquarium along with their real-life cousins. But wait, did you see that fish just swim in FRONT of Nemo? And come to think of it, how come they look like they're actually in the water, instead of just being an image projected on the glass? Well, the secret is actually quite simple; the characters are indeed projected on a clear screen, but that screen is actually inside the aquarium and not the exterior wall. It's a very subtle distinction, but that's why the characters appear to be in the tank, cavorting about with the other inhabitants of the aquarium. Well, all except Peach, that is. She's firmly stuck on the aquarium viewing window, telling you exactly how many Guests she's seen today, among other trivial tidbits.

6. Hydrolators

Speaking of the Seas pavilion, when it was known as the Living Seas, part of the experience involved you traveling down to SeaBase Alpha via the Hydrolators. What are Hydrolators? They were elevators built to take you down to the ocean floor, where you could explore the laboratories and observe the aquatic wildlife in the aquarium. Once you boarded your Hydrolator and the doors closed, the elevator would rumble, and you could feel yourself descending through the ocean depths, as evidenced by the bubbles rising on the other side of the viewing portals. Well, that's actually not what was really happening. SeaBase Alpha was, in reality, just on the other side of the door, and the rumbling and bubbles were merely sensory effects to create the illusion of your Hydrolator plunging to the ocean floor. Sure, it was pretty easy to figure out what was really going on, but it was a fun effect, and really went a long way to immersing you in the undersea world of the Living Seas.

7. Leaping Fountains

This whimsical water feature can be found near the Journey Into Imagination with Figment pavilion. There, graceful arcs of water playfully leap from one teal-colored pad to another, magically holding shape in flight. That is the science known as laminar flow. Consider the common garden hose. When in use, the water flow, based on the pressure, comes out spraying, perhaps in a narrow line, but nonetheless turbulent. Water droplets stray near and far from the intended path. On the other hand, consider how water released through a drinking straw will hold its form as gravity takes it downward. This is laminar flow, when all the water molecules are moving in synchronous order. It makes for a pretty cool effect, and a fun one too. (Admit it, you've spent many moments trying to "catch" those leaping fountains as they arced overhead!) The orientation and timing of the fountains are carefully synchronized to create the illusion of a single splash of water leaping about the various fountains.

8. Lights in the Ground at Future World

We saved one of the simplest, but most surprising effects for last. As the sun goes down at Epcot, Spaceship Earth and all the surrounding pavilions, including those in World Showcase, take on a whole new look as they are bathed in colorful lights. But the incredible lighting effects aren't limited to what's above the ground. As you walk through Future World at night, you'll find several groups of paving tiles brilliantly lit up by fiberoptic lights projected through tiny pinholes throughout the tiles. The lights form dazzling geometric shapes, and they swirl and change color right before your eyes. The best part of this effect is that it's totally unexpected, and you'll see many Guests stop in amazement when they realize what's underfoot. It's just another example of those great innovative touches that Disney's Imagineers infuse into everything we see, adding to the mood and ambiance of the surrounding area. And what a perfect way to say goodnight as you leave the world of the future.

Ten Creative Uses of Color at Walt Disney World

Colors play in important role in bringing that Disney magic to life, but sometimes in ways that you'd least expect. Here are some of our favorite examples of Disney's innovative use of color throughout the parks.

1. Pink Sidewalks for Parading

As you walk down Main Street, U.S.A., World Showcase in Epcot, or throughout Disney's Hollywood Studios, you may notice that the sidewalks are tinted pink. Why? Well, the pink hue of the sidewalks actually makes the surrounding landscaping appear brighter. How? Red and green are complementary colors, meaning they are opposite each other on the color wheel. Complementary colors provide the strongest contrasts to one another, and when placed alongside each other can make both appear brighter. The pinkish hue of the sidewalks contrasts nicely with the green grass and shrubbery, making both appear just a little bit brighter. The surrounding foliage would be somewhat more drab if the sidewalks were a standard gray.

2. Colors of Nature

Speaking of foliage, Guests often take the surrounding flowers and plants for granted, but they too play an integral part in establishing the mood of your surroundings. Note the contrast between the sculpted trees in Tomorrowland, which lend an air of geometric precision to the world of the future, with the natural appearance of the plantings in Adventureland and Frontierland that help to reinforce the untamed nature of these exotic lands. But just as important is the use of color. Adventureland is overflowing with lush greens that evoke the deepest and darkest jungles of Africa and South America, while over at Liberty Square and the American Adventure, you'll note that the plantings are comprised of red, white, and blue flowers.

3. A Landscape of Color

At the Land Pavilion, the surrounding landscape is planted in distinctive rows to represent the lushness of the natural environment, with the trees at the top sporting white blooms to evoke the clouds in the sky.

4. Magical Colors for a Magical Hat

Sometimes the effort to provide a unique colorscape results in new innovations, such as the paint treatment that was used to allow Mickey's Sorcerer Hat (the former icon of Disney's Hollywood Studios) to shimmer in a myriad of brilliant colors as you walked around it, an effect accomplished by using a specially formulated paint called chameleon paint.

5. All Grays Are Not the Same...

Cinderella Castle looks to have a simple two-color scheme during the day, but in reality seven different shades of gray are used at different elevations to enhance the grandeur of this magnificent structure.

6. ...And Neither Are All Whites

At the American Adventure, you'll note that the trim appears to be a uniform white, but such is not the case. Several different shades of white were carefully selected based on a variety of criteria. The first was the environment; the Florida sun can be quite strong and can greatly influence the perception of colors, including white. Another is the fact that the same shade of white can appear in different hues when placed next to different colors. On the American Adventure building, the white used in the trim on the building facade is a warm white so that it blends well with the color of the bricks. If you could compare them side by side, you would see that the white used in the trim on the roof is much cooler (bluer). That's necessary due to the dark blue tiles of the roof. If the same white were used in both places, it would look very different and would create a startling contrast.

7. Go Away!

On the other end of the spectrum, the Imagineers also developed a color dubbed "Go Away Green." This shade of gray green is rather nondescript, and that is precisely the point: it is used on fences, garbage cans, construction walls, and any other areas that are not meant to be a part of the action. The eye tends to gloss right over this color, and that is exactly what the Imagineers intended!

8. Jeweled Mosaics

But back to Cinderella Castle and its walk-through breezeway. What could have been a simple walkway from Main Street to Fantasyland is transformed into a magical journey via five immense mosaic murals depicting Cinderella's story. Five-hundred different colors can be found within the mosaics, which boast more than one million pieces of glass, in addition to accents of silver and 14-carat gold. A very special use of color can be found in the fourth mural, in which the prince slips the wayward glass slipper onto Cinderella's foot. Her step-sisters stand by in bitter, wide-eyed amazement: Anastasia's face has a reddish hue, symbolizing her anger at what has transpired, while Drizella's face is green, signifying envy.

9. The Colors of Space

Then there are the planetary orbs greeting Guests as they enter Mission: SPACE. The largest is red in keeping with the attraction's theme of traveling to Mars, and the vibrant colors, coupled with the abstract art of the structure, visually draw Guests in as they approach. The paint used for these planets is a unique "color-shifting" paint that provides Guests with different tints depending on the position of the sun as well as the angle from which the structures are being viewed. It's not exactly the kind of paint that you can pick up at your local home improvement store...this paint cost Disney more than $800 per gallon!

10. A Rainbow of Energy

While Mission: SPACE is arguably the most colorful spot in Future World East, at one time the Universe of Energy Pavilion featured a rainbow of colors – literally! The original pavilion boasted panels of reds, yellows, and oranges meant to evoke the idea of fire and ergo, energy. When the pavilion received an overhaul in 1996, these panels were repainted in the colors of the rainbow, with the idea of creating a sense of optimism and looking forward. The pavilion was returned to its former palette in 2009.

Ten Oft-Overlooked Details Found Underfoot

Even the casual Disney visitor is aware of the wealth of details that the Imagineers infuse into every corner of the parks, whether it's the authentic fortress in Pirates of the Caribbean (can you hear the pirates digging for treasure in a distant cave?) or the whimsical inventions and lab equipment at Journey Into Imagination (be sure to keep an eye out for the shrinking hallway!). But many might not be aware of the treasures to be found underfoot.

1. Cobblestones, Bricks, and More!

For example, in World Showcase, you'll discover a treasure trove of ground level detail. Each pavilion features courtyards and walkways constructed in a distinctive style unique to the host country. Look for cobblestones in the United Kingdom, stone slabs in Japan, and intricate brickwork in the American Adventure. Meanwhile, at Disney's Animal Kingdom, you'll find that the ground at Chester and Hester's Dino-Rama mimics the wear and tear of a well-worn parking lot, the perfect place for in impromptu carnival to set up shop!

2. Critter Tracks

As you wander around the grounds at the Wilderness Lodge, you'll find all sorts of critter tracks embedded in the pathways surrounding the resort. See if you can spot deer tracks, opossum, and even the occasional bear!

3. Biking to Everest

Over in Asia at Disney's Animal Kingdom, you'll find a mish mash of bicycle tracks criss-crossing the walkways, bicycles being a common form of transportation in this part of the world.

4. This Way Out

Speaking of tracks, here's an "under foot" detail that many people overlook. As you exit many attractions, you'll find yourself on a moving walkway that takes you out of the unloading area. The walkway will have footprints on it to let you know which way to go, but oftentimes the footprints are a bit unusual. For instance, those on the walkway at the Seas with Nemo & Friends feature a distinctive nautical design, while those at Pirates of the Caribbean include one shoe print and one dot. Why a dot? Why, that's the peg leg of the pirate that exited the fortress right before you of course!

5. Welcome to England!

At Epcot's United Kingdom pavilion, you may sometimes spot a playful hopscotch grid sketched out in chalk in front of the pavilion as well as a welcome message added by a friendly Cast Member.

6. The Art of...Water?

Speaking of Cast Member magic, keep your eyes open as you exit Epcot at night. You may catch a faint glimpse of a favorite Disney character in the walkway around Spaceship Earth.

Even more surprising, you may notice that the illustration fades out as quickly as it appears! A moment's study will reveal the source of these whimsical drawings; talented Cast Members armed with nothing more than a bucket of water and a special mop who wander around sketching Mickey and friends under the futuristic glow of the giant geodesic sphere.

7. Watch Out, Wet Cement!

Sometimes you'll spot some initials or footprints "left" in the wet cement as the area was being constructed. For example, over in the Magic Kingdom, look for the Lady and the Tramp heart engraved in the cement outside Tony's Town Square Restaurant. Meanwhile, over at Epcot...

8. Oh, Figment...

On a mischievous note, head way over to the right of the Imagination pavilion and take a peek around the corner. You'll find that Figment carved his signature into the wet pavement. Sheesh, didn't he cause enough trouble INSIDE the Imagination Institute?

9. Dino Tracks

In its heyday, you could once see giant dinosaur tracks in Echo Lake at Disney's Hollywood Studios. Not only would you find them in the landscaping leading away from the giant figure of Gertie the Dinosaur standing in the lake, you'd also find those footprints continuing into the nearby walkways, as well as cracks that resulted from all that dino weight!

10. Mickey's Sunset Surprise

Speaking of Disney's Hollywood Studios, see if you can spot the "Mortimer & Co. Contractors, 1928" stamp on the walkways along Sunset Boulevard. This is, a nod to Mickey Mouse's first major on-screen appearance in 1928's *Steamboat Willie*.

Five Disney "Firsts"

The history of Disney (whether we're talking films, parks, or technological innovations), is resplendent with notable "firsts." Many are well known, such as *Snow White and the Seven Dwarfs'* status as the first feature-length animated film, and the first use of a synchronized sound track in animation with the release of *Steamboat Willie*. But there are many other "firsts" to be discovered, some of which are rather obscure.

1. Mickey Mouse's First Words

As mentioned earlier, the first use of a synchronized soundtrack was for the 1928 animated short, *Steamboat Willie*. The film is also notable for being the public debut of Mickey and Minnie Mouse (although both had appeared a few months earlier in a test screening for the short *Plane Crazy*). However, even though the film featured numerous sound effects and a humorous rendition of "Turkey in the Straw," as well as the sounds of Mickey laughing and whistling, Mickey didn't actually speak. He also didn't speak in the follow-up shorts *The Gallopin' Gaucho, The Barn Dance*, or *Plane Crazy* (re-released after the success of the first films). In fact, Mickey wouldn't talk in any of his first eight films. It wasn't until the release of 1929's *The Karnival Kid* that audiences first heard Mickey Mouse speak (voiced by Carl Stalling, though Walt Disney himself would eventually provide the voice of the world's most famous mouse). And what were those immortal words? "Hot dogs, hot dogs!"

2. The First Walt Disney Company Stock Certificate

April 2, 1940 was an auspicious day in Disney history, as that was the day the first stock certificate was issued for Walt Disney Productions. Seventeen years later, the company went public in an IPO, with shares priced at $13.88. As of this writing, the price of a share was $104.73. Incidentally, when Disney purchased Pixar on May 5, 2006 (in an all-stock deal worth $7.4 billion), it simultaneously made Steve Jobs (then CEO of Pixar) the largest individual Disney shareholder, with 7% ownership of shares. Not too bad!

3. The First Use of Computer Animation in a Disney Film

This one is a little tricky, as it depends on how you define computer animation. The first totally computer animated feature length film was Pixar's *Toy Story* (1995), though since the film was produced by Pixar and distributed by Disney, it technically wouldn't be considered Disney's first computer animated film. For that distinction we'd need to fast forward to 2005's *Chicken Little*, which gets the nod as the first totally computer animated film produced by Walt Disney Pictures. But computer graphics had been utilized in Disney films before the release of either of those movies. *The Rescuers Down Under* (1990) was the first Disney film to utilize a new animation process called the Computer Animation Production System, or CAPS (which was actually developed by Pixar). The software replaced traditional hand-painted cels, and also allowed animators to simulate three-dimensional multiplane effects, used to great effect in *Beauty and the Beast* (the second film to use CAPS), particularly in the ballroom scene.

But even CAPS wasn't the first use of computer generated imagery in a Disney animated film. That honor goes to 1985's *The Black Cauldron*, which goes down in history as being Disney's first animated feature film to utilize computer generated imagery, which was used to animate various elements such as bubbles, a boat, a floating orb of light, and the cauldron itself. (Technically speaking, computer graphics were first put to use for 1986's *The Great Mouse Detective*, which was in production at the same time as *The Black Cauldron*. However, since *The Black Cauldron* was released first, it gets the gold medal.)

4. The First Guests to Visit Disneyland

It's a great thrill to be the first Guest to enter a Disney park. The streets are empty, and in the case of the Magic Kingdom, you get to behold the sight of Cinderella Castle towering at the end of Main Street U.S.A. with nary a soul in sight. But imagine being the first person to have EVER entered the Magic Kingdom. For that matter, imagine being the first Guest to enter ANY Disney park. That distinct honor goes to Dave MacPherson, a 22-year-old college student from Long Beach, who had waited all night to purchase that coveted first ticket. (Dave's ticket was actually "ticket number 2," "ticket number 1" having been pre-purchased by Roy O. Disney for posterity). The first children to enter the park were cousins Christine Vess Watkins and Michael Schwartner, who were five and seven years old at the time. Walt Disney posed for a once-in-a-lifetime photo with the pair, who (along with MacPherson) received lifetime passes. Christine and Michael were invited back to Disneyland in 1975 to help celebrate the park's 20th anniversary.

5. The First Disney Park Audio-Animatronic Figures

Audio-Animatronic figures have become synonymous with Disney, and for good reason. The first Animatronic figure was inspired by a mechanical bird that Walt Disney had gotten while on vacation (the inspirational bird eventually wound up on display at the "D23 Presents Treasures of the Walt Disney Archives" exhibit at the Museum of Science and Industry in Chicago, Illinois).

Soon after, the infamous "Dancing Man" (which used Buddy Ebsen as a real-life model) was created by Roger Broggie and Wathel Rogers. But the first Disney attraction to make use of this new technology was The Enchanted Tiki Room in Disneyland, which opened in 1963. The multitude of birds that performed during this whimsical tropical show were synchronized to a musical score via an ingenious method of using audio tape with prerecorded tones to vibrate a metal reed that closed a circuit to trigger a relay. The relay would send a pulse of electricity to a mechanism that caused a pneumatic valve to activate a specific part of the bird, whether it be an eye, a beak, or wing.

More Animatronic figures were unveiled at the 1964-65 New York World's Fair (and eventually relocated to Disneyland), including the Carousel of Progress and Great Moments with Mr. Lincoln. But the first Audio-Animatronic figures were the tiki birds, which continue to delight audiences to this day, and whose origins go back to a small souvenir that Walt Disney picked up on the spur of the moment.

Six Disney "Seconds"

So that completes our list of "Disney Firsts." But by the very definition of "first," there must be a "second," and as you might expect, the history of Disney is filled with a number of "next in line" instances...some of which are more significant than the "firsts" that preceded them. So, get out your red ribbons and your silver medals as we take a look at several notable Disney "seconds."

1. Disney's Contemporary Resort

Most fans know that when Walt Disney World opened in 1971, there were two resorts to accommodate Guests (even though there were plans for several more). The two, Disney's Contemporary Resort and Disney's Polynesian Village, both opened on October 1st of that year with much fanfare (along with the Magic Kingdom, of course). Opening ceremonies marked the beginning of a new era in Disney history, and Guests eagerly flocked to the resorts and the park to see what surprises awaited them. Most Guests, of course, headed towards the Magic Kingdom, but a large number were also on hand to witness the grand openings of the resort's signature hotels. Guests visiting the Polynesian Village were enchanted by the exotic tropical setting and lush foliage. They were just as eager to see what futuristic surprises awaited them at the nearby Contemporary but, unfortunately, they would have to wait. You see, the Polynesian was the first Disney resort to open, and it would be a while before the second resort opened its doors. And how long was this interminable wait? A grand total of 45 seconds.

2. Mickey Mouse

The world's most famous mouse (sorry Minnie!) has his own collection of "seconds." First and foremost is his very name...no, not the "mouse" part (we'll get back to that), but the "Mickey" part. You see, when Walt Disney dreamed up his new character on a train ride back from New York City, he not only conceived of the perfect character to build his empire around, but the perfect name as well! And what was that ideal moniker? Mortimer!

Wait...what? Morti-who?

That's exactly what Walt's wife Lillian said upon hearing the name (OK, those weren't the exact words she used but you get the point). She thought Mortimer sounded too stuffy and recommended "Mickey" instead. Walt agreed, and a star was born.

3. Mickey the Rabbit. Huh?

Well, now we get to Mickey's other infamous "second." The reason Walt was on the train in the first place was that he was returning from a disastrous meeting in which he lost the rights to his original animated creation, Oswald the Lucky Rabbit. Seemingly at the brink of ruin, Walt instead turned the potentially devastating news into an opportunity; an opportunity to create a whole new character that would propel Walt and his Studio to heights of which he had only dreamed and, more importantly, to take the hard lessons learned at that fateful meeting in New York and turn them into the foundation of an entertainment empire that continues and flourishes, to this day.

4. Walt's Second Business

The lessons Walt learned in the Oswald debacle bring to mind one of his more curious quotes: "I think it's important to have a good hard failure when you're young." It's a curious quote when you think of all the successes that Walt Disney enjoyed throughout his lifetime. His achievements may never be equaled, but they were all due to his perseverance and a fervent belief in himself. While one could attribute the quote to Walt's experiences that led to the creation of Mickey, he was actually referring to an earlier time in his life, the time when he lost his first animation studio.

While in Kansas City, Walt started up his own studio, Laugh-O-Gram, in 1922. After hiring several animators, the new studio began producing innovative animation shorts. Unfortunately, business was slow, and eventually the studio went bankrupt. However, rather than giving up, Walt picked himself up and set off for Hollywood to open a new studio (and as we all know, this one was a bit more successful!). It was a tough experience, but one which taught the young filmmaker much about business and life. As he further went on to say, "I learned a lot out of that. Because it makes you kind of aware of what can happen to you. Because of it I've never had any fear in my whole life when we've been near collapse and all of that. I've never been afraid. I've never had the feeling I couldn't walk out and get a job doing something."

5. Disneyland's Second Day

The opening of Walt Disney's dream park, Disneyland, was a much-anticipated event, with a buildup that included Walt using the new medium of television to introduce viewers to the park. After years of planning and construction, Disneyland finally opened its gates on July 17, 1955 for an invitation-only Media Preview. Not only would Guests get the chance to experience the wonders of Disneyland firsthand, but the entire nation was able to watch the proceedings on a special TV broadcast hosted by Art Linkletter, Bob Cummings, and Ronald Reagan. It should have been a cause for celebration, but unfortunately, the day turned out to be a disaster.

Well, disaster may be an over-statement, but things certainly didn't go as planned. For one thing, the crowd swelled to 28,000 people, despite only 11,000 invitations being issued. The in-coming roads were jam-packed, and to top it all off, California was experiencing a nasty heat wave, with temperatures climbing well in excess of 100 degrees. Water fountains failed to work, a gas leak closed much of the park, and the newly poured asphalt sank under the pressure of ladies' high-heeled shoes. Unfortunately, the confluence of all these incidences generated a lot of bad press, and that just wouldn't do. Walt Disney invited the media back the next day to experience the "true" Disneyland, and this was the day that all Guests were welcome. Things went much smoother (though the crowds were still massive, with an estimated 50,000 people in attendance), and it was on this day that the first official Guests were welcomed and given lifetime passes (those lucky individuals were profiled in the previous list).

6. Disney's First "Second" Film: The First Disney Animated Sequel

Walt Disney was never one to rest on his laurels. After he mastered one challenge, he was always looking forward to the next. While fans would gladly have lined up for another Seven Dwarfs adventure or some more high-flying hijinks from Dumbo, Walt had no interest in repeating something that he had already done. As he famously once said, "I've never believed in doing sequels. I didn't want to waste the time I have doing a sequel. I'd rather be using that time doing something new and different. It goes back to when they wanted me to do more pigs." That last part may require a bit of an explanation.

You see, one of Walt's earliest animated successes was the Silly Symphony cartoon *Three Little Pigs*, released in 1933. The cartoon short spawned a major hit song in "Who's Afraid of the Big Bad Wolf," and fans and theater owners alike were eager for a follow-up. Everyone, that is, except Walt Disney. With the pronouncement, "You can't top pigs with pigs," Walt had his sights set on even higher aspirations, and the rest as they say, was history. It would be another 57 years before the first full-length animated feature was released that could rightly be called a sequel (ignoring earlier shorts that were part of a larger series, like the Winnie the Pooh featurettes).

That film was *The Rescuers Down Under*, released on November 16, 1990 as a follow-up to 1977's *The Rescuers*, based on a series of books by Margery Sharp. *The Rescuers Down Under* also has the distinction of being the second film released during the Disney Renaissance (which began with *The Little Mermaid*), and the second Disney animated film that didn't include any musical numbers (can you name the first?). There would of course be many more sequels released in future years, both direct-to-video and for theatrical release (including such modern-day classics as *Toy Story 2* and *Toy Story 3*), but *The Rescuers Down Under* was the first, and it's important to remember that no full-length sequels were released in Walt Disney's lifetime.

Oh, that first non-musical film we mentioned? That would be 1985's *The Black Cauldron*.

Nine Disney Myths

Secrets. Legends. Little known facts. Walt Disney World is filled with all sorts of hidden details and stories, so many in fact that a big part of the fun of being a Disney fan is in discovering all those fun-filled tidbits. But like so many other legends, stories sometimes change over time. Perhaps it's the case of a few different tales being mixed together, or a tall tale that's repeated so often that it becomes believable. Sometimes it's nothing more than a classic case of "whisper down the lane," where stories and facts are distorted over time to create a whole new legend that sounds plausible but turns out not to be true. Myths and urban legends have been around as long as there were people to tell them, but in today's world of the Internet, blogs, and message boards, it doesn't take long for a falsehood to get legs and wind up being published everywhere. So it's no surprise that there are lots of Disney myths floating around these days, and in this list, we'll look at a few of them.

1. Walt Disney's Singing Graveyard Bust

Before we get into some of the lesser-known myths, we'll touch on a few that are fairly well known. These have been discussed so many times that most Disney fans are probably aware that they're not true, but nonetheless they're still fun to share. The first takes us to the Haunted Mansion (as we press forward you'll see that this attraction has quite a few myths associated with it). In the singing busts scene in the graveyard, one of the busts has fallen over. The face on the stone figure bears a striking resemblance to Walt Disney, and many people believe that it is in fact Walt warbling along with rest of the quintet. A cute story, but that's not Walt Disney. It's actually Thurl Ravenscroft, whose distinctive baritone can be heard quite clearly as the busts sing "Grim Grinning Ghosts." His voice may be familiar, he sang the classic Christmas song "You're a Mean One, Mr. Grinch" from the TV animated special "How the Grinch Stole Christmas," and he also performed the voice of Tony the Tiger.

2. Dismantling a Castle

Another popular Disney myth has to do with the very symbol of Walt Disney World, Cinderella Castle. Over time, a legend somehow grew that the Castle could be quickly dismantled in the event of a severe hurricane. That's not true, and a moment's reflection will show that doing so would be highly impractical (how would the necessary massive cranes may be moved into position?), not to mention dangerous. The Castle is, in fact, quite sturdy, and can easily withstand the fiercest winds that a hurricane can muster. It's not clear where this story began, but it may have started with the publication of photos of the Castle during construction, showing the individual turrets being lifted into place by large cranes.

3. Walt's Final Resting Place

No list of Disney myths would be complete without the bizarre tale of Walt Disney's final resting place. The story is a bit morbid, but it's become so prevalent and persistent that even today, misconceptions abound. Without going into too many details, the story goes that

Walt Disney was cryogenically frozen and is being kept "in stasis" beneath the Pirates of the Caribbean attraction in Disneyland. Aside from the fact that the first cryogenically frozen individual wasn't frozen until a month after Disney's death, it's doubtful that, according to his daughter Diane, Walt Disney was even aware of such a procedure. In any event, Walt Disney's final resting place is at Forest Lawn Cemetery, though the legend persists to this day.

4. The Pirates of the Caribbean Chessboard

Next up is the Pirates of the Caribbean attraction, and the legendary chess board that you can see in the queue. The legend goes that the two skeletons in the cell are locked in a perpetual stalemate; that the positions of the pieces on the chess boards are such that neither player can win, and they are destined to play for all eternity. This myth actually has a basis in fact, as the chessboard was originally set up in just such a position. Imagineer Marc Davis mapped out the specific positions for the stalemated chess pieces that Guests would see on the board when they looked through the bars.

Unfortunately, even though it may have been true at one time, such is no longer the case. If you have a photo of the chessboard, you can likely see it yourself. Set up the pieces, find your favorite chess opponent (or a good computer chess program), and see how it plays out. You'll likely find that one of the players can win very easily, and oftentimes, in just a few moves. So what happened? Probably nothing more sinister than Cast Members inadvertently moving the pieces as they "cleaned" the area. If you do a Google search on images of the chessboard, you'll see that the pieces have moved all over the place throughout the years. A few seem to be set in their proper squares, but others come and go and move all around the board.

Another related tale about the chessboard is that at one point the pieces were moved during a cleaning, and everyone realized that they had no idea how to put them back. Cast Members realized that there was a unique way in which the pieces were to be arranged, and after a long search, an original sketch of Davis' turned up, containing his exact instructions for placing the pieces. These instructions were taped underneath the board just in case they were moved again. Is this true? The last part doesn't appear to be true or else the pieces would always be in the proper place. But what of the rest? We'll go on record as maintaining that the origins of the story are likely true, but alas, the notion of a perpetually stalemated board has been lost in the mists of time.

5. The Carpet in the Hall of Presidents...

This myth centers around the Great Seal that's in the carpet in the entryway. Many people assume, and have written, that this is the Presidential Seal of the United States, and why not? This is the Hall of Presidents after all! But what you actually see on the floor is the Great Seal of the United States, not the Presidential Seal. Admittedly, the two are very similar, but they are subtly different.

6. ...And the Act of Congress That Allows it to Be Displayed

That's the easy part. The second part of the legend is a bit more uncertain. It is commonly stated that Disney had to obtain a special Act of Congress (or simply "special permission," depending on which version of the story you hear), in order to put the Seal on display. An addendum to the story is that the Seal is only on display in two places in the United States, here at the Hall of Presidents, and at the Capital itself (or the White House, or Independence Hall...you get the idea). But is it true? A call to the Library of Congress turned up no documentation from Congress regarding the Seal at the Hall of Presidents, and the researcher we talked to was skeptical that any such permission would need to be obtained. A reading of the actual laws pertaining to appropriate uses of the Seal doesn't shed much light on the subject, as they are varied and vague (and don't address this question specifically). This legend is so persistent that Cast Members routinely tell the tale to Guests as they wait for the next show to begin in the theater. It may very well be true, but in the course of researching the tale we have yet to find any actual documentation that any such permission was obtained or necessary. We're not quite prepared to say this one isn't true, so if any of our readers have information on this we invite you to share it with us. After all, it does make for a good story!

7. Walt Disney World's Geographic Center

We're going to switch parks for out next legend, and this is one we know to be false. When you exit the rear of the former Innoventions West building in Epcot, you'll find a courtyard filled with plaques commemorating significant events in science and discovery. It is said that when you stand in the center of the courtyard, you're actually standing in the geographic center of Walt Disney World. (Another variation says that you're standing in the center of Epcot itself). Even a casual look at a map will prove this tale to be false, as the center of Walt Disney World (as best as can be determined, due to the irregularity of its boundaries), is roughly to the east of the Epcot monorail line, right in the heart of an undeveloped patch of forest.

The center of Epcot, incidentally, would put you in World Showcase lagoon (hope you brought your snorkel!). The origins of this myth are rather mysterious, particularly since it's so easily disproved. Similar stories are told of the various survey markers that can be found throughout Epcot. While they are neat to find and do have a geographic significance (as it relates to surveying), the markers don't have anything to do with specific locations of significance in Walt Disney World itself.

8. Haunted Mickeys

Finally, we'll touch on a unique set of stories, those that began as myths but have since become true (hey, this is Walt Disney World, anything can happen!). Coincidentally, all of them have to do with the Haunted Mansion. The first involves one of the most iconic Hidden Mickeys that you can find at the Magic Kingdom, the three dinner plates on the table in the ballroom scene. This Hidden Mickey has been around for ages and continues to be a favorite for those visiting the happy haunts of Liberty Square. It has always been a great one to point out to Disney newbies, and was a wonderful introduction to the world of Hidden Mickeys. The only trouble was...it wasn't an official Hidden Mickey. When cleaning the set (or, to be more proper, "dirtying" the set), Cast Members would often arrange the plates in a Hidden Mickey. The problem was that that wasn't how they were supposed to be setup. There were specific instructions on how the different elements on the table were to be arranged, and officially, those three plates weren't meant to be arranged in that manner. That didn't stop Cast Members from creating the classic Mickey but it also didn't stop the next set of Cast Members from setting them back to their proper positions. What that meant was that when you toured the Haunted Mansion, you would usually be able to spot that Hidden Mickey...but sometimes you wouldn't (somehow that always disappointed me!). Over time though, the Hidden Mickey became so popular that it was finally made "official" and that's how the plates are arranged today. (Or perhaps not...in hushed corners you may hear whispers that even that is an urban legend, but the plates are now seemingly set in their permanent Mickey arrangement, so we may never know...unless a Cast Member or sympathetic ghost tells us for sure.)

9. The Bride's Ring

Speaking of Haunted Mansion spirits, the Mansion's most infamous resident is arguably the bride in the attic. Once upon a time, some remodeling at the exit of the attraction necessitated the removal of a small post, leaving an irregular ring in the ground. Legend quickly grew that this was the bride's wedding ring, which she flung out of the attic window in a fit of despair. This story was so persistent that Cast Members would point it out to you if you asked. Alas, it was just a legend, and in a subsequent minor renovation the "ring" disappeared. Fortunately, the tale didn't end there. The "bride ring" story was so popular that it was incorporated into the new interactive queue that was added to the Haunted Mansion in 2011. As you wander through the queue you'll find the bride's ring embedded in the ground, and this is the real thing, not a leftover post remnant.

Our Five Favorite Holiday Moments

Christmas is a wonderful time to visit Walt Disney World, when it's resplendent with beautiful decorations and all the holiday trimmings you could imagine. There are plenty of iconic sights and experiences to enjoy during the holidays, from Mickey's Very Merry Christmas Parade to the Cinderella Castle Dream Lights. But as with all things Disney, there are lots of little gems and tucked away surprises that add to the merriment.

1. Window Shopping on Main Street U.S.A.

A walk down Main Street during the holidays is a one-of-a-kind experience that brings back all the nostalgic memories of years gone by. From the giant Christmas tree in the heart of Town Square to the dazzling spectacle of Cinderella Castle rising like a giant ice sculpture in the distance, Main Street is filled with Christmas joy and is sure to fill your heart with that unique holiday spirit. But as you walk down Main Street, take some time to do a little window shopping. You'll find that many of the stores have put out all new displays just for Christmas. You'll find Mickey and Minnie with their own Christmas windows, done up in all their "Santa" fineness, Daisy Duck whipping up some delicious holiday treats by the Confectionery, overflowing toy boxes, nostalgic jewelry and poinsettia tree displays, not to mention a series of windows at the Emporium that bring Charles Dickens' "A Christmas Carol" to life with a Disney twist.

2. The Yacht Club Village

Visiting the Walt Disney World resorts is a favorite holiday tradition, especially since each one is decorated in the resort's theme. You'll find nostalgic Victorian splendor in the Grand Floridian, northwest rustic charm at the Wilderness Lodge, and a whimsical "under the sea" motif at both the Beach and Yacht Clubs. But it's at the Yacht Club where you'll find an oft-overlooked gem, the miniature Mickey's Village display in the lobby. The next time you visit, take some time to enjoy the many details that can be found throughout this tiny town. See if you can spot "Marcelene's Home Made Candy Sweet Shop," a tribute to the town that Walt Disney grew up in, Marceline, Missouri. (And yes, Marcelene is spelled with an "e" on the store sign.)

3. A Disney World Showcase...of Chocolate

Sweet treats and Christmas go hand-in-hand (at least in our house), and during this time of year the Disney confectioners and pastry chefs pull out all the stops to create several delightfully delectable displays. No, you can't eat them, but you can enjoy the incredible craftsmanship and expertise that went into creating these one-of-a-kind holiday scenes. Perhaps the most famous Walt Disney World "edible" edifice is the life size gingerbread house at the Grand Floridian. The BoardWalk and Contemporary also host their own gingerbread houses and Christmas trees, and you'll find a scrumptious chocolate carousel at the Beach Club. But there are many other confection creations to be found throughout the resorts and parks, with new ones popping up all the time. A frequently overlooked, but equally delightful display can be found in the upper level of the Land pavilion. Paying homage to Disney resorts around the world, this chocolate display features miniature candy versions of some famous Disney locations across the globe, including the Aulani resort in Hawaii, the Disney Cruise Line, and Disneyland's Matterhorn, not to mention Epcot's own Spaceship Earth. Yum!

4. Froehliche Weihnachten!

Speaking of World Showcase, one of the most rewarding experiences you can enjoy during the Christmas season is to tour the pavilions of World Showcase and see the presentations of each pavilion's storytellers. Each storyteller weaves a wonderful tale of the holiday traditions from his or her country. It's fascinating to hear about the different celebrations that occur around the globe, particularly in those countries that don't celebrate Christmas specifically, but have their own special holiday traditions. And, of course, you can visit Santa Claus (and Mrs. Claus) in the American Adventure pavilion. But for pure Christmas splendor, head on over to the Germany pavilion for some true holiday magic. In addition to the pavilion's storyteller, Helga (who shares the stories behind such traditions as the Christmas tree and the Advent calendar, which both have their origins in Germany), you can visit Die Weihnachts Ecke (The Christmas Corner), where you can see beautiful holiday decorations on display all year round. You can even find the legendary Christmas Pickle, and read about the origins of this German tradition. (Which actually leads us to another myth, but we'll save that for our next book!) During the holidays, be sure to check out the miniature train village next to the pavilion. You'll find that it's decked out in all its holiday fineness...all the way down to the tiny Christmas wreaths on the doors!

5. IllumiNations

OK, this one isn't really an overlooked holiday treat, but it's one of our favorites, and definitely one that's not to be missed. IllumiNations is a moving, spellbinding show any time of year, but at Christmas it truly transforms into something extra magical. At the conclusion of the regular show, get ready to enjoy the special holiday finale. A stirring message of peace and good will echoes across the lagoon, while each of the World Showcase pavilions are highlighted in turn, wishing Guests a festive holiday season in their native language. But it's the fireworks show that will really bring a tear to your eye. As "Let There Be Peace On Earth" plays throughout World Showcase, the sky is filled with a dazzling display of reds, greens, and shimmering pyrotechnics that will simply take your breath away. Just when you think they couldn't possibly shoot off any more fireworks, they do just that, and the jaw-dropping finale is something that you'll never forget! But it's the message that's at the heart of this wondrous nighttime show...the wish "that everyone, everywhere, share in the spirit of the season, peace on earth, good will to men."

Eleven Fun Facts About Disney's Fireworks

No evening at Walt Disney World would be complete without a viewing of one of the many spectacular nighttime shows featured throughout the parks. Here are some fun facts about our favorites, past and present.

Wishes

1. Boom Boom Boom

A total of 683 individual pieces of pyrotechnics were used during each show, requiring the triggering of 557 firing cues. (That's approximately one every 1.3 seconds. Better cover your ears!).

2. The Wishing Star

The show's highlight, the "wishing star," reached a height of approximately 290 feet in the evening sky.

3. Tinker Bell's Flight

Some 60,000 Guests were on-hand to witness the first flight of Tinker Bell; she flew down from the top of Cinderella Castle for the first time on July 3, 1985. The flight is about 850-feet-long and takes about 30 seconds to complete. (Thank goodness she has lots of pixie dust to spare!)

IllumiNations

4. The Earth Globe

The spectacular Earth Globe weighs 350,000 lbs., which is approximately the same weight as the blue whale, the largest known animal to have ever lived. The Globe has 187,200 LEDs (light-emitting diodes) that cover its surface, which are then used to bring the Globe to life to tell the story of how our world came to be.

5. Feel the Heat

The Inferno Barge holds 37 nozzles, capable of sending propane-fueled fireballs 60 feet into the air.

6. Holiday Magic Around the World

At Christmas, 1,195 individual pyrotechnic pieces are set off during a holiday showing of IllumiNations with 455 being devoted to the Holiday tag alone. The fireworks come from 34 locations around World Showcase Lagoon.

7. Unique Colors for a Unique Show

There are 14 different colors employed by the eight programmable Syncrolites used during the show. The color palette originally included four colors that were specifically created for IllumiNations: lavender, mint, pumpkin, and lagoon. In late 2011, some of the equipment was replaced with versions that were more environmentally-friendly. Unfortunately, the new equipment couldn't replicate the custom colors from the past, and they were replaced with more traditional orange, green, magenta, and yellow hues.

8. Lighting the Torches

There are 19 torches surrounding World Showcase Lagoon, each one individually numbered. A 20th torch, the Unity Torch, is revealed toward the end of the show when the Earth Globe opens and the Unity Torch rises from its center.

Happily Ever After

9. Movie Magic

The Magic Kingdom's newest nighttime spectacular features 25 Disney films shown throughout the projected portions of the show.

10. Lights Please!

There are 50 choreographed spotlights and lasers used throughout the show; more than any other show in Disney history.

11. Bringing the Castle to Life

Projection-mapping technology was first used at the Magic Kingdom in 2010, with the launch of "The Magic, The Memories & You," a nighttime show that combined Guest-submitted photos with different colorful layouts that were projected onto Cinderella Castle.

Our Ten Favorite Hidden Mickeys

For the few of you who don't know, the Hidden Mickey is a time-honored tradition throughout Walt Disney World. In its typical form, the Hidden Mickey is comprised of three circles (and yes, those two top circles should ideally be a bit smaller, in other words, ear-sized...so those three grapes in that centerpiece in your favorite restaurant don't count!). Imagineers have been hiding these little tributes through the attractions, lands, and resorts at Disney ever since the park opened; and new ones are arriving all the time. In fact, no one is really sure how many there are in total, but here are ten of our favorites:

1. Haunted Mansion Ballroom Dishes

We've talked about this Hidden Mickey in some of our other lists, but even though its official status (and existence) has changed over the years, it's always been one of our favorites. But since we've covered this particular Mickey elsewhere, we'll toss in an Honorable Mention for the sake of this list. In the graveyard, look for the ghostly apparition on your right as you exit the spooky cemetery. You'll find a silhouetted Hidden Mickey in his raised left hand. (This one is a little harder to spot than it had been in past years, but it's still worth seeking out!)

2. Spaceship Earth

There are many Hidden Mickeys in Spaceship Earth, but we think the cleverest one can be found in the Islamic scholars scene. As you pass by the solitary figure on the left, take a close look at the bookshelf. As you pass in front of it, you'll see that three of the scrolls that appear to be randomly sticking out actually form a Hidden Mickey when viewed from the front!

3. Journey Into Imagination With Figment

Similarly, you'll find all sorts of Mickeys in Journey Into Imagination With Figment, but our favorite is actually at the exit of the attraction. As you wind your way through the corridor leading to the ImageWorks section of the pavilion, take a close look at the lettering for the ImageWorks signs. You'll see that three of the circles behind the "I" and "M" form a tilted Hidden Mickey.

4. The Seas with Nemo & Friends

Again, our favorite Hidden Mickey at this attraction isn't on the actual ride, but in the post attraction area. Throughout this interactive undersea laboratory, you'll find many illuminated signs with lots of information about sharks and other creatures of the sea. Oftentimes, if you look hard enough you'll find a Hidden Mickey formed by the bubbles in the water. Here's a hint, look down in the corners...that's where they can usually be spotted (the best for little kids to find them). Additionally, (and this one's really cool), you can occasionally find a giant Hidden Mickey arranged in stones on the bottom of the aquarium. These Mickeys come and go and can pop up in different areas of the aquarium, but if you find one, it's a sight you'll never forget.

5. Soarin' Around the World

Soarin' Around the World features a few Hidden Mickeys that we especially love. The first is formed by the temporary juxtaposition of three hot air balloons in Monument Valley on the Arizona-Utah border. The second is even more spectacular. Look for the fireworks bursting over Spaceship Earth in the finale. Two of them simultaneously explode over the grand geodesic sphere, forming a perfect Hidden Mickey. (But look quickly or else you'll miss it!)

6. Mission: SPACE

In the gift shop at the exit of Mission: SPACE, you'll find a number of Hidden Mickeys. One of our favorites can be found in the craters on the painting of the Moon, and another can be spotted on the walls amongst the pipes and junction boxes. Oh, and while you're there, don't forget to check out the Mickey Nebula painted on the ceiling!

7. Gran Fiesta Tour

When Gran Fiesta Tour took over for El Rio Del Tiempo, Guests were anxious to see if any Hidden Mickeys were added (even though this was now Donald Duck's show!). Sure enough, as you approach the final scene in Mexico City, keep an eye out on the left for a boat floating in the water. On it you'll find three bongos, perfectly arranged in a Hidden Mickey.

8. Beach Club Resort

This one is a little more elusive, but it's well worth looking for it. The Beach Club features a beautiful sitting area called the Solarium, and as you make your way down the entrance hallway, you'll find a lovely painting on the left-hand wall depicting a nostalgic day at the beach. Up in the sky is a fanciful cloud in the shape of our favorite Disney mouse.

9. Splash Mountain

This is actually one of the first Hidden Mickeys I discovered, and also one of the cleverest. Early in your journey leading to the briar patch, you'll pass Br'er Frog lazily casting a fishing line in the water. Sitting nearby, perched delicately on a rock is a unique red and white fishing bobber with, you guessed it, two smaller fishing bobbers serving as Mickey's ears.

10. Tomorrowland Transit Authority PeopleMover

When you mention Hidden Mickeys and the TTA, most people think of the belt buckle worn by the woman getting her hair done at the futuristic salon. But another oft-overlooked Hidden Mickey can be found in Mickey's Star Traders, which you can see out through the windows on your right. The giant lamp hanging from the ceiling is in the shape of a classic Mickey, but that's not the one we have in mind. On the far wall is a mural of a busy highway, and at the heart of it is a cleverly-designed cloverleaf ramp system in the shape of, you guessed it, a Hidden Mickey!

Four Clever Hidden Numbers and Years

*S*even Dwarfs. One Hundred and One Dalmatians. Three Little Pigs. 20,000 Leagues Under the Sea. Numbers have certainly played a big part in Disney's cinematic history (quick, name all seven dwarfs!), but many folks don't realize that numbers play a significant (though oft-overlooked) role in the parks as well. And not just in attraction names (with all apologies to the Three Caballeros at Mexico's Gran Fiesta tour), but in the smallest of details found throughout all the parks; details that may seem innocuous at first but in fact are clever inside jokes or veiled references to an historic date.

1. More Than Just an Address

Let's begin with something as innocent as house numbers. Most of us have one, and by and large they don't mean anything. But at Walt Disney World it's a different story. Given that the Imagineers needed to put house numbers on many of the buildings throughout the parks (particularly the Magic Kingdom) and given that they'll never miss a chance to infuse some humor or historic authenticity into the smallest of details, you'll find that the house numbers you see actually carry some significance. Most famously, you'll find that the buildings that line the streets from Liberty Square all the way through Frontierland have numbers that are in fact years; indicating the time periods when those buildings would have existed. Walking from Liberty Square through Frontierland towards Splash Mountain is like traveling through time, with the buildings in Liberty Square numbered in the 1700s (beginning with the Hall of Presidents bearing the number 1787, the year the U.S. Constitution was ratified) and those in Frontierland representing those in the 1800s (many buildings have two-digit numbers, the trick is to put an "18" in front of it, and just like that you've traveled back in time!)

2. Emporium Secrets

You'll also find some references to significant dates in Disney history on Main Street U.S.A., such as a plaque over the door of the Emporium Gallery that reads "Established in 1901" (the year Walt Disney was born). According to its sign, the Emporium itself was established in 1863, but the derivation of that year is a bit more complicated. According to the fictitious back-story, that was the year the Emporium was established by its founder, Osh Popham. But why 1863? It turns out that Disney had released a film called *Summer Magic* in 1963 (one hundred years later), which told the story of a Boston widow and her children who took up residence in a small town in Maine. The film also starred Burl Ives (of "Have a Holly Jolly Christmas" fame) as...you can see where this is going... none other than Osh Popham.

3. Opening Dates

Over at the Casey Jr. Splash 'n' Soak play area, see if you can spot the numbers on the various train cars that represent the years that each of the four Disney parks opened. (Magic Kingdom in 1971, Epcot in 1982, Disney-MGM Studios in 1989, and Disney's Animal Kingdom in 1998, in case you forgot!)

At Buzz Lightyear's Space Ranger Spin, you used to be able to see a more obscure reference to a significant date. Before it was recently removed during a renovation, you could find a small painting of Stitch zipping through space in a tiny ship with some alien writing on the side. This writing (which used the same alphabet seen in Stitch's Great Escape! and on the newspapers being sold by the robot newspaper vendor at the entrance to the TTA) spelled out 1972, the year that the building that houses the attraction opened.

Over in Epcot, pay close attention to the flight announcements as you wait to enter the boarding area of Soarin' Around the World. You'll hear that you'll be embarking on flight 5505, which is a reference to the date that Soarin' first opened; May 5, 2005.

More humorously, a trip over to Chester & Hester's Dino-Rama at Disney's Animal Kingdom will uncover several road signs and license plates bearing the number 498, a reference to April 1998, the date the park opened.

4. Movie Math Magic

Next, let's head on over to Disney's Hollywood Studios and take a journey on Star Tours – The Adventures Continue. While you're making your way through the queue, see if you can hear the announcement saying "Will the owners of a red-and-black landspeeder, vehicle ID THX 1138, please return to your craft. You are parked in a no hover area." *THX 1138* is the name of George Lucas's first film, which of course set the stage for *Star Wars*, released six years later.

Another infamous movie reference is A113, which can be found in nearly every Pixar film, as well as many recent Disney films. (As mentioned earlier, A113 was the number of the classroom used by character animation students at the California Institute of the Arts.) Surprisingly, A113 isn't very prevalent in the parks, though you could find a poster of Donald Duck's nephews that included the image of a Disney Vacation Club travel ticket with the number A113 on one of the exterior facades of the Streets of America in Disney's Hollywood Studios.

Five Favorite Imagineering Tricks

Imagineers spend a lot of time and thought dreaming up all the things that make Walt Disney World such a magical place. As you might expect, they have a full arsenal of technology and talent at their disposal to bring these dreams to life, but they've also cooked up a variety of pranks and gags to fool Guests and to create masterful illusions, in a fun and magical way, of course. How so? Let's take a stroll through the parks and see what sort of mischief awaits you.

1. Things are Not Quite as They Appear

Sometimes you might be fooled into seeing things that are not really there, or at least aren't quite what they seem. A favorite trick of Imagineers is called forced perspective, which makes things appear bigger than they really are. How does it work? To understand forced perspective, you need to know how our eyes and brain work together. When you look at a distant object, your brain uses many subtle clues to help you judge how big it is, or relatively speaking, how far away it is. For instance, if you see a friend waving to you across a field, your brain instinctively knows how tall she is. Right now though, your friend might only appear to be an inch or two tall. (Hold up your hand and pretend to hold her between your thumb and forefinger to get an idea of how tall she appears to you. Don't squeeze though!) Of course, your friend isn't actually two inches tall. But that's one of the clues your brain uses to let you know that your friend is standing far away from you, as opposed to a few feet away. Similarly, if you see an object that you know is a certain distance away, such as across a football field, you have a pretty good idea of how big it really is, because you're used to how knowing big other objects appear at that distance. Confusing?

Well, let's go to Main Street, U.S.A., for a perfect example. Everyone has, of course, seen a two- or three-story house. So, you have a pretty fair idea of how big a window looks to you if it's at ground level, on the second floor, or even higher. The smaller the window, the higher it must be off the ground. The Imagineers used this perception to make the buildings seem taller than they really are. If you were to measure the second and third story windows on the stores of Main Street, you'll find that they're much smaller than the first story windows. Because the windows appear smaller to you, your brain tricks you into thinking that they're much higher than they really are.

How much smaller are they? The ceilings of the first floors of the Main Street shops are 12 feet tall, which is a perfectly reasonable height. But the second story is only 10 feet tall, while the third floor is only 8 feet tall! (Goofy would probably get his hat knocked off.) For comparison, look at the Town Square Exposition Hall, and you'll notice quite a difference. There, the floors are all the same height, just like a normal building.

Imagineers use the trick of forced perspective throughout the parks to give Guests a sense of grandness. You'll see it at Cinderella Castle (the stones actually get smaller and smaller the higher you go), the mountainside of the Canada pavilion in Epcot (where the trees are smaller at the top), the Eiffel Tower in the France pavilion (which in reality is only 1/10th the size of the real thing), and the Empire State Building facade that once stood in the Streets of America at Disney's Hollywood Studios.

Forced perspective isn't only used to make things appear bigger. In Peter Pan's Flight, the tiny buildings you see when you fly over London are much narrower at the bottom than they are at the top to exaggerate the illusion of height!

2. Mirror, Mirror

Imagineers use reflections quite often to make things appear and disappear. For instance, the disappearing butterfly illusion in the Journey Into Imagination With Figment is accomplished by a cleverly placed mirror in the middle of the cage. In the Haunted Mansion, the famous ballroom scene ghosts are reflections, not off a mirror, but off a large piece of glass that's positioned between you and the ballroom floor. (The Audio-Animatronics figures are actually beneath the balcony!) A similar technique was used in Spaceship Earth during one of the final scenes where you saw people communicating with each other across great distances, such as the mother singing a lullaby to her child. Some of the figures were actually above and behind you, and they were being reflected off of the glass in front of you to make them semi-transparent.

Another creative use of mirrors is to give the illusion of depth. The infinite corridor in the Haunted Mansion makes use of this technique. What you're actually seeing is a series of repeated reflections of the ghostly candelabra floating in the distance.

3. A Bit of Misdirection

A favorite prank of the Imagineers is to fool you into thinking something sinister is about to happen to you, and then at the last minute letting you off the hook. In Expedition Everest, for example, the initial part of your journey leads you to a pair of twisted railroad tracks that appear to be sending you hurtling off the mountain. Instead, you careen backward down the slope toward your fearsome encounter with the Yeti. (Though we're not sure that's actually a better situation.)

A similar trick is used on Big Thunder Mountain Railroad, where your train tracks appear to have been demolished by a cave-in.

In the former Maelstrom attraction in Epcot's Norway pavilion, your boat would change direction midway through your journey, and for those who didn't know better, you would think you were about to plunge backward over the waterfall that saw from the pavilion's courtyard. Thankfully, your boat soon started to move forward again, so you didn't actually tumble backward over the falls. (Though there was another ominous drop looming ahead...). The same ride mechanism still exists in Frozen Ever After, but this time there isn't any misdirection leading you to believe that you're about to take a backward plunge into the icy abyss of Elsa's castle.

4. Gotcha!

So far, these tricks have been used to create illusions or to confuse your expectations. But Imagineers aren't beyond giving you a nice, healthy scare! The attic in the Haunted Mansion was once filled with spooks that popped out at you unexpectedly, unleashing a shriek that would make you jump out of your seat. (Constance the Bride now takes up residence in the attic, and while she does wield an axe, at least she's not jumping out at you. Small comfort.) In Test Track, your leisurely(?) tour through the testing facility has a heart-jolting surprise as you round one of the bends. Watch out for that truck!

5. That Makes Scents

Finally, the Imagineers have come up with another way to have some fun at Guest's expense. As if fooling your eyes weren't enough, they decided to have some fun with your nose. While the smell of cinnamon-laced apple pie in Mickey's PhilharMagic is enchanting, you'll probably be less appreciative of the skunk odor in Journey Into Imagination, the stinkbug in It's Tough to be a Bug, or some gone-but-not-forgotten "favorites" including the acid smell in Test Track, or (my personal, um, favorite) Stitch's chili dog belch in Stitch's Great Escape!

Nine Favorite Rainy Disney Moments

When most people think of Walt Disney World and rain, they conjure up images of folks donning their ponchos and scurrying for cover. And while a Florida thunderstorm might put a damper on your day of touring in the parks (although we'll talk about why that could actually be a good thing later), you can discover all sorts of magical moments that are inspired by the rain. So, grab your umbrella and rain poncho as we take a look at the most magical rainy moments at Walt Disney World.

1. "it's a small world"

What better way to start our list than with a bit of whimsical magic. (This is Disney after all!) For the first part of your trip around the world, you're joined by children from countries around the globe as they sing that familiar song in their country's musical style. But soon you're transported to a magical tropical rain forest where the children are replaced by whimsical animals, some of whom are carrying spectacularly colored umbrellas to protect themselves from the "rain." Magical!

2. Carousel of Progress

Ah, the age of electricity! As Valentine's Day draws near, you'll hear a small, um, disagreement between Mother and Father about an approaching rain storm. (Mother insists one is approaching, while Father disagrees. His lumbago isn't acting up after all. Who do you think is right?) Take a quick peek outside the window as the storm approaches – before the thunderstorm hits and the lights go out!

3. Walt Disney's Enchanted Tiki Room

This serene musical show is not always lighthearted and festive. At one point, the entire theater is plunged into semi-darkness as a fierce thunderstorm rages outside. Look out the theater windows as the lightning flashes; you'll really think it's raining! Don't worry though, the storm soon passes, and just as quickly it's back to the festivities. When the Tiki Room was under "new management," the storm occurred when Iago angered the Tiki gods, unleashing their fury and the ensuing storm. Thankfully, Iago quickly learned his lesson and made peace with the Tiki gods, and the show returned to its familiar festive self.

4. Norway Pavilion/Maelstrom

We're going to back in time with our next stop, and you actually used to get a double dose of wet weather here. On Maelstrom, one of the most spectacular scenes was the North Sea Oil Rig, where raging winds and crashing waves swirled around as you as you rode beneath the breathtaking spectacle of a colossal deep-sea oil rig lighting up the night sky. You didn't get wet (not much anyway), but you definitely felt a chill. After the ride, you could see a five-minute film about Norway that took you on a stunning tour of that beautiful country. During the film, you got a brief glimpse into the life of the Vikings as you joined them aboard a ship while they fought their way through a raging sea storm. (Bet they could have used one of those wonderful heavy sweaters from the gift shop!)

5. Jungle Cruise

Not every rainy magical moment at Walt Disney World is courtesy of the Imagineers. Mother Nature is quite capable of providing a few wonderful rainy moments herself! One of the best is on the Jungle Cruise. If it's nighttime and a light rain is falling (or better yet, if there's the distant rumble of an approaching thunderstorm and you're still dry), take a ride on the Jungle Cruise for a unique experience. Instead of the leisurely daytime tour through the jungle that you usually enjoy, riding the Jungle Cruise at night with a bit of rain transforms it into an eerie and spooky adventure! As you leave the boarding docks, you'll be plunged into a dark and rainy jungle, with nothing but your boat lamp to light the way. And of course, the temple is even eerier after dark. You'll really feel like you're in the deepest and darkest corners of the jungle, but fortunately your guide is still with you with those punny jokes to keep the mood light! (Just hope your seat is under cover, it's possible you could be the unlucky Guest who gets dripped on the whole time! Good thing you have your Mickey poncho...)

6. Living with the Land

As your boat tour starts, you'll visit a desert, a prairie, and even a barnyard. But the most spectacular scene is the tropical rain forest, filled with cool mist, lush vegetation, and wonderful visual effects that make you feel like you're really there. Good thing your boat has a canopy.

7. Haunted Mansion

It might require a bit of luck to experience this magical moment (and some cooperation from Mother Nature), but if you happen to be in the Magic Kingdom during an evening thunderstorm, head over to the Haunted Mansion. If you think it's creepy inside, just wait until you approach the Gothic mansion during a dark and scary storm! The claps of thunder and the howling of the distant wolf combine to create an experience you'll never forget. Take your time approaching the Haunted Mansion (thank goodness for the extended canopy!) to check out the graveyard. Somehow, Madame Leota's tombstone is even spookier during a thunderstorm. And when you've finished your ghoulish tour, what better way to leave the Haunted Mansion than by walking by the black hearse as it's lit up by a flash of lightning! I get the chills just thinking about it...

8. Pirates of the Caribbean

Okay, we're almost there, one away from the most magical rainy moment at Walt Disney World. However, next up is our top candidate for the creepiest rainy moment: the opening pirate scene in Pirates of the Caribbean. After you pass through the misty waterfall, you'll come across a group of pirates (well, their skeletons anyway) standing eternal guard in an underground cavern. Not creepy enough for you? Then just wait for the next scene, where... well, we'll save the rest for our next list, the Scariest Attraction Scenes in Walt Disney World. For now, we'll get things back to a more whimsical mood with our final entry.

9. The Many Adventure of Winnie the Pooh

Here we are, our pick for the most magical rainy moment at Walt Disney World, the Blustery Day scene in the Many Adventure of Winnie the Pooh. The sequence starts with a wonderful visual of Winnie the Pooh's dream-self floating up and away, followed by the wacky and bizarre world of heffalumps and woozles. But then the rain arrives, and you find yourself in a magical rainstorm, complete with stunning visual effects (watch for the little rain drops in the puddles!) and the familiar song from the beloved animated short. Ah, I feel a rumbly in my tumbly and a strange craving for hunny!

Here's one last touring tip: Don't be discouraged if it starts to rain during your day at the parks. Most of the attractions are inside, and the rain often chases quite a few people away, so you'll actually have more of the attractions to yourself, particularly in the evening. And as we've seen, the rain can provide lots of magical moments that you might not ordinarily get the chance to experience.

Have fun, and don't forget your poncho!

Eleven Scariest Attraction Scenes

1. Pirates of the Caribbean

Let's first finish our discussion about that rainy scene in Pirates of the Caribbean. What could be more frightening than a raging thunderstorm? How about a raging thunderstorm out at sea with a skeleton or two thrown in for good measure? This is exactly what you'll find in Pirates of the Caribbean, right as you pass the beach scene strewn with the skeletons of the less-fortunate pirates who tried to make off with the treasure ages ago. This scene appears on your right and is filled with thunderous explosions of lightning and a torrential downpour. At the helm is the skeletal remains of a notorious pirate, and the scene is so convincing that you'll swear you're getting drenched by the raging storm. Though you actually don't get wet here, don't fret...you just might get your wish on the drop through the darkness looming ahead.

2. Haunted Mansion

During its development, there were two schools of thought on how the attraction would be realized. Some of the Imagineers wanted to have a suitably creeping setting, while others wanted to take a more lighthearted approach. While several of the scenes, most notably in the graveyard, have their whimsical moments, the attic is most definitely themed to be creepy and frightening. A thumping heartbeat can be heard as you make your way through the cobweb strewn attic, and the images of the bride's husbands disappearing from their portraits (signifying their unfortunate demise) leads you to the knife wielding bride herself, who wickedly recites her wedding vows...with a curious emphasis on the "till death do us part" section.

3. Twilight Zone Tower of Terror

This attraction is frightening from start to finish, beginning with your journey through the decaying remains of the lobby, left in the state that it was in when lightning struck the tower in 1939. But surely the most frightening part of your journey into the unknown is that uneasy moment before your elevator takes its initial faster-than-gravity plunge down the elevator shaft. Even more terrifying (for those with sensitive stomachs) is the rapid ascent back to the top. To make things worse, you'll drop again...and again...and...well, you'll never know quite how many times you'll drop or when your journey to the Twilight Zone will end due to the random nature of the drops. Just hang on tight (and be sure to scream when the elevator doors open at the top so the whole park can hear you).

4. The Great Movie Ride

This is the first of our entries that reference attractions that have since closed, but these scenes still put a chill in our hearts when we think back upon them. In the Great Movie Ride, things started off happily enough as you got a glimpse of the musicals made back in the heyday of Hollywood glory. But things took a turn when you found yourself in the midst of a gangster-filled shootout, and things definitely hit the top of the scary-meter when you found yourself aboard the Nostromo from the classic sci-fi film, *Alien*. As you saw an Animatronic version of Ripley nervously looking around, armed with her flamethrower, the alien itself suddenly sprang out at you with teeth gnashing and claws bared. And just when you thought you'd escaped, it descended upon you from overhead. Yikes! At least now you were off to Munchkinland. What could be scary about that?

6. Ellen's Energy Adventure

Another scene from a now-closed attraction, this one makes our list not because it was intentionally frightening, but just because it was loud! As we watched the universe explode into existence with the Big Bang, galaxies, solar systems, and planets quickly formed. Before we knew what was happening, we found ourselves racing over a newly-formed planet Earth, where we took a sudden turn and crashed into the primordial forest. And boy, did we crash! The thunderous boom that rocked the theater was ear-splitting, and quite scary if you weren't expecting it! But then came the dinosaurs, and at least they weren't so scary.

7. DINOSAUR

Perhaps the dinos from Ellen's Energy Adventure weren't overly frightening (unless you consider getting sneezed on frightening), but the creatures in the Animal Kingdom's DINOSAUR attraction definitely are. The ride itself is treacherous enough, but it's that final encounter with the Carnotaurus that will leave you screaming...if you can hear yourself, that is. The ear-splitting roar of this fearsome prehistoric predator leaves Guests trembling, and lest you thought you were brave enough for it not to bother you; you'll see evidence to the contrary as you disembark the ride to find the souvenir photo taken of you just as the Carnotaurus roared. Yep, that's you cowering in your seat, hands tightly covering your ears. And we're not sure but...yep, we can definitely see you screaming. Brave indeed.

8. ExrtraTERRORestrial Alien Encounter

Soon to be home to a Wreck-It Ralph-themed attraction, this theater was once home to one of the most frightening attractions every to be found at Walt Disney World, the Extra-TERRORestrial Alien Encounter. Don't let the early appearance of the lovable and cuddly Skippy fool you; the show itself brought you face to face (or teeth, or, well, whatever it was) with a fearsome alien, who proceeded to break loose from the teleportation tube to wreak havoc throughout the theater...in total darkness mind you. Wait, was that blood you felt dripping down from ceiling? And you thought Stitch's chili dog burp was bad...

9. Expedition Everest

This one is a bit subjective, for if you like roller coasters you'll love Expedition Everest. The frightening moment we're referring to isn't the encounter with the Yeti (though that's pretty scary enough). No, it's the backward portion of the ride, which sends you hurtling UP a hill at breakneck speed. It's scary enough going forward, but racing along backward with no idea where you're going can be rather unnerving for the faint of heart!

10. Snow White's Scary Adventures

This seemingly innocent dark ride that once resided in Fantasyland did contain one truly terrifying scene; the moment the Queen turns to reveal herself as the evil witch. While you may have been expecting a whimsical jaunt through the woods with Snow White and those lovable dwarfs, this was an unexpected fright...and the one that definitely put the "Scary" in "Scary Adventures!"

11. Maelstrom

Now home to the charming (and dare I say tear-jerking) Frozen Ever After, this attraction was formerly known as Maelstrom and took you on a journey through the Norse world of Vikings and trolls. In actual fact, that attraction wasn't all that frightening, but for first-timers who were hurtling backward toward an apparent backward plunge down a waterfall, this was definitely a "hold your breath" moment! Of course, when you were traveling with a first-timer, you didn't tell them that they wouldn't actually fall backwards, did you? No, we thought not.

Six Favorite Secret Paths

The prospect of getting from point A to point B at Walt Disney World can be a magical adventure in its own right. Part of the fun in exploring the parks and resorts is in discovering different ways to get to where you're going. Whether it's a little-known shortcut, a route to avoid the crowds, or even a longer path that offers a new experience, there are many roads to take as you wander around Walt Disney World. Here are a few of our favorites:

1. Main Street U.S.A.

One of the best ways to avoid the crowds on Main Street U.S.A. is to make your way through the shops on either side, rather than down the main thoroughfare. Not only is it a good way to avoid the congestion outside, but it's also a great way to beat the heat. (If you really want to cool off quickly, make your way to the exit doors of the Plaza Ice Cream Parlor at the end of Main Street on the Tomorrowland side. Here you'll find an air curtain – giant blowers that blast cold air straight down just inside the doorway that will cool you off in no time. Just be sure you're not standing in the way of your fellow Guests. This is a doorway, after all!) But if you do go through the shops, just don't race through as there's plenty to see here. Even if you're not in mood for shopping or already have your souvenirs, you'll still be rewarded by taking your time and exploring your surroundings.

On the Tomorrowland side, make your way to the back of the Crystal Arts shop. Look around to discover a wealth of antique artifacts, including an antique time clock from the early 20th century (complete with time cards!), as well as a collection of authentic glass blowing tools like tweezers, sheers, and jacks (the things that look like giant tweezers with two blades). The details here are amazing and well worth the visit. Outside of Uptown Jewelers, you'll find a quaint little cross street that's frequently empty.

On the Adventureland side of the street, take a moment to pause as you enter the Emporium Gallery. Most people are entranced by the wide selection of merchandise on display here, but the real treasure is up above you. You'll find a wealth of Victorian era artifacts, a beautifully detailed mural, and a magnificent chandelier.

2. To Tomorrowland...

If you're heading toward Tomorrowland from Main Street U.S.A., take a right at the Plaza Ice Cream Parlor and head on through the Tomorrowland Terrace. This will take you right into the heart of Tomorrowland, bypassing the normal path through the hub and across the bridge (don't forget that this path works just as well as you're heading out). Surprisingly overlooked, this path not only allows you to avoid the crowds making their way to Tomorrowland via the hub, but it's much shorter as well.

3. And Beyond...

From Tomorrowland, you can take a quiet path over to Storybook Circus and Fantasyland that starts to the left of Space Mountain. It's a bit longer perhaps (depending on the crowds), but the walk is tranquil, and you'll actually get some wonderful views of the Walt Disney World Railroad as it chugs around the tracks. Get your cameras ready...this is one of the best places to snap photos of this iconic attraction!

4. The Path to the Future(s)

There are three main thoroughfares in Epcot once you enter the courtyard beyond Spaceship Earth. These are the two walkways leading on either side to the West and East sides of Future World, and the promenade that leads to World Showcase. These can get quite busy as you may expect, though typically not exceedingly so. Still, there are alternate ways to get around them, and again, these paths offer their own set of surprises. If you're making your way toward Soarin' Around the World and the other attractions on the West side, take a stroll through the former Innoventions West building (home of the Epcot Character Spot and Club Cool) and head towards the rear exit. Not only will you bypass the main walkway, but you'll discover one of the great "secret spots" in Epcot, a large open space (nice and cool!) that is rarely visited. It's not a bad place for a bathroom break either. Continuing on, as you exit the building, you'll find yourself in a courtyard filled with plaques in concentric circles on the ground. These plaques commemorate different milestones in science and discovery and are a frequently overlooked detail in Future World.

If you're heading toward Mission: SPACE and Test Track, take a detour through MouseGear. Not only will you discover one of the best gift shops in all of Walt Disney World, but you'll get a welcome break from the Florida sun. Exit at the rear of the store and you'll find yourself right in front of Test Track.

5. Off to See the World

Heading to World Showcase? Here you have two alternative paths you can take. These paths offer their own unique views, and while they don't save you much time versus the main pathway along the promenade, you will bypass much of the crowds. The paths start in their respective East and West sides of Future World, so if you're enjoying the attractions on either side, these two paths will definitely save you some steps. On the West side, look for a path heading away from the Imagination pavilion. This tranquil path not only leads you to the Canada side of World Showcase, but it's also home to several rose gardens that you can stop and enjoy. (Yes, you can literally stop and smell the roses!)

On the East side, seek out the bridge that leads from Test Track around the lagoon toward the Odyssey restaurant. This area was once home to a flock of beautiful pink flamingos, but even though they're gone, you can still enjoy some peaceful water views as you make your way toward the Mexico pavilion. It's also a great place to watch the tree lighting ceremony at Christmas. Most people will gather in the main promenade, but you can find a secluded spot along the Odyssey walkway and enjoy this holiday spectacular in relative calm.

6. On to Hollywood

Finally, if you're in Epcot or visiting the Epcot resorts, don't forget that there's a walkway that will take you to Disney's Hollywood Studios. The walkway follows alongside the boat canal and is surprisingly tranquil. You'll also be afforded spectacular views of the Swan and Dolphin resorts, and yes, that's the Tower of Terror you see looming in the distance!

Ten Unusual Dates in Disney History

The history of Walt Disney World, and of Disney in general, is filled with notable dates, including everything from the Walt Disney's birthday to the opening dates of today's parks and attractions. These dates are so important that they're often immortalized in clever ways within various attractions. But Disney history is also filled with some unusual dates, and these are some of our favorites.

1. November 15, 1965

Ending months of public speculation, Walt Disney and Roy Disney join then-governor of Florida W. Haydon Burns at a press conference to publicly announce the plans for Walt's "Florida Project." Up until then, Disney had been quietly buying up parcels of land in the Orlando area, hoping to keep the process a secret lest the prices skyrocket.

2. December 29, 1974

Inside one of the rooms of the Polynesian resort, holiday celebrations are set aside briefly as a stack of legal papers requiring a signature were delivered to the room's occupant. The papers were dutifully signed, and the resort Guests got back to their vacation. And so, with that simple signature, John Lennon officially broke up the Beatles.

3. January 15, 1975

Astronauts Scott Carpenter, Gordon Cooper, and Jim Irwin appeared in Tomorrowland for the grand opening of Space Mountain. Carpenter and Cooper were part of the famed

Mercury 7 astronauts and were among the first astronauts to fly into outer space. Irwin was the eighth person to walk on the Moon as part of the Apollo 15 crew.

4. June 20, 1976

How does going for a swim at Pop's Willow Grove sound? Construction for this old-fashioned watering hole began this day on the shores of Bay Lake, and Walt Disney World's first water park soon opened under its new name, Disney's River Country (later closing in 2001).

5. January 25, 1987

After defeating the Denver Broncos in Super Bowl XXI, New York Giant's quarterback Phil Simms is the first to utter the now-iconic phrase, "I'm going to Disney World!" as part of the "What's Next?" marketing campaign launched by Disney that year. The phrase has been a part of every Super Bowl since then (with the exception of Super Bowl XXXIX in 2005).

6. January 1, 1994

Nearly everyone has seen the famous film of Walt Disney outlining plans for his Florida venture, and telling us what those five little letters, E-P-C-O-T signified ("Experimental Prototype Community Of Tomorrow"). But actually, EPCOT doesn't refer to Epcot anymore. Huh? As time went by, Epcot became recognized as a word unto itself, and was no longer seen as an acronym. It was also clear that Epcot had not become the community of Walt's original vision. And so the decision was made that year to make EPCOT Epcot; and the park has been known as Epcot (big "E," little "pcot") ever since.

7. September 14-15, 1999

For the first time in its history, Walt Disney World closed its gates due to extreme weather conditions. Hurricane Floyd, a category 4 storm that forced massive evacuations up and down the U.S. eastern seaboard, seemed poised to slam into central Florida, but at the last minute veered up the coast.

8. October 8, 2003

While Mickey had gone through numerous transformations throughout the years, he had never been rendered in full 3D until now. It was on this day that Mickey's PhilharMagic made its Magic Kingdom debut. While it's Donald Duck that steals the show, Mickey is the true star, and for the first time fans got to see him in all of his fully-rendered, 3D glory.

9. November 18, 2003

Mickey Mouse celebrates his 75th anniversary with the unveiling of 75 Mickey statues at Walt Disney World. The statues, each weighing 700 pounds and standing six feet high, were designed and/or inspired by a select group of Disney legends, artists, actors, and athletes.

10. November 16, 2004

Everyone's favorite alien, Stitch, lands in Tomorrowland as the star of his new attraction, Stitch's Great Escape! The night before the attraction opened, Stitch apparently snuck into the Magic Kingdom and did a bit of "redecorating" of Cinderella Castle with some toilet paper and graffiti. There was no doubt to Guests the following morning, Stitch had arrived!

Nine Underrated Attractions

Walt Disney World is well known for its famous and classic attractions, but sometimes that means Guests will pass by some of the lesser known attractions on the way to the big headliners. While you may not have time to visit every attraction in the parks, if you find yourself with some extra time on your hands, these are definitely worth a visit.

1. The Aquarium at the Seas with Nemo & Friends

Nemo may seemingly be the star of the show at this Epcot pavilion, yet many new Guests don't realize that there's much more to this pavilion than the ride-through attraction. No, the real stars are the aquatic animals that reside in the main aquarium; one of the largest in the world. While you may be tempted to exit straight through the gift shop and back out to Future World, you should instead take the escalator leading to the second floor and marvel at the sea life that surrounds you as you venture into the viewing area. You'll see fish of all sorts, a few sharks, and even a sea turtle or two. You'll even find a pair of manatees off in their own pool, happily cavorting among the leaves of chewed up lettuce.

2. Journey Into Imagination With Figment

This attraction may be overshadowed by its nearby neighbors Test Track and Soarin' Around the World, but this whimsical delight (which you can often ride without a wait), has a unique charm all its own. Fans of the original version may miss certain elements of the old show, but Figment is still his mischievous self, doing his best to disrupt your tour of the Imagination Institute every chance he gets. If you keep your eyes out, you'll find some clever jokes and puns scattered throughout the attraction.

3. Tomorrowland Transit Authority PeopleMover

I can hear many of you screaming now. "What do you mean? This is one of my favorite attractions in all of Walt Disney World!" And we're right there with you. Oddly though, this attraction is often passed over by first-time Guests, which is understandable if they have a FastPass+ for Space Mountain or other headliner attractions. But Guests in the know realize that this is one of the best attractions to be found at the Magic Kingdom. Not only is it relaxing and filled with wonderful details, it actually gives you the feeling that you really are living in the world of the future, riding aboard the latest in state-of-the-art transportation. And who can forget that page for "Mr. Tom Morrow..."

4. The Monorail

"Wait, that's not an attraction?" Well, technically you're right, but nothing says "Disney" more than the monorail, and no visit to Walt Disney World is complete without a ride aboard this futuristic conveyance. Once you enter those doors, you'll feel that your stepping into a whole new world and touring the Seven Seas Lagoon aboard the highway in the sky is an experience you'll never forget. And in case you forgot, ""¡Por favor, manténgase alejado de las puertas!"

5. Maharajah Jungle Trek

With the opening of Pandora, Disney's Animal Kingdom has truly become a park to be enjoyed day and night. Along with other headliner attractions like Expedition Everest and Kali River Rapids, there's a lot to do in Disney's newest park. But tucked away amongst the animals and foliage are quite a few hidden gems, and our favorite is the Maharajah Jungle Trek. This walk-through outdoor exhibit takes you to the exotic world of Asia, and along the way you'll see tigers, bats, and even a Komodo dragon. But it's the tranquility that's the real draw here; you can take your time and stroll through at your leisure, and even rest on a bench by a beautiful jade fountain. The theming throughout the trails is incredible, and there are lots of surprises waiting to be discovered. And there's no better way to pass the time if you happen to be waiting for your FastPass+ time to arrive for the nearby Expedition Everest.

6. Living with the Land

This attraction was once quite popular and was, in fact, at one time one of the most popular attractions in Epcot, with wait times typically well over 45 minutes. But as Test Track and Soarin' opened, Guests started to migrate away from Living with the Land in favor of its larger cousins. Today, that means you'll often find little or no wait for this attraction (except on the busiest days). But don't let the lack of line fool you; this is a wonderful attraction, and along with the aquarium at the Seas pavilion, perfectly embodies the original concept for Epcot.

7. "it's a small world"/Walt Disney's Enchanted Tiki Room/Carousel of Progress

We're going to combine these three entries into one because they're all on the list for the same reason. Many is the Guest (and occasional guide book) who dismisses these three attractions as "corny" and "outdated." And thusly misinformed, the first-time visitor quickly crosses them off their to-do list. But all these attractions also share something in common; they all have strong connections to Walt Disney. They were all near and dear to Walt's heart, and if there are any attractions that typify that true Disney ideal, it would be these three. Sure, they may be idealistic, and some say a bit naive in their central message, but that's the true magic of Disney - to be able to be naive and to let yourself believe that we can live in world filled with peace, dreams, innovation, and good old-fashioned fun. So, if you routinely pass over these attractions in favor of big thrills, do yourself a favor and go check them out with a new frame of mind. You just may find your eyes opened up to a whole new world, and for a moment – even a brief one – you can get back in touch with that innocent child that lives in each one of us.

And that's the true magic of Disney.

Made in the USA
Lexington, KY
18 April 2018